digital
photography:
an introduction

digital
photography:
an introduction

TOM ANG

LONDON, NEW YORK, MUNICH,
MELBOURNE, DELHI **DK**

Contents

To Wendy

Project Editor Nicky Munro
Project Art Editor Jenisa Patel
DTP Designer Vânia Cunha
Production Controller Sarah Sherlock

Managing Editor Stephanie Farrow
Managing Art Editor Lee Griffiths
Americanizer Christine Heilman

Produced on behalf of Dorling Kindersley by
Sands Publishing Solutions
4 Jenner Way, Eccles, Aylesford, Kent ME20 7SQ
Project Editors David & Sylvia Tombesi-Walton
Project Art Editor Simon Murrell

Original edition produced on
behalf of Dorling Kindersley by
HILTON/SADLER
63 Greenham Road, London N10 1LN
Editorial Director Jonathan Hilton
Design Director Peggy Sadler

First published in the United States
in 2002 by DK Publishing
Second edition published in the United States
in 2007 by DK Publishing,
375 Hudson Street, New York, NY 10014

06 07 08 09 10   10 9 8 7 6 5 4 3 2 1

Copyright © 2002, 2004, 2006
Dorling Kindersley Limited
Text copyright © 2002, 2004, 2006 Tom Ang

A Cataloging-in-Publication record for this book
is available from the Library of Congress.

ISBN-13: 978-0-7566-2601-3

DK books are available at special discounts for
bulk purchases for sales promotions, premiums,
fund-raising, or educational use. For details,
contact: DK Publishing Special Markets,
375 Hudson Street, New York, NY 10014
or SpecialSales@dk.com

Printed by Star Standard in Singapore
Reproduction by GRB Editrice s.r.l. in Italy

Discover more at
www.dk.com

Introduction

One hundred and sixty years after the invention of photography, an enemy rose above the horizon. Digital imaging threatened to sweep away film, make the darkroom redundant, and exile the hard-won craft skills of picture-making. In a short time, the threat grew as numerous new enemies appeared, in the shape of more and more digital cameras, scanners, image-manipulation software, and the Web, all banding together to raze conventional photography to the ground.

Photographers watched with steadily increasing apprehension, but the threat turned out to be the best friend photography could have hoped for. Instead of opposing conventional photography, digital technologies have in fact revitalized whole swaths of photographic practice. Traditional techniques—in use of both the camera and lens, as well as darkroom manipulations—fully retained their relevance as the foundation upon which many digital advances were based; this is reflected in references to film-based techniques throughout this book. Indeed, the union of conventional photography with digital technology has turned out to be incredibly fertile, providing us with new worlds of practical, creative, and enjoyable potentialities.

Digital Photography: An Introduction celebrates the maturing of digital photography as a force to be reckoned with. So here you will find all the love and enthusiasm I have for conventional photography and its subtle craft skills for creating telling, effective, and rewarding images. At the same time,

I hope to share with you my thrill and wonder at the flexibility, power, and economies that are possible with digital photography. Photographers are, today, working at the leading edge of image-making, contributing to the ongoing development of what is nothing less than a visual powerhouse of as-yet-undreamed-of potential.

This book's aim is to help you get the most from this powerhouse. It brings together a vast amount of technical information and practical advice and reveals numerous tips and tricks of the trade, all in one compact volume. It is offered in order to help you improve, enjoy, and understand the medium of communication that is photography.

This revised edition of *Digital Photography: An Introduction* is intended as your photographic companion. I hope it will help you on your own journey of visual, technical, and creative adventures, leading to personal discovery. Ultimately, I hope this book will give you the knowledge and inspiration to surpass its teachings. For you to do so will be the best compliment you could give—at which point you should be sure to congratulate yourself.

Total photography

1

Photographic pathways

People who have made a large investment in film-based photography will wish to keep their legacy work but also fully participate in digital photography. With the proliferation of digital SLR cameras (*see p. 17*), many old lenses by the likes of Pentax, Nikon, Olympus, and Leica can (with some restrictions) be used on digital cameras. In addition, developed films—prints, negatives, or transparencies in color or black and white—can all be scanned to create full-fledged digital images that may be worked on in a computer.

Something magical happens when you combine the pathways through film-based and digital photography. A world of unimagined opportunity opens to you, with more than one way to achieve nearly any end—and from every fresh option arise yet more new creative opportunities. In short, total photography (the combination of analog with digital) gives you the best of both worlds. By increasing your options, it can inspire as it empowers. It is no exaggeration to say that the only limit is your imagination.

Digital route

Subject

Digital camera
Anything you can photograph using a film camera can also be recorded as a digital representation of the subject by using a digital camera.

Memory cards
A digital camera uses memory cards to store the digital representation of the subject.

Film-based route

Print

Negative   **Slide**

Film camera
A film camera records an analog representation of the subject, with each image being recorded on an individual frame of film.

Film
Once exposed to light from the subject, minute changes take place in the composition of the image-carrying emulsion layers of the film. At this stage the image is invisible and is known as a latent image.

Processing
Processing the film in special chemicals amplifies the latent image so that a recognizable image of the subject appears. Depending on the film used, you could have a positive image (or slide) or a negative, which requires printing, in color or black and white.

Analog and digital

Analog representation of the world is the one we are most familiar with, since it is based on a perceptible relationship between the representation (the movement of the hands of a clock, say) and the thing itself (the passage of time). Map locations possess relationships similar to the real places, so the map is an analog representation. Digital representation uses arbitrary signs whose meanings are predefined but bear no obvious relation to the thing. A digital watch could show the time in Chinese characters or Arabic numerals. Your ZIP code uses numbers arbitrarily to define a location. To know what the code refers to, you need a code book. Similarly, computer files (strings of symbols) may digitally represent the analog image you see as a print or negative. But a point on the negative corresponds to—is an analog of—a real thing in the original subject.

Storage
Once you are satisfied with the results of your work, you can store digital images on any of a range of removable media, including CDs, DVDs, and Zip and Jaz disks.

Processing in the computer
Images are downloaded directly into your computer as digital files. Now, using image-manipulation software, the digital adventure can begin.

Publish on the Internet
If you are connected to the Internet, you can send your digital images anywhere in the world as an attachment to an email. Equally, if you have a website, you could exploit the Internet to reach a potentially enormous audience.

Scanning
Taking a print or a film original as your starting point, you can use a scanner to create a digital representation of your analog image. Each scan is an individual digital file and you can work on it as if it had been taken with a digital camera.

Printing
In the time it takes to prepare chemicals to print in a darkroom, you could run off several prints from a desktop printer—all in normal room light. And even with readily affordable printers, print quality easily comes close to photographic papers.

Digital camera features

Many features of digital cameras are based on those of film cameras. The main handling difference is that instead of loading film, you slot in a memory card. Nearly all digital camera features require electrical power, while many film-camera features can be mechanically governed.

When you are choosing a camera, don't be put off if there seem to be too many features for you. It is not expected that you use them all; the manufacturer is simply trying to please as many people as possible by providing all the most popular features. Before purchasing a camera, you should ensure that the model you like is comfortable for you to use—some are very small, which can make them awkward for people with large hands. Many cameras are smaller than they look in promotional literature, so check the physical dimensions.

Another important consideration is the menus. Make sure they are easy enough for you to read—some screens require very good eyesight.

Shutter control
The shutter button on a digital camera is in reality a switch that triggers a whole series of complicated electronic operations.

Windows
You view the subject through the viewfinder window, but it does not accurately represent the framing of the subject.

Flash
A built-in flash is handy for working informally in low-light conditions.

Zoom lens
Many digital cameras offer a zoom lens so you can easily change the field of view. But extreme wide-angle effects are harder to obtain.

Digital zoom
This feature takes the image produced by the lens's longest focal length setting and then enlarges the central portion of it. The digital camera thus offers a zoom range that appears to be longer than that offered by the lens alone.

Transferring images
The camera's capacity to record images is limited by the capacity of the memory card in use. You can slot in a new card as the first fills up, or transfer files to other storage devices or a computer. Some cameras connect directly to a printer, allowing you to print without any intervening computer.

Longest zoom setting

Digital zoom enlargement

Focusing in the dark

In one method, a beam of infrared (IR) light is projected from the camera. The beam scans the scene and reflects back from any object it meets. A sensor on the camera measures the angle at which the beam returns, translates this into a subject distance, and sets the lens accordingly. However, this method is prone to interference from, say, an intervening pane of glass, which reflects the beam prematurely. The other method uses a pattern of light from the camera or flash unit, which directly assists the focus detectors to assess the image itself.

Subject

Sensor

Beam transmitter

Controls
Switches and buttons set different modes of operation, such as the image-quality settings.

Setting buttons
Combinations of buttons and LCD information allow a large range of settings to be made, adding to the camera's versatility.

LCD screen
The LCD can be used for viewing the subject, displaying pictures taken, and providing information on camera settings.

Viewfinder systems

Four viewfinder systems (to enable you to frame and focus an image before recording it) can be found in digital cameras. The simplest uses a liquid crystal display (LCD) screen to present a low-resolution image of the subject. Most cameras offer in addition a direct-vision viewfinder. This is a small lens (separate from the image-taking lens) through which you view the subject. Having this allows you to turn off the LCD and so save battery power, but since you are not viewing the subject through the image-taking lens, subject framing is prone to inaccuracy.

The best system is the single lens reflex (SLR) arrangement, identical to that in a film camera. It gives you an accurate view of the subject and makes focusing very easy (*see p. 17*). An alternative is what appears to be an SLR system, but the traditional focusing screen is replaced with an LCD screen viewed through the eyepiece. This screen is sufficient for framing but resolution is not high enough for precise focusing.

Digital cameras

The digital camera that is best for you depends on what you want to do with the images, how much equipment you wish to carry around, and how much money you have at your disposal.

Certainly, it is possible to obtain images that are suitable for all but professional reproduction from the vast majority of beginners' cameras, which means it is not necessary to spend a lot of money. Furthermore, older models and second-hand cameras can offer superb value.

First, calculate your budget; then decide which features you cannot live without. Finally, be prepared to make some compromises.

Beginners' compacts

At one time, the natural way to classify digital cameras was by their resolution or megapixel count. However, pixel count alone no longer determines how good or versatile a camera is. It makes more sense to look at the features, capabilities, and design goals of a camera.

Beginners' compacts are not only small, they also are easy to use, offer fewer options to control (and are therefore less confusing), and, despite their low cost, are capable of producing surprisingly good to very good results. All cameras offer a modest zoom of, usually, a long focal length

Tried and tested
Models based on best-selling lines are highly evolved, with tried-and-tested design and features. This model is smaller than its predecessors, but offers a 4x optical zoom lens and uses two AA batteries instead of four.

The viewfinder can be used instead of the LCD monitor.

A rotating dial is used to select shutter programs.

The flash is linked to the camera's zoom function.

Real resolution

In photographic terms, resolution is a measure of how well an optical system is able to discern, or separate out, fine subject detail to a "visually useful" extent—in other words, so that there is usable contrast to distinguish one detail from another. Camera manufacturers may make claims that their 2.5-megapixel sensor can produce files equivalent to a 4-megapixel sensor through pixel interpolation; however, the fact is that while an image cannot reveal more information than was captured in the first place, it is certainly possible to process the basic information of an image file in different ways

in order to give the impression that there is more information than is really present. But the final arbiter of any such claim is your subjective check of the image itself. Not only should you confirm that you can see more detail and see it more clearly, you should also make sure that subject colors are true, that contrast is realistic, and that the file-size output is appropriate to the task in hand. Why handle a 12-MB file, for example, when all the detail you need is contained in 8 MB? Note, however, that one form of interpolation, that of color, usually takes place in the capture of the image by handheld digital cameras (some cameras work in a different way).

three times longer than the wide angle, which itself is limited to the equivalent of 35 mm or a little longer. All beginners' compacts will also offer a tiny flash for dark conditions. Pixel counts range from 3 megapixels to as high as 6 or 7 megapixels.

Lifestyle compacts

The flexible form of the digital camera, which does not need to accommodate a roll of film, makes it possible for the camera's designers to create a stylish look, and has led to the production of so-called "lifestyle" compacts. These models sacrifice little capability, if any, to allow for their sleek shapes, ultra-slim and eminently pocketable designs, and superb finishes that simulate finely turned metals. The performance level of these cameras compares well with beginners' compacts, but their cost is somewhat higher, in return for which you obtain a piece of modern technology that is also a fashion statement. Before parting with your money, however, check that the camera you want is not too small for your hands to operate comfortably.

Within this category of cameras you can even find models that are waterproof, up to a depth of 5 ft (1.5 m) for 30 minutes—ideal for water sports.

Up periscope

Cameras that use a periscopic design for their lenses are almost as slim as a case for business cards: they are the ultimate pocketable camera. Yet models such as this can carry a 5-megapixel sensor, and offer a 2½-in (6.3-cm) LCD viewing screen.

This model has a 3x optical zoom with ISO 800 sensitivity.

The shutter release is always sited for the right index finger.

Always make sure the flash can be turned off if required.

Moiré patterns

One problem that can affect the quality of images recorded by a digital camera is known as "moiré." This occurs when the regular pattern of the sensor array in the camera interacts with some regular pattern in the image area, such as the weave of the cloth worn by your subject. The overlapping of two regular patterns, which are dissimilar and not perfectly aligned, leads to the creation of a new set of patterns—the moiré pattern—which is sometimes seen as bands of color or light and dark. Some digital SLR cameras (see p. 17) offer a sophisticated optical solution—the so-called "anti-aliasing" filter—while some other manufacturers use a filter—known as a "low-pass" filter—that very slightly softens the image by cutting out detail.

The appearance of the moiré pattern is readily discernible in the open weave of this fabric.

Digital cameras continued

Enthusiast compacts

For the avid photographer on a relatively tight budget, enthusiast digital compact cameras offer a winning combination of high performance, excellent versatility, and affordability. Cameras in this range may offer wider angles of coverage (up to 24 mm unaided), longer focal length zooms, the ability to record images in raw format, synchronization with accessory or studio flash, sturdier construction, and a larger range of accessories than is available for simpler cameras.

Most important, the majority of these cameras offer a full range of photographic controls over exposure, color balance, and focus. More attention is given to lens and image processor design, with a resulting improvement in picture quality. Allied with typical pixel counts of 6 megapixels and more, these cameras are certainly capable of a fair range of professional work.

When selecting a camera, try to ensure that the features you commonly use are easy to access—preferably with one click of a button. The size of many cameras can be hard to gauge just by looking at pictures, so check the dimensions before you make a purchase. If speed of operation is important, test it on the camera itself, because some models are still not quick to start up or to take a photograph.

"Prosumer" cameras

Cameras that are able to produce results to professional standards but may lack professional standards of sturdiness, durability, and range of accessories are called "prosumer" models. For the avid nonprofessional photographer, these cameras offer the best balance between quality and cost. They are easily capable of all but the most demanding professional tasks, but they are, on the whole, compact and lightweight, full-featured, and some can take a wide range of accessories. There are broadly two types of prosumer camera: bridge cameras are substantial, with inflated feature counts, but are based on a fixed lens; while digital single-lens reflex (dSLR) cameras offer interchangeable lenses.

Bridge cameras

The viewfinders of bridge cameras are both their weak and strong points: you view your subject on an LCD screen that is housed under an eyepiece—an electronic viewfinder (EVF); additionally, there is usually a larger screen built into back of the camera. The LCD image will not seem strange to those used to using a video camera, but to photographers, it will appear coarse, with unnatural colors. The advantage of the EVF is that it keeps the camera relatively compact. Another

Functionality and quality
Certain designs have evolved to highly refined standards in the years since affordable digital cameras first hit the mass market. On this model, every feature is tried and tested, offering superb functionality and image quality. It features a 28–100-mm zoom, an 8-megapixel chip, a 2½-in (6.3-cm) LCD monitor, and much more.

Feature-packed bridge
Many bridge cameras look larger than they are in reality; yet, despite their compact dimensions, they can pack a 9-megapixel sensor with wide-angle to very long focal length zoom (28–300 mm in some cases), an extensive ISO range of 80–1600, an LCD screen, and a 640 x 480-pixel movie mode.

advantage of the bridge form is that the fixed lens ensures no dust gets onto the sensor.

Bridge cameras often feature zoom lenses with very large ranges—focal lengths may reach 420 mm. To make the most of these focal lengths, it is helpful if the camera offers optical image stabilization, which reduces unsharpness caused by camera shake. However, the wide-angle end of the zoom is often limited to 35 mm equivalent; for wider views, you will need to fit a wide-angle converter—usually a rather bulky optic.

dSLR cameras

Prosumer digital SLR cameras are smaller, lighter, and generally have lower pixel counts than their professional equivalents. However, their imaging abilities mean they are likely to sustain an experienced photographer through to a professional level. In fact, professionals often use these cameras as backups. Cameras by some manufacturers allow you to use relatively ancient lenses with the appropriate mounts, although there may be limitations with exposure modes or autofocusing.

Digital SLR

Some fully interchangeable SLR cameras are significantly smaller than bridge cameras with fixed lenses. Models such as this offer good image quality with APS-sized chips of 6 megapixels, rapid response, and the versatility available only to cameras with interchangeable lens mounts.

Hot-shoe mounts accept the fitting of supplementary flash.

Many buttons and dials on dSLRs do similar jobs to those on film SLRs.

Interchangeable lenses give the best versatility.

Sensor size and field of view

Sensor area	Projected image

A camera lens projects a circular image. The sensor or film captures a relatively small rectangular area at the center of this projected field of view. If the rectangle extends to the edge of this circle of light, the sensor is able to capture the full field of view. If the rectangle falls short of this, then the field of view is reduced. Many dSLR cameras of the type that accept conventional 35 mm format lenses use small sensors—thus, the field of view available to the sensor is reduced. As a result the 35efl (35 mm equivalent focal length) is multiplied: in other words, the field of view is equivalent to that of a lens with a longer focal length. For example, on the Nikon D1, focal length is increased by about 50 percent compared with the 35 mm format coverage; while the Contax, with its large sensor, does not increase effective focal length at all.

35 mm film area

Context is key
This view of the Taj Mahal, taken with
a 24–28-mm lens, places it in context,
rather than making it dominant. The
natural light fall-off darkens the corners,
~ulling the composition into shape.

Memory cards

Rather than moving parts, memory cards have banks of memory registers that hold their state—on or off—without needing power, yet are easily changed. When an image is written to them, the registers are rapidly flipped on or off according to the data they must hold. To read off the memory, the registers are turned into a stream of data bits. Modern cards hold vast amounts of information and can read or write very rapidly.

For a time, it seemed that there would be just three types of digital-image memory cards. Unfortunately, there are now several systems all vying for pole position. For the photographer, the main consideration is compatibility between personal equipment: if you own only one camera, there is no problem: you can download images directly to your computer. But as soon as you have another camera or you want to use another device, you must ensure compatibility. In this respect, the most versatile memory card is the CompactFlash. But cards from other manufacturers promise higher transfer rates, or better capacity, economy, or size.

All cards have to be slotted into the camera so that recorded images can be saved onto them. The first time you use one, it may have to be formatted (structured to receive data) by the camera. Unlike film, you can remove the card at any stage before it is full and slot it into a reader to transfer files to a computer. You can also erase images at any time to make room for more. However, do not try to remove the card while the camera or reader is accessing it: wait for the lights indicating card activity to go out before removing the card.

CompactFlash

This is the most widely used and available memory card, with a choice of card readers and a variety of capacities to suit different budgets. Capacities range from 8 MB to at least 2 GB—with the best-value cards being those offering 128–256 MB capacity. Some types offer faster operational speeds: this is worthwhile for improving camera response.

Secure Digital and MultiMedia cards

One of the newest standards, Secure Digital is based on the MultiMedia card: it combines very small size with the promise of large capacities (at least 2 GB), yet with low draw on current. They are also sturdy, both electrostatically and physically, and are in increasingly widespread use for a range of electronic equipment. The cards feature a mechanism to prevent accidental writing or erasure.

Memory card slots in behind a dust cover

Using the memory card

Memory cards are easily replaced in a camera, but do not try to change cards when the camera is reading from or writing to the card—usually, a light warns you when the card is in use.

Card care

- Keep memory cards well away from magnetic fields, such as magnets, television monitors, audio speakers, and so on.
- Keep cards cool: do not leave them in a car on a hot day or lying around in bright sunshine.
- Keep cards dry: do not take them out into warm, humid conditions immediately after coming out of an air-conditioned room, for example.

- Insert memory cards into cameras or card readers gently. Too much force may damage the contacts.
- Keep memory cards dust-free: the contacts are extremely fine and can easily be damaged by small particles of dirt or grit. In sandy or dusty conditions, do not remove a card from the camera unless you are safely sealed inside a tent or car.
- Keep cards in protective cases when not in use.

xD-Picture Card

These are some of the fastest-working cards for digital photography, with capacities protected to an astonishing 8 GB. Despite these features, power consumption is low, robustness and reliability are very good, and the price of average-sized units (128 MB) is comparable to that of other cards.

Microdrive

This is an ultra-miniature hard disk drive that fits into CompactFlash type II slots. It is used in professional-quality digital cameras because it is relatively robust, fast, and offers very high capacities, from 170 MB to 8 GB, with good economy.

MemoryStick, and MemoryStick Duo

Introduced by Sony, this format is used on a variety of digital equipment, including Sony video cameras, thus allowing interchange. But independent card readers are scarce, and compatibility with other makes of digital camera is poor. Capacities of the Pro version may reach as much as 2 GB. The smaller Duo format was created for use in compact and mobile devices.

Memory card readers

There are two ways of transferring images taken on your digital camera. First, you can connect the camera to your computer and instruct the camera's software to download images. Second, you can take the memory card out of the camera and read it to the computer. To do this, you need a memory card reader, a device with circuitry to take the data and send it to the computer, usually via a USB cable (though some use a FireWire interface).

The card reader you buy needs to be compatible with the type of card that your camera uses, and there are many types available. However, there are now many models of card readers on the market that can read several different types of memory cards.

Multitype card reader

Using a reader

When slotted in, the reader opens the card as a volume or disk. You can then copy images straight into the computer.

CompactFlash card reader

Choosing a scanner

Today's scanners are so powerful and capable that professional-quality results are achievable even by those on a fairly modest budget.

Flatbed scanners

Flatbed scanners work somewhat like photocopiers: you place an original print face down on the glass and a sensor runs the length of the original to make the scan. If your print is large enough and good enough, even inexpensive scanners can produce publication-quality images. These scanners can also be used as a type of close-up camera for taking images of flat subjects at full size or high magnification.

Flatbed scanners can be adapted for transparent originals using a transparency adapter (*see right*). Check that the adapter is supplied with the scanner, since a separate one can be expensive.

If you plan to scan flat originals of about letter size, an entry-level scanner offering resolutions in the region of 600 ppi (points per inch)—often quoted as 600 dpi (dots per inch)—will be fine.

For scanning artwork up to tabloid size, you will need a tabloid-size scanner, which is far more costly. Scanning a large original in sections and blending the parts is not recommended with entry-level machines: unevenness around the edges is likely to make a poor match.

Well-known manufacturers offer machines that cater to a range of needs, from the home-office worker upward. In general, it is true that the more you pay, the better performance you can expect—in terms of mechanical operation, reliability, and quality of software interface.

Transparency adapters

Should you need to scan medium- or large-format films, you need a scanner with a transparency adapter. This is simply a light source that shines light through the transparency or film onto the scanner's sensor. The area for scanning transparencies is almost always smaller than that for artworks or prints, which are scanned by reflected light. Many scanners use a light panel something like a light-box; others a light that traverses the length of the glass platen. Yet others use a sliding tray arrangement.

Transparencies require a higher scan resolution than prints. So-called repro-quality scanners offer resolutions of at least 1,200 ppi in one direction, and their maximum density ratings should equal or exceed 3.5.

Buttons to launch applications and initiate scanning make the machine easy to use.

Easy, quick, reliable
Typical of numerous flatbed scanners, this model produces excellent results from prints, is easy and quick to operate, and is reliable.

Specialist film scanners

For the digital photographer, a specialty film scanner represents the best balance of features and quality. Modern film scanners can provide excellent-quality results at a very reasonable cost.

The principal manufacturers all offer film scanners capable of producing results that, with a little work, are suitable for professional use.

Most scanners accept 35 mm both as cut film strips and mounted transparencies, using film carriers or slide holders that are inserted into a slot on the front of the machine. For the medium-format, all scanners accept cut film strips but some also accept mounted transparencies. Some scanners are available with an adapter suitable for APS (Advanced Photo System) film cartridges.

Points to consider

Resolution Choose a machine that offers an optical resolution of at least 2,700 ppi (points per inch). This will create files around 20 MB in size, which should be enough for fair-quality tabloid inkjet prints or for magazine reproduction up to about letter size.

Maximum density Look for a machine offering a maximum density of at least 3.6—this will allow you to scan color transparencies to fair quality.

Quality of film carriers Some carriers are flimsy, and you may find others awkward to use.

Film formats An APS adapter is usually an extra cost. For a panoramic format 35 mm, you are likely to need a medium-format scanner. These offer up to eight film carriers but many will be optional items at extra cost.

Driver interface On many scanners, you have no choice but to use the manufacturer's, and some are far easier to use than others. VueScan scanner drivers work with many machines and may be superior to the manufacturer's own.

Oversampling Some scanners can sample an original more than once, combining information so that differences are averaged. This has the effect of keeping genuine, repeatable information—and because unwanted data or noise is random, oversampling strips out image-degrading artifacts.

Computer connection The best option is FireWire (which is also known as IEEE 1394 or iLink). USB is a low-cost option, while USB 2 is faster; SCSI is used by older equipment.

Easy connectivity

This modern desktop film scanner offers remarkably good optical performance—sufficient for many professional tasks, as well as convenient features and easy connection to the computer.

A spring-loaded door accepts film and slide carriers while keeping dust out. It also accepts adapters for APS film.

Choosing software

It is likely that all the software you need to make a start in digital photography will be provided with the digital camera, scanner, or computer that you purchase. In addition to the utility software that enables your computer to "talk to" and control the digital camera or scanner, you will need an image-manipulation application. The best known and by far the most widely used is Adobe Photoshop. But that does not mean you must have it: many digital photographers do a great deal of satisfying work using much less costly, easier-to-learn software.

Beginners' software

Entry-level image editors are all easy to use. For PC only, consider Ulead PhotoImpact or Roxio PhotoSuite, both of which offer many features at a very low cost, while Corel Paint Shop Pro has a very good suite of features that are broadly easy to use, although costing slightly more than PhotoImpact or PhotoSuite. For Mac, Adobe Photoshop Elements is easy to use and offers a feature set that will take you a long way; it also provides a good place from which to progress to the complexities of Photoshop. This group of applications offers not only image-manipulation features but also gives help with projects such as creating albums, calendars, and websites.

Adobe Photoshop

The most costly of widely available digital photography software, Photoshop is one of the most powerful software applications on the planet—let alone for digital photography. Its range of features is so extensive and powerful that

Adobe Photoshop
While Photoshop is not easy to use, it offers unrivaled manipulation of layers and masks. Its plus points far outweigh its few limitations, which is why the application remains highly recommended.

Checklist

When purchasing software, particularly the professional applications with more advanced feature sets, you should check the following:

Operating system required If you do not have the latest computer, check that your version of the operating system—for example, Mac OS 9.1 or Windows 98—will run the software.

Minimum RAM Check how much RAM the software needs to run efficiently. One advantage of entry-level software is its modest demands for RAM.

Minimum hard disk space Check how much hard disk space the software needs. In addition to the space for the software itself, it will need space to store temporary working files—the larger your files, the greater the space needed.

Additionally, you will need at least a CD reader to install files, but some software is delivered on DVDs. An Internet connection may be needed to unlock or register software and to download updates or fixes.

not even the busiest professionals could say they regularly use, and are familiar with, all of the tools and controls. Ease of use is not the first quality that Photoshop is noted for. However, what experienced users most appreciate is the ease with which Photoshop can be customized, so that working with its numerous features can be highly streamlined and efficient.

The power of Photoshop is also greatly increased by the numerous software plug-ins that are available for it. These can extend its every feature—from specialized saving of JPEG files, to lens-distortion correction, and an almost infinite number of filter effects. Its ability to manipulate numerous layers and masks is also unrivaled by any software. As a result, despite limitations that remain unimproved after many revisions, such as limited brushes and tonal controls, Photoshop continues to top any recommendation list.

Beware that Photoshop, like any other image editor, benefits from having access to ample amounts of RAM (*see above*).

Other image editors

Corel Painter for Mac and PC offers many paintlike effects together with image-editing tools, some of which are more powerful than those in Photoshop. Corel PhotoPaint is part of a suite of graphics software and offers very good power for the money. Equilibrium DeBabelizer is designed for image processing in batches, and its tools for making global changes to an image are extremely powerful. Finally, Binuscan PhotoRetouch can apply changes such as contrast or levels through precisely localized brushes; the DigiCam version is a cut-down, lower-cost option worth exploring.

Corel Painter IX
This application can be used to create paintlike effects on both PC and Mac computers.

Digital asset management

When you build up a collection of more than a few hundred images, you will be very grateful for software that helps you organize it by presenting each folder's contents as a series of thumbnail images. You will also be able to add captions, including camera details. Some will help you build webpages, too. The fastest and easiest to use is Camerabits Photo Mechanic; while Extensis Portfolio and FotoWare FotoStation are large and powerful, they are fairly costly and much slower than Photo Mechanic. All work in Windows XP and Mac OS X. Lower-cost options include ACDSee, Adobe Album, and Corel Photo Album (PC only).

Raw file conversion

Photographers looking for the utmost quality from their images will record in their camera's raw format (*see p. 87*), which then needs to be converted to a standard such as TIFF or JPEG. Camera manufacturers provide their own raw converters, but these are often poorly written. One of the most highly regarded is that found in Adobe Photoshop. There are also raw converters in Photoshop Elements and Paint Shop Pro. Capture One from Phase One (PC and Mac) is a standalone converter that produces excellent images, but it is not the easiest to use. Other converters include Bibble (PC and Mac), BreezeBrowser, and RawShooter (PC only).

Plug-in applications

Plug-ins are programs in their own right, but they make use of another application's core program, or "engine." Photoshop comes with many of its own. PhotoTools from Extensis is exceptional in adding a good range of tools, including convenient buttons to supplement the standard menu. Another popular Extensis plug-in is Intellihance, used for making quick, overall image improvements. The most popular plug-ins are those that produce special effects such as sunbursts, metallic and beveled text, blurs, and so on. Corel KPT and Alien Skin offer a wide range of effects—between them, more than anyone would ever need.

Installing software

It is easy to choose which software will be most useful to you, since you can easily find demo or trial versions—for example, in books on Photoshop and on the Web—that you can experiment with before you buy. To avoid problems that often occur with newly installed software, follow these tips.

● Read the instructions—you may have to install items in a specific order or make sure a system file is up to date before the software works properly.

● Turn off virus protection.

● Always install via the installer or install shield program: to do otherwise may make it very difficult to uninstall correctly.

● If the software does not work properly, it may be easiest simply to reinstall from scratch—existing files belonging to the software will be overwritten.

● If the computer crashes when you first run the software, there may be a conflict. Try starting the software with no other software running. Check the "Read Me" files or the manufacturer's website.

Printers: Choosing and using

Digital printers place inks or pigments at precisely determined points on a substrate, such as paper or cardboard. The dominant printer technologies in use are the inkjet and the laser; other types, such as dye-sublimation, are far less common.

Inkjet printers

Modern inkjet printers produce excellent print quality at low prices. They work by squirting minute quantities of ink onto the substrate. They are generally reliable, and most are easy to use. The only downside is the cost of inks and good-

quality paper. However, while the inkjet is the dominant technology, it is not the only one. When near-photographic quality is required, there are dye-sublimation printers, and for graphics-heavy pages, the color laser is more suitable. Features to consider in an inkjet printer include:

Paper handling Some printers detect paper size and make settings to suit. Others take a large range of papers, from ordinary weight to cardboard. Some models also accept paper on a roll, allowing small posters to be printed (*see pp. 180–1*).

Inkjet printer
Typical of modern inkjet printers, this model takes a variety of papers on a nearly straight paper path and is simple to use, but good prints need several minutes to output.

Being able to change ink tanks separately is an economic arrangement.

A paper-thickness-adjustment control is a useful feature.

Checking printer output

Today's desktop printers can outperform the quality of many digital cameras. But to ensure that you produce the best possible image, color settings have to be correctly made (*see pp. 176–9*).

● Examine closely any areas of very dark tones in your test print: do the dots of color appear to run together into uneven clumps or puddles? If so, the paper is unsuitable. Produce another test print on better-quality paper (*see pp. 180–1*).

● Examine any large areas of even midtones, such as blue sky or evenly painted walls. Do they appear banded (as if painted in strips with tiny gaps between) or uneven in any way? If so, reject the print.

● Examine closely any small areas of what should be smooth, even transitions in tone, such as the side of a face falling into shadow or the bodywork of a car. Do they look mottled or banded? If so, reject the print.
See pp. 182–3 for help with printing problems.

Resolution In general, higher-resolution printers deliver better-quality results, but the issue is not simply about resolution. The difference between 2,000 dpi (dots per inch) and 2,880 dpi is of no practical significance: the precise way in which the printer software uses the dots available is far more important (*see right*). Looking at results when comparing printer quality is better than reading technical specifications.

Four or six inks In general, printers using six colors for printing are more likely to produce photographic quality than those using only four.

Separate ink cartridges Most desktop printers keep all color inks in an integrated cartridge (the black is usually separate), so you have to change the cartridge when the cyan has run out even if there is still plenty of magenta and yellow. Choose printers with separate tanks for each color.

Printers with card readers This is convenient for basic proof-printing—to check the quality of images from a shoot—or if you repeatedly need to make prints to order, since you can store prepared files on a card and print them off as needed.

Laser printers

These printers work on the same principle as photocopiers: electrical charges on the surface of a drum alter according to the light falling on it. The drum picks up toner or not, according to the pattern of the charge, and deposits the toner onto the paper. The toner is then fused onto the paper by heat and pressure. However, where laser printers differ from copiers is in the fact that the charge is built up dot by dot and line by line. A laser beam reflects off a mirror that spins around: as it turns, the beam of light scans across the drum. By rapidly turning the laser on and off, a series of dots is applied to the drum. Color printers use colored toners to build up the image, usually one at a time, so a full print needs four passes. Laser printers are useful for rough proofing and good-quality text output.

Halftone cells

Printers can lay more than 2,000 dots of ink per inch (dpi) but since no printer can change the strength of the ink and not all can vary dot size, not all dots are available for defining detail. Thus, printers use groupings of dots—halftone cells—to simulate a grayscale. At least 200 gray levels are needed to represent continuous tone. Therefore, a printer must control a large number of ink dots just to represent gray levels, reducing the detail that can be printed. In practice, detail resolution above 100 dpi meets most requirements. Now, if a printer can lay 1,400 dpi, it has some 14 dots to use for creating the effect of continuous tone. If you multiply together the four or more inks used, a good range of tones and colors are possible.

Filling in cells
Each cell accepts up to 16 dots—counting a cell with no dot, 17 grayscale levels are thus possible. Cells should be randomly filled. Here, they have a regular pattern, so when cells are combined a larger pattern emerges. The device resolution is used to place more dots in each cell.

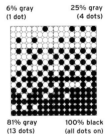

6% gray (1 dot) 25% gray (4 dots)

81% gray (13 dots) 100% black (all dots on)

Multipurpose laser
For a small business or home office, a laser machine that can print, scan, fax, and copy—all in one unit—is an economical, space-saving solution. However, be aware that a serious breakdown will leave you with all functions out of order.

Computers: Choosing and using

The serious digital photographer will spend at least as much time at the computer as actually out and about taking pictures. The computer has, in effect, replaced the darkroom. For most users, how a computer works is irrelevant to obtaining results. But remember: the computer is only as good as the instructions given to it.

What to look for in a computer

All Apple Mac computer models G3 and higher are capable of digital photography work, but they may need extra RAM. All Windows machines with Pentium series chips and higher are also suitable but are also likely to need a boost in RAM. You should consider 256 MB to be the minimum.

However, less-obvious features, such as the quality of the mouse and keyboard, can also make a significant difference to your enjoyment and comfort. If the keyboard action is not to your liking or if you find the mouse uncomfortable, then do not hesitate to change it: these replacement accessories are inexpensive, and if you ask for the exchange at the time of purchase they may be even cheaper.

Desktop computer
Modern computers at their best combine style with tremendous computing power. Despite its very compact form, this iMac is capable of professional-quality image manipulation, as well as video and music editing.

Built-in webcam

Slot-loading CD drive

LCD screen

Casing contains everything—no separate hard-drive "tower" is required

iMac ports
Your computer should offer at least two FireWire (IEEE 1394) ports, two USB ports, and Ethernet for networking.

Apple iMac

Stand with tilt adjustment

Computer care

Computers are usually built to run continuously for years in an office and so they should be very reliable when used in a domestic environment: most problems have to do with the software. You can safeguard your computer's useful life by following some simple rules:
- Connect your computer to a surge-protected power supply or power strip.
- Do not jolt or attempt to move the computer when it is working.
- Ground yourself before opening the computer and touching any internal part, or before picking up a component for installation. A grounding strap that attaches to your wrist is readily available.
- Once a year, open the computer and carefully vacuum away the accumulated dust—usually worse on the cooling fans and around the drives.
- Use virus-checking software and keep them up-dated, particularly if you are a Windows user.
- Keep ample free space at the back of the computer for the air to circulate and keep the machine cool.

Software packages

When budgeting, do not forget software costs. A full suite of software for image manipulation as well as desktop and Web publishing can cost more than a computer, so use modest applications until your skills develop. Professional software can be very hard to master, while simpler, cheaper packages still produce good results (*see pp. 24–5*).

Computer interfaces

When buying a computer, make sure its interfaces match those of the equipment you wish to use. Note that you may need to install some software to make a connector work.
• Universal Serial Bus (USB) is easy to install and use, with data-transmission speeds adequate for printers, removable drives, and digital cameras. USB 2 is faster but generally not as fast as FireWire.
• FireWire (IEEE 1394), also known as iLink, is a high-speed standard suitable for professional work. It offers an excellent choice for removable drives, extra hard disks, and digital cameras.
• Small Computer Systems Interface (SCSI) is generally used by older equipment.

Laptop or desktop?

Modern laptops have more than enough power for digital photography. Some, like the Apple laptops, are not only more powerful than most desktop types, the screen is of sufficient quality and large enough for serious work. Against the premium cost of miniaturizing is the convenience of a computer that takes up no more desk space than an open magazine.

Laptop computer
Laptops running Windows software are very numerous and similar to each other. Modern examples, such as this, are perfectly capable of image manipulation.

Mac versus PC

The first question for anyone wishing to buy a computer is "Do I buy a PC or a Mac?" In fact, you can work for your entire life on one machine or the other without being aware of any substantial differences between them. It is easy and natural to compensate for features that you find awkward, and you will naturally make full use of features that suit you. There is no single difference between PC-compatibles and Apple Macs that makes for a clear choice. Modern computers, if well built, are very reliable and perform extremely well. Modern operating systems are superbly powerful and generally highly stable, with few of the crashes that used to be part of the computing experience.

However, independent market surveys have shown that workers on Apple Macs are more productive and profitable, possibly because the design of the interface allows smoother workflows. Added to these factors is

the Mac's relative immunity to virus attacks. In the first two years of Mac OS X, there were no reported viruses, and it attracted only a fraction of a percent of hacking attacks—during the same period, there were literally thousands of viruses and attacks on Windows machines. Apple Macs seem to accept new peripherals such as cameras, scanners, or drives with more ease than do Windows machines. And if you wish to create a network, Macs of nearly any vintage will network within seconds of being connected.

Another advantage of the Mac is that it can easily read Windows disks. (With special software such as Virtual PC, a Mac can even run some Windows programs, though this is not recommended for graphics-intensive applications or games.) While nearly everyone in the world uses a PC-compatible machine, most creative people producing content for webpages, magazines, photography, books, and advertising are Mac users.

Computer accessories

As your expertise in digital photography increases, you may wish to invest in accessories that will make life easier and increase your enjoyment.

Graphics tablets

These input devices are an evolutionary step up from the mouse. Comprising a flat tablet, like a solid mouse mat, and a penlike stylus, graphics tablets give you excellent control over hand-drawn lines because of their high spatial resolution—that is, they can detect tiny changes in position. They also allow you to increase the width of a line or the depth of a color by varying the pressure of the stroke—something that is impossible to do with a mouse. A tablet can be small, about the size of a mouse mat, or large enough to need a desk to itself. It is good practice to alternate the use of graphics tablet and mouse to help avoid repetitive strain injuries—for example, by using the graphics tablet for image manipulation and the mouse for the Internet and word processing.

Removable media

Digital photography produces huge amounts of data, and removable media provide the essential storage space you need. In general, the bigger the capacity, the cheaper it is per megabyte of data. The smallest you should work with is the 100 MB or 250 MB Zip disk: these are inexpensive, and the 100 MB size is very widely used by both Mac and Windows owners. However, for digital images, even the 250 MB disk is limited in capacity.

Although not strictly removable media, portable hard disk drives are, all around, the best solution for the digital photographer. Not only are their capacities ample for most workers—offering from 40 GB to 120 GB—they are also cost-effective. Models of about the size of electronic personal organizers are extremely portable and ideal for working on location with a laptop computer, since they can be powered from the laptop. Larger, desktop hard disk drives are the fastest and can offer capacities up to 500 GB, yet—at the size and weight of this book—are still relatively portable; however, this type does need an AC power supply.

DVD-RAM technology offers remarkable capacities for the lowest cost: a disk holding 9 GB of data (9.4 GB nominally) will cost less than three DVD movies. The disadvantage is that reading and writing speeds are relatively slow. The best choice of all are the DVD-RAM drives that can also write CDs. DVD-R disks can be written to only once.

Graphics tablet
Graphic tablets come in a range of sizes—starting with models smaller than a mouse mat—to suit different ways of working. Large sizes can take up the entire desk area. The pen and mouse tools also cover a range, from simple devices to those sporting several buttons to access various functions.

Portable drives
Small portable hard disk drives are lightweight and offer a surprisingly high capacity for backups. Additionally, most can be powered from your laptop via its USB or FireWire port. This makes them ideal for location work, since you won't need to track down a power outlet.

Compact discs (CDs)

The best option for exchanging files with other people is the CD. It holds up to 700 MB of data, and once written, the content on it cannot be changed. Rewritable CDs (CD-RW) are also available: these can be written, erased, and rewritten many times; however, inconvenience and compatibility concerns mean that this is not a recommended option. CD writers are relatively inexpensive accessories, although many new computers now have them built in as standard.

CD writers with the fastest write speeds do not cost much more than slower writers—a 52x write speed is not unusual—and they will save you time in the long run. So-called "burn-proof" writers are more reliable at writing disks than those without this feature. Also, there is evidence that gold-plated discs are more reliable than dye-impregnated ones, which appear bluish on the writing side.

UPS, surge protectors, adapters, and cables

Computer systems are highly susceptible to even very small fluctuations in the amount of electrical current powering them. Because of this, you may want to consider protecting your equipment from power surges and outages—something that is even more worthwhile if you live in areas with uncertain power supplies. Saving your work frequently as you go ensures that, if the worst happens and your machine does crash, then at least not too much of it will be lost. However, apart from the frustration and wasted time involved in restarting your computer, an uncontrolled shut-down does carry with it the risk of damage to your hard drive. To safeguard against this, an uninterruptible power supply (UPS) is essential, although it can be expensive to buy. This is a battery that powers the computer and monitor for a short period in case of a power loss, giving you time to quit the application and shut the computer down safely.

Another useful piece of equipment is a surge protector, which prevents sudden rises in power from damaging your delicate equipment. This is well worth its relatively low cost.

Other accessories that you will accumulate are cables to connect devices to your computer and to each other, and adapters that allow older equipment, such as those based on SCSI, to be used with newer systems, such as FireWire.

USB peripheral port and connector

USB computer port and connector

Parallel printer port and connector

SCSI computer port and connector

Adapters

You can adapt SCSI to FireWire or USB, serial to parallel, and so on. Most incompatibilities with equipment can be resolved with an adapter, though conflicts with other devices may result.

USB ports

USB (Universal Serial Bus) is a widespread protocol allowing devices to be plugged straight into a working computer and be recognized and connected.

Parallel ports

Connectors that use parallel technology are complicated and can be less reliable than other fittings. As a result, their use is in decline.

SCSI ports

The SCSI interface is an older type of connection that used to be seen on professional-grade scanners and studio digital cameras.

Setting up a workroom

A workroom for digital photography has the huge advantage over the traditional darkroom used by film-based photographers in that it does not need to be light-tight—any spare room, or just a corner, is suitable. Nor are chemicals, trays, timers, safelights, or running water required.

The ideal environment

The key requirement of a digital workroom is comfort: you are likely to be spending long hours sitting in the same position, so don't allow the computer to become a source of ill health. Take note of the following points:

• Ventilation should be adequate to dissipate the heat produced by the computer and monitor during hot weather.

• You should be able to subdue the lighting with heavy curtains or blinds to help screen contrast.

• There should be sufficient electrical outlets for your equipment needs.

• The desks you work on should be stable and capable of taking the heavy, static weight of a large monitor without wobbling.

• The desk/chair should be at the correct height so that, when seated, your forearms are horizontal or inclined slightly down when at the keyboard.

• There should be ample space underneath the desk for your legs.

• The chair should support your back and legs.

• Arrange desk lamps so they do not shine onto the monitor screen. Some lamps are especially designed for computer use, illuminating the desk without spilling light onto the screen.

• Keep an area free for drinks and food. Make sure anything spillable is kept well away from electrical equipment or disks.

• Arrange the monitor so the top of the screen is about level with your eyes, or slightly higher.

• Your monitor's screen should not face any light source, such as a window or a lamp.

• You can make a hood at least 8 in (20 cm) deep from black cardboard to block unwanted light from reaching the screen and degrading the image.

• Arrange a picture-editing area, containing a lightbox and your files, away from the computer and monitor.

The digital photographer's desk
The ideal desk area has all the equipment within easy reach. The arrangement of equipment will vary, depending on precisely what you are doing and your own preferences, but everything should be conveniently close to hand. It is a good idea to locate the monitor in the middle, preferably in the inside corner of an L-shaped or curved desk.

Laptop computer

Printer

Slide scanner

Removable drives

Monitor

CD burner

Zip drive

Keyboard

• Be sure you have safe storage for data files—any magnetic-based media, such as Zip, Compact-Flash, and so on, should be stored at least 12 in (30 cm) away from the strong magnetic fields produced by monitors, speakers, and electric motors. In addition, keep magnetic media away from direct sunlight and other heat sources.

Electrical arrangements

Most computer peripherals draw low current at low voltages compared with domestic appliances. This is fortunate, since the peripherals for even a modest workroom could easily sprout a dozen power cords:

• If you are in any doubt about electrical safety, seek advice from a qualified inspector.

• Never overload extension cords—check the label for the maximum load.

• Don't stretch cords across walkways.

• Don't plug a device into a computer or a peripheral that is switched on unless you know it is safe to do so. Even then, never unplug a device that is halfway through an operation.

Avoiding injury

It is unlikely that you will work the long hours at high levels of stress that lead to repetitive strain injury, but you should still take precautions:

• At least every hour, get up and walk around and take a few minutes away from the screen.

• After two hours in front of the screen, take a longer break—stretch your limbs and look out the window at distant objects to exercise your eyes.

• Listen to your body: if something starts to ache or is uncomfortable, it is time to make adjustments or to take a break.

• Keep your equipment clean and well maintained—sticky mouse rollers or a streaky or dirty monitor screen or keyboard can all add, in more or less subtle ways, to stress levels.

• Install software that times how long you have been working and blanks the screen at regular intervals—say, every 15 minutes—to encourage you to take a short rest of 10 seconds or so. Every hour, it suggests you take an even longer rest.

Computer

Desk lamp turned away from monitor

CDs

Backup disks

Flatbed scanner

Mouse

Graphics tablet

Lightbox and slide viewer

Photography for the digital age

2

Picture composition

Much of the advice found in specialty photographic books and magazines concerning picture composition is often treated in a very proscriptive fashion—as if the adherence to a few "rules" can somehow bring about satisfactory outcomes. It may be better to think of any rules simply as a distillation of ideas about features that photographers—and, of course, painters and other artists in the centuries before the invention of the camera—have found useful in making pleasing pictures.

Any photographic composition can be said to work if the arrangement of the subject elements communicates effectively with the image's intended viewers. Often, the most effective way to achieve a striking composition is to look for the key ingredients of a scene and then organize your camera position and exposure controls to draw those elements out from the clutter of visual information that is the ruin of many photographs.

If you are new to photography, it may help to concentrate your attention on the scene's general structure, rather than concentrating too hard on very specific details—these are sometimes only of superficial importance to the overall composition.

Symmetry
Symmetrical compositions are said to signify solidity, stability, and strength; they are also effective for organizing images containing elaborate detail. Yet another strategy offered by a symmetrical presentation of subject elements is simplicity. In this portrait of a Turkana man, there was no other way to record the scene that would have worked as well. The figure was placed centrally because nothing in the image justified any other placement; likewise with the nearly central horizon. The subject's walking stick provides the essential counterpoint that prevents the image from appearing too contrived.

Radial
Radial compositions are those in which key elements spread outward from the middle of the frame. This imparts a lively feeling, even if subjects are static. However, in this family portrait, taken in Mexico, the radial composition is consistent with the tension caused by the presence of a stranger (the photographer), combined with the transfixing heat. The composition suggests that a modest wide-angle lens was used; in fact, it was taken with a standard focal length.

Diagonal

Diagonal lines lead the eye from one part of an image to another and impart far more energy than horizontals. In this example, it is not only the curve of the palm's trunk, but also the movement of the boy and his dog along it that encourage the viewer to scan the entire picture, sweeping naturally from the strongly backlit bottom left-hand corner to the top right of the frame.

Overlapping

Overlapping subject elements not only indicate increasing depth perspective, they also invite the viewer to observe subject contrasts. In the first instance, distance is indicated simply because one object can overlap another only if it is in front of it. In the second, the overlap forces two or more items, known to be separated by distance, to be perceived together, with any contrasts in shape, tone, or color, made apparent as a result. In this example, shot in Spain, overlapping architectural elements jostle for dominance.

The golden spiral, or "Rule of Thirds"

This image, overlaid with a golden spiral—a spiral based on the golden ratio—as well as with a grid dividing the picture area into thirds, shows that, as photographers, we almost instinctively compose to fit these harmonious proportions—the proportions that "look good."

Tall crop

The opposite of a letterbox composition (*right*) is a tall and narrow crop, which emphasizes an upward-sweeping panorama—a view that can be taken in only by lifting the head and looking up. As with all crops based on a high aspect ratio, it usefully removes a lot of unwanted detail around the edges.

Letterbox composition

A wide and narrow letterbox framing perfectly suits some subjects, such as these prayer flags in Bhutan. Such a crop concentrates the attention on the sweep of colors and detail, cutting out unwanted—and visually irrelevant—material at the top and bottom of the image.

Picture composition continued

Framing

The frame within a frame is a painterly device often exploited in photography. Not only does it concentrate the viewer's attention on the subject, it often hints at the wider context of the subject's setting. The colors of the frame may also give clues about where the photograph is set. In this portrait, the colors of the painted wood suggest Central or South America, while the structure of the building and the subject himself lead you to expect the unexpected. In fact, the house is in an "African" village built in Mexico populated by descendants of escaped African slaves.

Geometric patterns

Geometrical shapes, such as triangles and rectangles, lend themselves to photographic composition because of the way they interact with the rectangle of the picture frame. Here, in this shuttered store in Spain, shapes from squares to thin rectangles and narrow triangles are all at work. In parts, they are working harmoniously (the gaps between the shutters); in others (the thin wedges created by the sloping road), they create tension in the composition.

Irregular pattern

The imperfectly regular rows of sacks left out to dry in the hot Mombassa sunshine lead your eye inexorably to the man who has authored the work. Both the pattern and the repetition are obvious, but the more thoughtful photographer learns to work with these elements rather than using them as the actual subject.

TRY THIS

Look out for various types of patterns—squares, circles, triangles, swirls, and so on—whenever you have a camera handy. When you find an interesting example, take several shots, shifting your camera position slightly between exposures. Examine the pictures carefully and you may discover that the shot you thought most promising at the time does not produce the best result. Try to think why this might be the case: often, it is because our response to a scene is an entire experience, while photographs have to work within the limits of the viewfinder and the proportions of the format.

Triangles

The windows of a building reflected in the curved glass of the front of a parked car in Andalucia, southern Spain, appear strongly distorted within the triangle implied by the frame of the windshield itself. The overall shape is not immediately apparent, but it is the framework on which all the elements—the repeated lines and rectangles, for example, and the bands of light and dark—are organized. The triangular shape in composition is most often encountered in scenes where parallel lines seem to converge, such as the sides of a road or the rails of train tracks, as they recede into the distance. In the two-dimensional photographic print or computer monitor image, this is powerfully suggestive of both depth and distance.

Image orientation

Since most camera formats produce rectangular pictures, you can change the way you hold the camera to give either horizontal or vertical results. Image orientation produces different emphases and can alter the whole dynamic of a shot.

Picture shape should normally be dictated by the natural arrangement of subject elements—in other words, by the subject's own orientation. In portraits, for example, the subject will usually be sitting or standing, and so the camera most often is turned on its side to give vertical framing. As a consequence, vertical picture orientation is often called "portrait." Landscapes scenes, however, with their usually horizontal orientation, have given their name to horizontally framed pictures.

Landscape-shaped images tend to emphasize the relationship between subject elements on the left and right of the frame, while portrait-shaped pictures tend to relate foreground and background subject elements. And bear in mind that picture shape strongly influences what is included at the periphery of a scene, so you can use image orientation as a useful cropping device.

Breaking the "rules"

If you decide to move away from these accepted framing conventions, or "rules," you then have an opportunity to express more of an individual vision. Simply by turning the camera on its side you could create a more striking picture—perhaps by increasing the sense of energy and movement inherent in the scene, for example. Using an unconventional picture orientation may, therefore, reveal to the viewer that you are engaging more directly with the subject, rather than merely reacting to it.

Think ahead

Another factor to consider is that since most printed publications are vertical in format, pictures are more likely to be used at full size if they are vertically framed. As a safeguard, commercial photographers often take vertically framed versions of important views or events, even if an image's natural orientation is horizontal.

A potential problem with vertical framing occurs with cameras with swiveling LCD screens. Even if the camera has a viewfinder, if you attach any type of lens accessory, you then have to use the LCD screen exclusively for viewing and framing.

If, however, your images are intended for publication on the Web, bear in mind that the monitor's format is more horizontal in shape, and so appropriately framed images will then be easier to use at full size.

Reclining figure
The strong horizontal lines of both the bench and the metal siding on the wall behind, as well as the elegant, reclining pose of this Fijian woman, all suggest that horizontal framing is appropriate here.

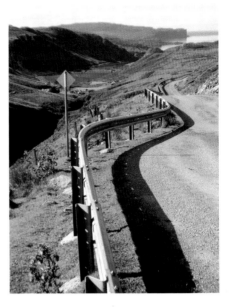

Landscape scenery

A horizontal, or "landscape," view (*above*) is often an obvious choice for a landscape subject. However, vertical, or "portrait," framing (*right*) can effectively suggest space, especially when some natural feature in the scene—the snaking crash barrier in this example—leads the eye right from the foreground through to the background.

Still-life

Different sets of lines that may be contained within a picture can be given additional prominence, depending on the framing you decide to adopt. Horizontal orientation (*above*) allows the strong, diagonally slanting plant stems to make a visual statement, while the vertical image orientation (*right*) makes more of the parallel slats of the blind.

Image proportions

As you take more pictures, you may start to notice that the proportions of an image have a subtle effect on the picture's ability to communicate. A square image, for example, more often than not evokes a sense of stability and balance. However, an image that is just slightly rectangular can communicate a sense of indecision or make subject matter look uncomfortable within its frame. This type of framing is, therefore, best avoided unless you have clear reasons for it.

Panoramas

The "panoramic" picture was popularized most recently by the obsolescent APS (Advanced Photo System) cameras launched in 1996. In reality, this system simply cropped the top and bottom off an ordinary image, changing it into a narrow one, and so it is not a true panoramic image.

Digital cameras, however, can produce true panoramas (in which the camera swings through the scene, from side to side or up and down), so

True panorama
A true panoramic camera uses a swinging lens to project its image onto a curved piece of film. The movement of the lens causes the typical curvature of lines away from the middle of the frame, as you can see in this example taken at an exhibition in a picture gallery.

Horizontal cropping
As you can see, the sofa pattern here competes strongly with the child and her collection of much-loved toys (*left*). A severe crop more clearly defines the image content (*below*).

Vertical cropping
An attractively framed, if conventional, shot of a lake in Scotland (*above*) has been transformed into a sharper, more challenging composition (*right*) simply by cropping it into a narrower, more vertical shape, in imitation of a traditional silk wall hanging.

that the field of view of the image is greater than the field of view of the lens. This is achieved by taking a number of pictures that overlap and "sewing" them together (*see pp. 172–3*).

To achieve best results, pivot the camera around a fixed point, such as a tripod, so that as you rotate the camera the image does not appear to move. To aid you, some digital cameras have a "panorama function," which indicates where the next pictures should be taken by showing you on the LCD screen the previous image as a guide.

Taking time to select just the right view to experiment with pays dividends with panoramic images. For example, you need to be aware that panoramas made up of individual pictures that include subjects positioned close to the camera, or even in the near middle-distance, will show a perspective distortion that makes the scene appear bow-shaped once images are combined.

Exposure is another consideration when taking panoramas. If you swing your camera across a scene, you will see that the exposure settings in the viewfinder readout alter as different areas of light and shade influence the changing picture area. If you were to take your panorama like this, you might find that, say, the foreground area fluctuates between dark and light from frame to frame. To prevent this, take the camera off automatic and set the exposure manually.

Cropping

One of the simplest, and often one of the most effective, changes you can make to image proportions is to crop them—in other words, slicing portions from the sides, top, or bottom of the picture area. This can change the whole emphasis of a shot by, for example, removing unnecessary or unwanted subject matter, or changing the relationship between various subject elements and the borders of the frame. This can turn a mediocre picture into a truly arresting image.

Composition and zooms

Zoom lenses let you change the magnification of an image without switching lenses. Zooms are designed to change the field of view of the lens while keeping the image in focus. When the field of view is widened (to take in more of the subject), the image must be reduced in order to fill the sensor or film area. This is the effect of using a short focal length lens or a wide-angle setting on a zoom. Conversely, when the field of view is narrowed (to take in less of the subject), the image must be magnified, again in order to fill the sensor or film area. This is the effect of using a long focal length lens or a zoom's telephoto setting.

Working with zooms

The best way to use a zoom is to set it to the focal length you feel will produce the approximate effect you are aiming for. This method of working encourages you to think about the scene before ever raising the camera to your eye to compose the shot. It also makes you think ahead of the picture-taking process, rather than zooming in and out of a scene searching for any setting that seems to work. This is not only rather aimless, it is also time-consuming and can lead to missed photographic opportunities.

A professional approach

Many professional photographers use zooms almost as if they were fixed focal length, or prime, lenses, leaving them set to a favorite focal length most of the time. They then use the zoom control only to make fine adjustments to the framing. Zooms really are at their best when used like this—cutting out or taking in a little more of a scene. With a prime lens, you have to move the camera backward or forward to achieve the same effect. Depending on the type of subject you are trying to record, you could leave the zoom toward the wide-angle or telephoto end of its range. On some digital cameras, however, zooms are stepped rather than continuously variable, so they cannot be used for making small adjustments.

Zooms for framing

Zoom lenses come into their own when you find it difficult or time-consuming to change your camera position, since they allow you to introduce variety into what would otherwise be similarly framed images. In this large outdoor performance, one shot was taken at 80 mm (*top*), one at 135 mm (*middle*), and the other at 200 mm (*above*), all from approximately the same camera position.

Zoom movement

Color and movement literally seem to explode out from this photograph of a simple tulip—an effect achieved by reducing the zoom lens's focal length during a long, manually timed exposure. And in order to emphasize the flower's blurred outlines, the image was also slightly defocused before the exposure was made.

Zooms for composition

Zooming from 80 mm (*above left*) to 200 mm (*above right*) produced an intriguing abstract image by allowing patterns of light and dark, color and non-color, to reveal themselves. But as the focal length increases, depth of field also diminishes, so select the lens apertures with care.

POINTS TO CONSIDER

Distortion Most zoom lenses distort the image by making straight lines look curved. This is especially the case at wide-angle settings.

Camera shake At the very long effective focal lengths some digital cameras offer—such as a 35efl of 350 mm—there is a great danger that camera shake during exposure will reduce image quality. Make sure you hold the camera steady, preferably supported or braced, and use a short shutter time.

Lens speed As you set longer focal lengths, the widest available aperture becomes smaller. Even in bright conditions, it may then not be possible to set short shutter times with long focal lengths.

Lens movement Some lenses may take a few seconds to zoom to their maximum or to retract to their minimum settings. Don't be tempted to rush the action by pushing or pulling at the lens.

Digital zooms

The term given to a computer-generated increase in apparent focal length is "digital zoom." Although the lens focal length does not increase, the image continues to be magnified.

It works by taking a central portion of an image and enlarging it to fill the format, using a process called "interpolation"—extra pixels are added, based on existing ones, to pad out the space. This does not add information; indeed, it may even mask it. Clearly, you can obtain the same effect—sometimes even superior effects—by altering the picture using image-manipulation software, and this is very often a better option.

Long focal length settings on a zoom lens come into their own when you want to magnify a small part of a scene: a 35efl of 135 mm is ample for most purposes. This produces the characteristic "telephoto perspective," in which distant objects look compressed, or backgrounds in close-up shots are thrown strongly out of focus.

Nonetheless, many digital cameras now offer the equivalent of focal lengths of 300 mm and more. Some models reduce the effects of camera shake by using image-stabilization technology. Even so, it is worth making every effort to reduce unwanted camera-movement problems at source.

Telephoto perspective
Even a modest telephoto shot of a distant scene depicts well-separated objects as if they are compressed and piled on top of each other. This is because the relative differences in distance within the picture are small when compared with the distance between the subject and the camera. In this photograph, houses that were in fact hundreds of yards apart look squashed together, and depth of field extends throughout the image.

Image stabilization

Technology to reduce the effect of camera shake takes two forms. One uses a motion sensor to control a lens or thin prism that shifts the image to counter camera movement. This form, pioneered by Canon, is most suitable for still images and is available in several of their 35-mm format lenses. Olympus offers image-stabilized digital cameras and it is likely to become standard in more sophisticated, higher-end equipment. The other method analyzes the signals from the sensor and filters out the slight repetitions in image structure typical of camera shake. This system is used mostly in video cameras.

Secondary image / Corrector lens elements

Focal plane recording blurred image

Sharp image at focal plane

Corrector shift

How it works
A blurred secondary image, represented by the dotted lines here, can result if the lens moves while the picture is being exposed (*upper diagram*). A corrector group of lens elements within the lens hangs from a frame, which allows these elements to move at right-angles to the lens axis. Motion sensors tell the frame which way to shift the corrector group to compensate for any movement of the lens (*lower diagram*).

Camera movement

While the accepted wisdom is that you should hold the camera completely steady when taking pictures, so that camera shake does not introduce unwanted movement that might spoil your image, there is a place for pictures that display a thoughtful or creative use of subject blur.

Experimentation

Since the effects of movement are unpredictable, it is essential that you experiment with this technique. They are, in fact, unique, and no other recording medium represents movement in quite the same way. However, in order to produce the occasional winning shot, you must be prepared to make a lot of exposures, and here the digital camera's ability to delete unwanted frames gives it a distinct advantage over film-based cameras.

While taking pictures from a moving vehicle is generally not recommended, it is nevertheless a technique that can produce interesting results. In a fast-moving car or train, for example, even a short shutter time will not be able to prevent motion blur, especially of foreground objects. But you can introduce blur in almost any situation simply by setting a long shutter time—at least ½ sec—and then deliberately moving the camera during the exposure. Another possibility is again to set a long shutter time and then zoom the lens during the exposure. This gives the resulting image a characteristic "explosive" appearance (*see p. 47*).

As a bonus, digitally produced motion-blur images compress to a very high degree with little additional noticeable loss in clarity because of their inherently lower image quality.

Moving camera
The blur produced by taking a photograph from a speeding car streaks and blends the rich evening light in a very evocative and painterly fashion in this example. To the eye at the time of taking, the scene was much darker and less colorful than you can see here. It is always worth taking a chance in photography, since you never know what might come of it.

Digital close-ups

In the past, true close-up photography required specialty equipment and fiddly accessories. However, this situation has entirely changed thanks to the introduction of digital cameras. These cameras work at close-up subject distances as if they were designed for the job.

Digital's ability to handle close-ups is due to two related factors. First, because the sensor chips are small (*see p. 17*), lenses for digital cameras need have only short focal lengths. Second, short- focal-length lenses require little focusing movement in order to bring near subjects into focus. Another factor, applicable to digital cameras with zoom lenses, is that it is relatively easy to design lenses capable of close focusing by moving the internal groups of lens elements.

In addition to lens design, there is another feature common to digital cameras that also helps: the LCD screen. This provides you with a reliable way of framing close-ups with a high degree of accuracy, all without the complex viewing system that allows traditional SLRs to perform so well.

There will be occasions when you need to keep a good distance between yourself and the subject—a nervous dragonfly, perhaps, or a beehive. In such cases, first set the longest focal length on your zoom lens before focusing close up. In these situations, an SLR-type digital camera (one that accepts interchangeable lenses) is ideal, due to the inherent magnification given by the small sensor chip working in conjunction with lenses designed for normal film formats.

Simple subjects
Learning just what to include and what to leave out of a picture is a useful skill to master—not only is the image itself usually stronger for being simpler in visual content, as in the example shown here, but it is also often easier to use it for a range of purposes, such as compositing. Subject movement is always a problem with close-ups, especially plants outdoors, where they can be affected by even the slightest breeze. If you cannot effectively shield the plant from air currents, then set the shortest shutter time possible, consistent with accurate exposure, to freeze any subject movement.

Avoiding highlights
One of the secrets underlying good close-up photography is avoiding unwanted highlights intruding on the image. These usually appear as insignificant out-of-focus bright spots when you frame the shot, but in the final image they can appear far more prominent and be very distracting. To take this shot, I moved slowly around the subject, watching the LCD screen continually, and released the shutter only when the highlights were positioned just as I wanted.

Long close-up
A long-focal-length lens with close-focusing ability allows you to get close to small, nervous subjects, such as this dragonfly, and so obtain a useful image size. In addition, the extremely shallow depth of field with such a lens throws even nearby image elements well out of focus. The central bright spot is in fact a flower.

Safe distance
It was dangerous to get too near this constrictor, so a close-focusing long lens was the best way to obtain good magnification in this case.

Normal close-up
With static or slow-moving subjects, a normal focal length lens used at its macro setting will suffice.

Digital depth of field

On one hand, the closer you approach your subject, the more rapidly depth of field diminishes, at any given lens aperture. On the other, depth of field increases rapidly as focal length decreases. So the question is whether the increase in depth of field with the short focal lengths typical of digital cameras helps make close-up photography easier than with film-based equipment. The calculations are not straightforward, partly because in order for the shorter-focal-length lens to produce a given magnification, it must approach closer to the subject than a longer lens, which works

against the increase in depth of field. Another confusing factor is that digital cameras, with their regular array of relatively large pixels, cannot be treated in the same way as film-based cameras, whose images are based on a random collection of tiny grains of light-sensitive silver. With many digital cameras, you do not have the option of setting apertures at all, and, even when you do, the minimum aperture may be relatively large—say, f/8. Nonetheless, taking all these factors into account, depth of field often appears greater with digital photographic equipment than with conventional cameras.

Staying focused
Subjects viewed in close-up reveal their graphic forms, but you then have a very narrow depth of field. When stopping down to increase this, make sure neither camera nor plant moves during the shot.

Quick fix Image distortion

Anybody whose photography involves taking accurate pictures of buildings or any other prominent architectural, or even some natural, features is likely at some stage to come up against the problems associated with image distortion.

Problem

When using an extreme wide-angle lens, or an accessory lens that produces a "fish-eye" effect, the straight lines of any subject elements—such as the sides of buildings, the horizon, or room interiors—appear to be bowed or curved in the image. With ordinary lenses, this effect (known as distortion) is usually not obvious, though it is a feature of many zooms. Don't confuse this problem with converging verticals (*see p. 113*).

Problem...

Analysis

Distortion is caused by slight changes in magnification of the image across the picture frame. Lenses that are not symmetrical in construction (in other words, the elements on either side of the aperture are not similar) are particularly prone to this type of imaging distortion, and the asymmetric construction of zoom lenses means that they are highly susceptible.

Barrel distortion
In the original shot (*top*), a wide-angle attachment led to barrel distortion. Using Pinch filter, to squeeze the image from all sides, with the Shear filter engaged has helped correct the problem.

Solution

Corrections using image-manipulation software may be possible, but turning curves into straight lines is more difficult than adjusting straight lines. Try using the Spherize distortion filter; the degree of flexibility in Photoshop is not very great, but some other software packages offer more control and a better chance of correcting distortion. You could try applying a succession of filters—first, slight Perspective Distortion, then Spherize, then slight Shear—or apply filters to just a part of, rather than the entire, image.

...solution

How to avoid the problem

● Don't place straight lines, such as the horizon or a junction of two walls, near the frame edges.

● Avoid using extreme focal lengths—either the ultra-wide or the ultra-long end of a zoom range.

● Use a focal length setting that offers the least distortion, usually around the middle of the range.

● Place important straight lines in the middle of the image—this is where distortion is usually minimal.

Quick fix Lens problems

Although many lens problems can be solved, or at least minimized, using appropriate software, prevention is always better than cure.

Problem: Lens blurring

The image looks unsharp, blurred, or smudged. Contrast is not high and the highlights are smeared.

Analysis

A dirty lens or lens filter, lack of sharp focus, damaged optics, camera shake, or subject movement may separately, or in combination, be the cause of blurred pictures.

Solution

You can increase contrast to improve image appearance using the Levels or Curves controls of image-manipulation software. Applying a Sharpen or Unsharp Mask filter is also likely to improve the image. The main subject can be made to appear adequately sharp if the background is made to look more blurred. To do this, select areas around the main subject and apply a Blur filter.

Camera movement
While trying to catch the light on the dust raised by a running zebra, the camera slipped a little, giving this blurred image—most evident in the highlights on the zebra's back and in the grass. However, blur can suggest mood and setting.

How to avoid the problem

Clean the lens or lens filter if it is marked; use a tripod to steady the camera for long shutter times or when using a telephoto lens or setting; if available, use an image-stabilization lens.

Problem: Lens flare

Bright spots of light, sometimes fringed with color, can be seen in the image. Spots can be single occurrences or appear in a row, and stretch away from a bright point source of light in the scene. Similarly, a bright, fuzzily edged patch of light, known as veiling flare, fills part of the image area.

Analysis

These types of faults are most likely the result of internal reflections within the lens. Stray light entering the lens from a bright light source has reflected around the lens and then been recorded on the film or picked up by the sensor of a digital camera.

Solution

Working with a digital file, small spots of light can easily be removed by cloning or rubber-stamping adjacent unaffected areas of the image onto them. Large areas of flare, however, are more difficult to correct, since they cover a significant area of the picture and contain no information to work with.

Flare
An unobstructed sun in the frame causes light to reflect within the lens, resulting in flare. By changing camera position, it was possible to mask the sun with a column of the building, while allowing a little flare through to suggest the brilliance of the light. Some of the reflections may be removed, but probably not all of them.

How to avoid the problem

Use a correctly designed lens-hood to stop light from entering the periphery of the lens; and avoid pointing the lens directly toward bright light sources. If shot framing demands that you include an intense light source in the image, select a small aperture to reduce the size of any resulting internal reflections.

Quick fix Lens problems continued

Problem: Black skies

A blue sky is rendered almost black. This type of effect seldom looks realistic or believable.

Analysis

This is probably the result of a polarizing filter on the lens combined with underexposure. This can reduce the sky to the point where most, or even all, color is removed.

Solution

First, highlight the problem sky area and then use Replace Color in Photoshop, or a similar software package, to restore the color. The best way to work is by making small changes repeatedly rather than a single, large change. Check that you do not introduce banding, or artificial borders, in the areas of color transition. You can also try using a graduated layer (*see below*).

How to avoid the problem

Don't set a polarizing filter to produce maximum darkness: in the viewfinder, you may still be able to see the blue of the sky, but the recording medium may not have sufficient latitude to retain color if the image is then underexposed.

Problem...

...solution

1 Original image
The skies of Kenya seldom need a polarizing filter in order to emphasize their color—indeed, it may even cause a portion of the sky to turn too dark, as you can see here in the top left-hand corner of the image.

2 Gradient Fill
To correct this, you must remove the dark gradient while leaving the rest of the image unaffected. This calls for a transparent-to-solid gradient that runs counter to the darkness. Here a Gradient Fill of black-to-transparent, with its Blend mode set to Screen, was applied. The gradient was adjusted until the dark corner was neutralized.

3 Sky correction
Once the new layer was applied to the image, the carefully positioned Gradient Fill restored the natural color of the sky. Once you have made one adjustment, you may find the image needs more work—for example, the top right-hand corner may now seem too dark. With digital photography it is easy to create perfect tonal balance.

Problem: Dark image corners

Corners of the image are shadowed or darkened, with a blurred edge leading to blackness, or the middle of the image looks significantly brighter than the periphery.

Analysis

Images showing dark corners with a discernible shape have been vignetted. This is usually caused by using a filter with too deep a rim for use with a (usually) wide-angle lens, by stacking too many filters on a lens, or by using an incorrectly aligned or overly deep lens-hood.

Solution

If the areas affected are small, vignetting can be corrected by cloning adjacent portions of the image. Light fall-off may be corrected using a Radial Graduate or Gradient Fill (*see opposite*)—experiment with different values of darkness and opacity.

Darkened corners It is easy not to notice a lens-hood interfering with the image. The shadows in the corners here were not spotted until after film processing. Small apertures give deeper, sharper shadows.

How to avoid the problem

Vignetting is easy to avoid if you are careful with your filters and lens-hoods. Light fall-off, as an optical defect, can only be reduced, not eliminated altogether: use either smaller working apertures or a higher-quality lens.

Problem: Poor-quality close-ups

Images taken at the closest focusing distances are not sharp or lack contrast.

Analysis

Lenses usually perform best at medium or long distances: the degree of close-up correction depends on lens design.

Solution

Poor image sharpness may be improved by applying Sharpness or Unsharp Mask filters. Contrast will be improved with Levels or Curves. Try localized burning-in to improve contrast, which will also increase apparent sharpness without increasing visual noise.

How to avoid the problem

Small apertures are likely to improve sharpness. Try using different focus and zoom settings—there will be a combination that gives the best possible quality. An alternative solution is to attach a close-up lens to the main lens. This acts as a magnifying glass and can improve close-up performance.

Improving close-ups
The original image (*right*) shows the features characteristic of a low-quality close-up: poor sharpness and reduced contrast. Applying an Unsharp Mask filter and an increase in contrast significantly improves results (*far right*).

Problem... ...solution

Influencing perspective

You can exercise control over the perspective of a photograph by changing your camera position. This is because perspective is the view that you have of the subject from wherever it is you decide to shoot. Perspective, however, is not affected by any changes in lens focal length—it may appear to be so, but in fact, all focal length does is determine how much of the view you record.

Professional photographers know perspective has a powerful effect on an image, yet it is one of the easiest things to control. This is why when you watch professionals at work, you often see them constantly moving around the subject—sometimes bending down to the ground or climbing onto the nearest perch; approaching very close and moving farther away again. Taking a lead from this, your work could be transformed if you simply become more mobile, observing the world through the camera from a series of changing positions rather than a single, static viewpoint.

Bear in mind that with some subjects—still-lifes, for example, and interiors or portraits—the tiny change in perspective between observing the subject with your own eyes and seeing it through the camera lens, which is just a little lower than your eyes, can make a difference to the composition. This difference in perspective is far more pronounced if you are using a studio camera or waist-level finder on a medium-format camera.

Using zooms effectively

One way to approach changes in perspective is to appreciate the effect that lens focal length has on your photography. A short focal length gives a

Alternative views

This classic wide-angle view (*above left*) tells of a flock of sheep grazing on the rolling moors of Scotland. It is a simple, effective, but essentially commonplace interpretation of the scene. However, when I stepped back a little and crouched down, I noticed tufts of wool caught on a wire fence (*above right*), which had been there all the time, literally right under my nose. A switch to a long focal length setting on my zoom lens entirely changed the perspective and delivered a very different, and entirely more engaging, account of this attractive rural scene. (*For another treatment of this view, see pp. 104–5*) perspective that allows you to approach a subject closely yet record much of the background. If you step back a little, you can take in much more of the scene, but then the generous depth of field of a wide-angle tends to make links between separate subject elements, since there is little, if any, difference in sharpness between them.

A long lens allows a more distant perspective. You can look closely at a face without being nearby. Long lenses tend to pull together disparate objects—in an urban scene viewed from a distance, buildings that are several blocks apart might appear to crowd in on top of each other. However, the shallow depth of field of a long lens used at close subject distances tends to separate out objects that may actually be close together (*see p. 48*) by showing some sharp and others blurred.

Perspective effects

Wide-angle lenses
- Take in more background or foreground.
- Exaggerate in close-ups the size of near subjects.
- Exaggerate differences in distance or position.
- Give greater apparent depth of field and link the subject to its background.

Telephoto lenses
- Compress spatial separation.
- Magnify the main subject.
- Reduce depth of field to separate the subject from its background.

Telephoto perspective
Overlooking the action there is a sense of the crush of people at this festival in mountainous Tajikistan (*above*). Two children holding hands complete the scene. The long-focal-length version (*above right*) focuses attention on the dancer, but excludes all sense of setting beyond the crowd watching the traditional performance.

TRY THIS

For this exercise, leave your zoom lens at its shortest focal length setting. Look for pictures that work best with this focal length—ignore any others and don't be tempted to change the lens setting. This will help to sharpen your sense of what a wide-angle lens does. You may find yourself approaching subjects—including people—more closely than you would normally dare. The lens is making you get closer because you cannot use the zoom to make the move for you. Next, repeat the exercise with the lens at its longest focal length setting.

Changing viewpoints

Always be on the lookout for viewpoints that give a new slant to your work. Don't ignore the simple devices, such as shooting down at a building instead of up at it, or trying to see a street scene from a child's viewpoint rather than an adult's.

Your choice of viewpoint communicates subtle messages that say as much about you as they do your subject. Take a picture of someone from a distance, for example, and the image carries a sense that you, too, were distant from that person. If you photograph a scene of poverty from the viewpoint of a bystander, the picture will again have that distant look of having been taken by an aloof observer. Lively markets are popular photographic subjects, but what do they look like from a merchant's position? If you enjoy sports, shoot from within the action, not from the sidelines.

Practical points

Higher viewpoints enable you to reduce the amount of foreground and increase the area of background recorded by a lens. From a high vantage point, a street or river scene lies at a less acute angle than when seen from street or water level. This reduces the amount of depth of field required to show the scene in sharp focus.

However, from a low camera position, subjects may be glimpsed through a sea of grass or legs. And if you look upward from a low position, you see less background and more sky, making it easier to separate your subject from its surroundings.

Less can say more
At markets and similar types of locations, all the activity can be overwhelming—and the temptation is often to try to record the entire busy, colorful scene. If you look, however, at your feet there could be images showing much less but saying so much more. In Uzbekistan I noticed next to a fruit stand a lady who had nothing to sell but these few sad tulips.

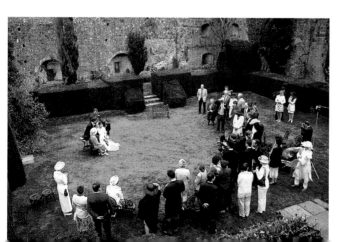

Subjects and setting
By climbing up to a convenient vantage point overlooking the lawn, I could leave the classic wedding group pictures behind and record a more complex image, one that revealed not only the wedding party and guests, but also the romantic setting of a ruined castle.

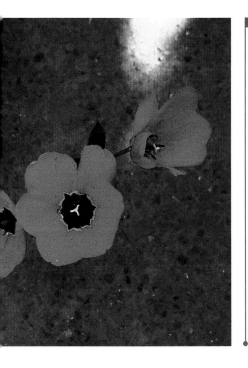

● In some parts of the world, it is a good idea to avoid drawing attention to your presence. Your search for an unusual camera viewpoint could attract the unwanted interest of officialdom. Even climbing onto a wall could get you in trouble in places where strangers are not a common sight or photographers are regarded with suspicion.

● As well as being discourteous, it might also be illegal to enter a private building without permission in order to take photographs. You may be surprised at how cooperative people generally are if you explain what you are doing and why, and then ask for their assistance.

● Try to be open and friendly with people you encounter—a pleasant smile or an acknowledging wave is often the easiest, and cheapest, way to elicit a helpful response from strangers.

● Prepare your equipment before making your move. Balancing on the top of a wall is not the best place to change lenses. With manual cameras, preset the approximately correct aperture and shutter time so that if you snatch a shot, exposure will be about right.

Changing viewpoint

This conventional view of the Mesquita of Cordoba, Spain (*above*), works well as a record shot, but it is not the product of careful observation. Looking down from the same shooting position, I noticed the tower of the building reflected in a puddle of water. Placing the camera nearly in the water, a wholly more intriguing viewpoint was revealed (*right*). An advantage of using a digital camera with an LCD screen is that awkward shooting positions are not the impossibility they would be with a film-based camera.

Quick fix Leaning buildings

Buildings and architectural features are always popular photographic subjects, but they can cause annoying problems of distortion.

Problem

Tall structures, such as buildings, lampposts, or trees, or even people standing close by and above you, appear to lean backward or look as if they are about to topple over.

Analysis

This distortion occurs if you point the camera up to take the picture. This results in your taking in too much of the foreground and not enough of the height of the subject.

Solution

● Stand farther back and keep the camera level—you will still take in too much of the foreground, but you can later crop the image.

● Use a wider-angle lens or zoom setting, but then remember to hold the camera precisely level—wide-angle lenses tend to exaggerate projection distortion.

● Take the picture anyway and try to correct the distortion by manipulating the image.

● Use a shift lens or a camera with movements. This equipment is specialized and expensive, but technically it is the best solution.

● Exaggerate the leaning or toppling effect to emphasize the height and bulk of the subject.

Problem...

Tilting the camera
An upward-looking view of the spires of Cambridge, England, makes the buildings lean alarmingly backward.

...solution

Using the foreground
By choosing the right camera position, you can keep the camera level and include foreground elements that add to the shot.

Problem...

Losing the foreground
To record the red flags against the contrasting blue of the building, there was no option but to point the camera upward, thus dismissing much of the foreground. As a result, the nearest building appears to lean backward.

...solution

Alternative view
Keeping the camera level, a shift lens was used, set to maximum upward movement. This avoided the problem of converging verticals. Although this is the best solution to optimize image quality, it does require a costly professional lens.

Quick fix Facial distortion

Distorted facial features can be a problem with portraits. To make the subject's face as large as possible, the temptation is to move in too close.

Problem

Portraits of people taken close-up exaggerate certain facial features, such as noses, cheeks, or foreheads.

Analysis

The cause is a perspective distortion. When a print is viewed from too far away for the magnification of the print, the impression of perspective is not correctly formed. This is why at the time you took the photograph, your subject's nose appeared fine, but in the print it looks disproportionately large.

Solution

- Use a longer lens setting—a 35efl of at least 80 mm is about right, so that for a normal-sized print viewed from a normal viewing distance, perspective looks correct.

- Use the longest end of your zoom lens. For many, this is a 35efl of 70 mm, which is just about enough.
- If you have to work close-up, try taking a profile instead of a full face.
- Avoid using wide-angle lenses close to a face, unless you want a distorted view.
- Don't fill the frame with a face at the time of shooting. Instead, rely on cropping at a later stage if you need the frame filled (*see pp. 44–5*).
- Don't assume you will be able to correct facial distortions later on with image-manipulation software. It is hard to produce convincing results.
- If you have a digital camera with a swiveling lens, it is fun to include yourself in the picture by holding the camera at arm's length—but your facial features will then be so close they will look exaggerated.
- Make larger prints. With modern inkjet printers, it is easy to make letter-size images (substantially larger than the usual photographic snapshot), and at normal viewing distances they are far less prone to perspective distortion.

Profile
Taking portraits in profile avoids many of the problems associated with facial distortion in full-frontal shots. Make sure you focus carefully on the (visible) eye—other parts of the face may appear unsharp yet be acceptable to the viewer.

Full-frontal
To emphasize the friendly character of this man, several "rules" were broken: a wide-angle lens was used close-up; the shot was taken looking upward; and the face was placed off in one corner, thus exaggerating the distortion already present. But the total effect is amiable rather than unpleasant.

Color composition

Successful color photography means learning to use color as a compositional tool—as a form of visual communication in its own right—rather than just reproducing a scene or subject that happens to be in color.

The importance of color

Color is far from being merely incidental, any more than is the surface texture of a subject or, indeed, the quality of the light illuminating it. Color is an integral part of our experience of the subject, helping to determine both the mood and the atmosphere of the scene and our emotional responses to it. One way to come to terms with this is to record colors as if they were distinct entities, separate from the things displaying them.

Mental focus

Once you have made this change in mental focus, you could, for example, start evaluating scenes not in terms of vistas or panoramas, but in terms of color content. Look at, say, the greens—are they as intense as you want? Is the light too contrasty for them to have real depth? Is your shooting position right in relation to the light in order to give the color impact you want to record? Look at a city scene not because it is full of activity but because there, among the drabness, are flashes of red, or blue, or green. And if a neighboring color is distracting, change focal length or crop the final image to exclude it.

Working digitally

An advantage digital photographers have over their traditional counterparts is that it is easy, using image-manipulation software, to alter the colors of the recorded image. Not only are broad-stroke changes possible—such as whole areas of sky or foreground—but you can also select very precise parts of a scene for the software to work on. And if radical changes are not appropriate, then it is just as easy to alter color contrast, saturation, or brightness to emphasize one particular part of the image or suppress another.

Color saturation
Red is such a strong color that it inevitably draws attention to itself. In this image (*right*), the reds coupled with the green reflections in the water are so strong that the fish almost seem to blur before your eyes. Using the image-manipulation software's Color Picker option, however, all manner of color adaptations become possible (*far right*).

Bright/pale contrast
A simple subject—floral table decorations in a restaurant (*below*)—has been transformed by an overhead camera angle and the contrast provided by the bright colors of the flowers with the far subtler tones contained in the rest of the image.

Color wheel

Strictly speaking, the color wheel displays only hue and saturation: in the middle are the desaturated colors (those containing a lot of white); on the perimeter of the wheel are the most saturated colors. The colors are organized in the order familiar from the spectrum, with the degree marks around the rim being used to help locate different hues.

Perception of color

If a pale subject is seen against a complementary-colored background, its saturation seems to increase. Similarly, a neutral gray changes its appearance according to its background color, appearing slightly bluish green against red, and magenta against green. If you compare the gray patches in the two colored panels here (*below right*) you can see this at work. If you cut small holes in a piece of white paper, so that only the four patches are visible, you can see that the blues are, in fact, identical, as are the grays.

Strong color contrasts

Color contrasts result when you include hues within an image that are well separated from each other on the color wheel (*see p. 65*). While it is true that strongly colored picture elements may have initial visual impact, they are not all that easy to organize into successful images. Often, it is better to look for a simple color scheme as part of a clear compositional structure—too many subject elements can so easily lead to disjointed and chaotic pictures.

Digital results

Modern digital cameras are able to capture very vibrant colors that look compelling on your computer's monitor screen. Because of the way the screen projects color, these are, in fact, brighter and more saturated than those film can produce. However, one of the advantages of using computer technology is that the color range offered by film can be enhanced with image-manipulation software, giving you the opportunity, first to create, and then to exploit, an enormous range of vibrant colors.

Distracting composition
Combine strong colors with an unusual and an appealing subject, and you would think that you have all the important elements for a striking photograph (*above*). In fact, there is far too much going on in this picture for it to be a successful composition. The painting in the background distracts attention from the man—himself an artist, from Papua New Guinea—while the white edge on the right disturbs the composition. A severe crop, to concentrate attention on the face alone, would be necessary to save the image.

Lighting for color
The unbelievably strong colors seen in this image, taken on an isolated Scottish shoreline, are the result of shooting in the bright yet diffused light from an overcast sky, which has had the effect of making all the colors particularly intense. The palette of contrasting dark reds and blues not only looks good on screen, it also reproduces well on paper. This is because the particular range of colors in this image happen to be those that print well. A range containing, say, bright purples or sky blues would not be so successful.

Simple composition

Bright colors are attractive in themselves, but they tend to be most effective when they are arranged in some type of pattern or sequence. This arrangement imposes a structure on them and thus suggests a meaning or order beyond the mere presence of the color itself. The main problem I encountered when taking this photograph of brightly colored umbrellas was avoiding the reflections from the store window in front of them.

Color gamut

The intensity of computer-enhanced colors gives them real appeal, but it is in this strength that problems lie. Strong colors on the page of a book or website will compete with any text that is included; they are also likely to conflict with any other softer image elements. In addition, you need to bear in mind that even if you can see intense, strong colors on the screen, you may not be able to reproduce them on paper. Purples, sky blue, oranges, and brilliant greens all reproduce poorly on paper, looking duller than they do on screen. This is because the color gamut, or range of reproducible colors, of print is smaller than that of the monitor.

Of the many ways to represent a range of colors, this diagram is the most widely accepted. The rounded triangle encloses all colors that can be perceived. Areas drawn within this, the visual gamut, represent the colors that can be accurately reproduced by specific devices. The triangle encloses the colors

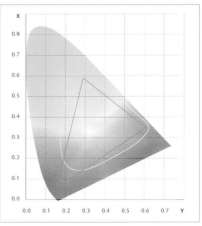

(the color gamut) of a typical RGB color monitor. The quadrilateral shows the colors reproduced by the four-color printing process. Notice how some printable colors cannot be reproduced on screen, and vice versa.

The appeal of rain
Rainy days are ideal for color shots because hues are more saturated due to low lighting contrasts (narrow luminance range). But you still need contrasts of color, as in this scene in Kolkata, India.

Quick fix Color balance

Correct color rendition depends on many different factors, one of which is ensuring that the recording media and light sources match.

Problem

Pictures taken indoors have a distinct color cast—either orange or yellow—and images appear unnaturally warm-toned. A related problem occurs in outdoor shots—there is a blue cast and images appear unnaturally cold. In other situations, pictures taken under fluorescent lamps appear greenish overall. Problems are compounded if you work in mixed lighting, such as daylight from a window and light from a table lamp. If you correct for the orange cast of the lamp, the window light looks too blue; if you correct for the window light, the lamp looks too orange.

1 Orange domestic tungsten
Photographs taken of rooms by domestic tungsten light often display an orange cast because the film used is intended to be exposed by daylight, which has a higher color temperature.

Analysis

All imaging systems, whether film-based or digital, assume that the light falling on a scene contains the full spectrum of colors. This produces the "white" light of daylight, often called 6,500 K light—a reference to its color temperature (see p. 116). If, however, the light is deficient in a specific band of colors, or is dominated by certain color wavelengths, then everything illuminated by it will tend to take on the strongest color component. We do not experience indoor light, for example, as being unduly orange because our eyes adapt to the dominant color and our brains "filter" it out. Likewise, we seldom notice the blue color cast that is often present in the shadows on sunny days because our eyes and brains compensate for the color cast—and so we see the colors we expect to be there.

2 Color Balance screen shot
Tones lighter than midtone are strongly yellow-red. To correct for this, "Highlights" was selected in Color Balance, and blue increased using the lowest slider.

Solution

There are various solutions, depending on whether you are using a film-based system or digital technology.

Film-based systems
● Use the correct film type for the principal source of illumination in the scene. For indoor photography, shooting under incandescent lights, use tungsten-balanced film. This advice, and that following, applies principally to slide film, as the film image is usually the final result. With color negatives, however, at least some color correction can often be made at the printing stage

3 Corrected color
Notice that the corrected image has retained a hint of the orange cast—removing it completely would have destroyed the mood of the shot.

- Attach a color-balancing filter to your lens so that the light reaching the film corresponds to that film's color balance. Use an 85B for daylight-balanced film exposed indoors under tungsten light; an 80B for tungsten-balanced film exposed in daylight. Pink or light magenta filters help to correct the color casts produced by fluorescent lamps.

Scanned images

- Scanner software can make corrections while it is scanning. If you have many images to correct, apply the settings that give the best results to all of them.
- Or make corrections using image-manipulation software. This may be more accurate, since you will then be working with the full image data.

Digital cameras

- Most digital cameras automatically correct for the white balance—they analyze the colors of the light and remove the color cast. In some situations, however, you will obtain more accurate results if you present the camera with a neutral color and set white balance manually.
- Images recorded by a digital camera showing an unwanted color cast can be corrected using image-manipulation software (*see pp. 112–13*).

    It is worth bearing in mind that you may not always want to correct a color imbalance, or at least not fully correct it. In some situations, the color cast may be helping to set the atmosphere of a scene or providing the viewer with additional information about the subject.

How to avoid the problem

- **Don't choose to photograph in mixed lighting conditions unless you specifically want the image to display unpredictable colors.**

- **Don't take color-critical shots under fluorescent lamps—it is very difficult to correct precisely the resulting cast.**

- **Don't rely on color-balancing filters—they make only approximate corrections. But partial correction does make later refinements—when printing or**

1 Blue dawn light
Taken at dawn, this shot displays a distinct blue suppressing the warm colors I perceived at the time film, the blue cast would have been more pronoun but, as you can see, even the digital camera's whit balance did not fully compensate for the distortion.

2 Levels screen shot
The quickest way to correct the image was t Levels. The Highlight Dropper (far right tool) was a to the area to be rendered a neutral white (the wh walls of the foreground building). The Shadow Dro was then selected and a deep shadow chosen.

3 Corrected color
The finished result shows greatly improved c overall, but note that the blue hills in the far dista

Silhouettes/backlighting

Although the results may look different, silhou-etted and backlit shots are variations on the same theme. In terms of exposure, they differ only in how much light is given to the main subject.

Silhouetted subjects

To create a silhouette, expose for the background alone—whether the sky or, say, a brightly lit wall—so that foreground objects are recorded as very dark, or even black. Make sure the exposure takes no account of the foreground. For this technique to be most effective, minimal light should fall on the subject, otherwise surface details start to

record and the form loses impact. Your aim is to exploit outline and shape, and to help this, a plain background is usually best.

When taking pictures into the light, you need to be aware of bright light flaring into the lens. As a rule, try to position yourself so that the subject itself obscures the light source, though it can be effective to allow the sun to peep around the subject to cause a little flare. Using a small aperture helps reduce unwanted reflections inside the lens.

Backlit subjects

The classic backlit subject is a portrait taken with a window or the sky filling the background, or fig-ures on a bright, sandy beach or a ski slope.

The challenge in terms of exposure in these types of situations is to prevent the meter from being overinfluenced by the high levels of back-ground illumination. If you don't, you will end up with a silhouette. To prevent this, either override the automatics or manually set the controls to "overexpose" by some 1½–2 f/stops.

Another approach is to set your camera to take a selective meter reading. Alternatively, with a center-weighted averaging meter reading, fill the viewfinder with the shadowy side of your subject, note the reading, or lock it in, move back, and recompose the image.

Backlit scenes are prone to veiling flare—non-image-forming light—which is aggravated by the need to increase exposure for the subject. In strong backlighting, however, it is hard to prevent light from spilling around the subject edges, blurring sharpness and reducing contrast.

Conflicting needs
In this strongly backlit portrait of a Kyrgyz shepherd (which has been cropped from a wide-angle shot), I positioned myself so that the subject shielded the lens from the direct rays of a bright sun. It is very difficult to achieve the right balance of exposure—if the horse is fully exposed, the sheep will be too light. This is clearly the type of situation that would benefit from a little fill-in flash (pp. 74–5). However, there was just enough light to pick out the color of the horse when the sheep were correctly exposed.

Dealing with flare

As the sun sets on a market in Tashkent, Uzbekistan, the dust raised by street cleaners fills the air, catching and spreading the still-bright sunlight. The lower the sun is in the sky, the more likely is it to become a feature in your composition. In the example here, the flare has been caused as much by the atmospheric dust as by any internal reflections within the lens itself. A normal averaging light reading taken in these conditions would be massively overinfluenced by the general brightness of the scene, and so render the backlit subject as featureless silhouettes. Therefore, what may seem like a gross overexposure—an additional 2 f/stops—is needed to deal with this type of lighting situation.

Sky exposure

Strong light from the front and a symmetrical foreground shape immediately suggest the potential for a silhouette. A passing windsurfer, in the Penang Straits of Malaysia, completes the picture. Simply by exposing for the sky, all the other elements fall into their correct place—the black, shadowy palm, the sparkling water, and the surfer are transformed. Using a catadioptric (mirror) lens produces the characteristic "hollow" look of the out-of-focus palm.

Virtue of necessity

When shooting into a fierce tropical sun, you may have no choice other than to produce a silhouette. If so, the strategy then becomes a search for the right type of subject. Here, on Zanzibar, dhows and beachcombers are complementary in terms of tone, yet contrasting in shape. Notice how the central figure seems diminished in size as his outline is blurred by the light flaring all around his body.

Accessory flash

Digital cameras, almost without exception, are equipped with a built-in electronic flash. What makes the modern flash so universal is that it is both highly miniaturized and "intelligent." Most units, for example, deliver extremely accurate computer-controlled dosages of light that suit the amount of available, or ambient, light in the scene.

Making flash work for you

Whatever you might gain in terms of convenience by having a ready source of extra light built into the camera, you lose in terms of lighting subtlety. To make flash work for you, you need to exploit what limited control facilities your camera offers.

First, use the "slow-synch" mode if your camera offers it. This allows the ambient exposure to be relatively long, so that areas beyond the range of the flash can be recorded as well as possible, while the flash illuminates the foreground (*see below*). This not only softens the effect of the flash, it can also give mixed color temperatures—the

cool color of the flash and the often warmer color of the ambient light—which can be eye-catching.

Second, try using a reflector on the shadow side of the subject. If angled correctly, it will pick up some light from the flash and bounce it into the shadows. Any light-colored material can be used as a reflector—a white sheet of paper, a white sheet, or a shirt. Professional photographers like to use a round, flexible reflector that can be twisted to a third of its full size. It is very compact, lightweight, and efficient, and it usually has two different surfaces—a gold side for warm-colored light and a matte side for softly diffused effects.

Third, an advanced option is to use slave flash. These are separate flash units equipped with sensors that trigger the flash when the master flash (built into or cabled directly to the camera) is detected. If you have a flash unit, then adding a slave unit is not expensive. However, you need to experiment with your camera to check if the synchronization of the multiple flash units is correct.

Flash limitations
Dusk in Istanbul, Turkey, and traditional musicians gather. The standard flash exposure used for this image lights only the foreground subjects, and the rapid light fall-off, characteristic of small light sources, fails to reach even a short distance behind the first musician. Adding to the problems, camera exposure is not long enough for the low ambient, or available, light levels prevailing at the time. As a consequence, the background has been rendered black. This type of result is seldom attractive, nor does it display any sound photographic technique.

Effective technique
When illumination is low, make the most of what light is available rather than relying on electronic flash. Here, exposure was set for the sky: this required a shutter of ¼ sec, giving rise to the blurred parts of the image. At the same time, the flash was brief enough to "freeze" the soldier in the foreground, so he appears sharp. Utilizing all ambient light ensures that the distant part of the scene is not wholly underexposed—some color can even be seen in the background building. Compare this with the image in which flash provided all the illumination (*above left*).

Using any setup with more than one flash means trying out different levels of flash output to discover the best results. Start by setting the slave to its lowest power output, bearing in mind that the task of this unit is to relieve subject shadows, not act as the main light. Some models of camera are designed for multiple-flash photography.

Flash synchronization

Because the pulse of light from electronic flash is extremely brief, even compared with the shortest shutter time, it is crucial that the shutter is fully open when the flash fires. Only then will the entire film area be exposed to the flash light reflected back from the subject. There is usually a limit to the shortest shutter time that synchronizes with the flash, often known as "x-synch." For most SLRs, this is between ¹⁄₆₀ and ¹⁄₂₅₀ sec. In some cameras, x-synch corresponds to the shortest available shutter time, which may be ¹⁄₈,₀₀₀ sec. To obtain this, however, you must use flash units made for that particular camera model.

Flash exposure

All flash exposures consist of two separate processes occurring simultaneously. While the shutter is open, or the light sensor is receptive, light from the overall scene—the ambient light—produces one exposure. This ambient exposure takes on the color of the prevailing light, it exposes the background if sufficient, and it is longer than that of the flash itself.

The second exposure is in addition to the ambient one. The burst of light from a flash is extremely brief, possibly less than ¹⁄₁₀,₀₀₀ sec (though studio flash may be as long as ¹⁄₂₀₀ sec) and its color is determined by the characteristics of the flash tube (which can be filtered for special effects).

The fact that there are two exposures means that it is necessary to balance them in order to produce good results. But it also allows you to make creative use of the process by, for example, allowing the flash exposure to freeze subject movement, while the longer ambient exposure produces blurred results.

Without flash
Bright, contrasty sunshine streaming in through large windows relieve the subjects—a troupe of young singers dressed in traditional costume from Kyrgyzstan— produced a strongly backlit effect. Without the use of flash, the shadows would appear very dark, but in this case a wall behind the camera position reflected back some light from the windows to relieve the contrast a little, and so retain some subject details.

With flash
In this interpretation of the previous scene (*above left*), flash has been used. This produced enough light to fill most of the shadows. Now we can clearly see the girls' costumes, but note the shadows that still remain on the carpet. It is important to set the camera to expose the background correctly: since in this example it was very bright, a shutter time of ¹⁄₂₅₀ sec was needed. The f/number dictated by the exposure meter was set on the lens, and the flash was set to underexpose by 1½ stops. This ensured that the foreground was exposed by both the flash and by the available window light.

Quick fix Electronic flash

Modern electronic flash units are versatile and convenient light sources, ideal for use when light levels are low (and the subject is relatively nearby), or when image contrast is high and you want to add a little fill-in illumination to the shadow areas. However, due to the intensity of their output as well as their limited range and covering power, obtaining naturalistic lighting effects and correct exposure can be problematic.

Problem

Common types of problems that are encountered when using electronic flash include overexposed results—particularly of the foreground parts of the image—and underexposed results—particularly of the image background. In addition, general underexposure of long-distance subject matter is very common, as is uneven lighting, in which the corners or foreground are less bright than the center of the image.

Analysis

Modern electronic flash units have their own light-sensitive sensor to measure automatically the light output from the flash or the amount of light reflecting back from the subject and reaching the film or camera sensor. As a result, they are as prone to error as any camera exposure meter. Furthermore, the light produced by a flash unit falls off very rapidly with distance (*see above right and p. 74*).

Overexposed flash-illuminated pictures are usually caused by positioning the flash too close to the subject or when the subject is the only element in an otherwise largely empty space.

Flash underexposure is caused by the unit's having insufficient power to cover adequately the flash-to-subject distance. For example, no small flash unit can light an object that is more than about 30 ft (10 m) away, and even quite powerful flash units cannot adequately light an object that is more than about 100 ft (30 m) distant.

Uneven lighting is caused when the flash is unable to cover the angle of view of the lens—a problem most often experienced with wide-angles. And another problem occurs when an attached lens or lens accessory blocks the light from a camera-mounted flash.

Light fall-off

Light from a flash unit mounted on the camera falls off, or loses its effectiveness, very rapidly as distance increases. This is evident in this close-up image of a bride holding a posy of flowers. The subject's hands and the roses nearest the flash are brightly illuminated, but even just a little bit farther back, the image is visibly darker. This is evident if you look at the back edge of the wedding dress, for example. The effects of this light fall-off can be greatly minimized by using a light source that covers a larger area—hence the very different lighting effect you get when using bounced flash (*opposite*).

Solution

For close-up work, reduce the power of the flash if possible. When photographing distant subjects in the dark—landscapes, for example, or the stage at a concert—a flash is usually a waste of time and is best turned off. A better option is to use a long exposure and support the camera on a tripod or rest it on something stable, such as a wall or fence. With accessory flash units—not built-in types—you can place a diffuser over the flash window to help spread the light and prevent darkened corners when using a wide-angle lens.

Mixed lighting

The result of balancing flash with an exposure sufficient to register the ambient light indoors delivers results like this. The lighting is soft but the color balance is warmed by the ambient light. Also, the background is bright enough for it to appear quite natural. If a greater exposure had been given to the background, there would have been an increased risk that subject movement would spoil the image.

Bounced flash

Direct flash used at this close distance would produce a harshly lit subject and a shadowy background. In this shot, the flash was aimed at the wall opposite the child. In effect, the light source then becomes the wall, which reflects back a wide spread of light. Not only does this soften the quality of the light, it also reduces the rapid light fall-off characteristic of a small-sized source of light. But bounced flash is possible only if you use an auxiliary flash unit. Note, however, that the background is rather darker than ideal—to overcome this, there must be sufficient ambient light to mix with the flash illumination to provide correct exposure overall (*above right*).

How to avoid the problem

The best way to obtain reliable results with flash is to experiment in different picture-taking situations. With a digital camera, you can make exposures at different settings in a variety of situations to learn the effects of flash without wasting any film. Some flash units feature a modeling light, which flashes briefly to show you the effect of the light—this is a useful preview, but it can consume a good deal of power and is likely to disturb your subject.

Uneven light

On-camera flash typically delivers these unsatisfactory results. The lighting is uneven, the shapes the flash has illuminated look flat, and there are hard, harsh reflections on all shiny surfaces. In addition, the flash has created unpleasant shadows (note the shadow of the lip-brush on the background woodwork). Always be aware of any flat surfaces positioned behind your subject when using flash from the camera position.

Radical
conversions

Scanning: The basics

Scanning is the bridge that carries film-based negatives and transparencies or printed images into the digital world. The process converts all color, brightness, and contrast information into digital data for your software to use. The quality of the scanner and the skill with which it is used are the key factors that determine the quality of the digital information and, hence, the quality of the image you have to work with (*see pp. 84–5*).

Scanning steps

You can think of scanning as a three-stage process:
• Gather together originals for the job. You may have to make prints of family portraits, say, or collect images for your club's website.
• Next is the actual scanning. To do this, the scanner makes a prescan to allow you to check that the original is correctly oriented, or to set the scanner to scan only as much of the original as you want, or to set the final image size and resolution. You then make the real scan and save the result onto the computer's hard disk.
• The final stage is basic "housekeeping"—put your originals somewhere safe, somewhere you can readily find them again, and, if the work is critical, create a backup copy of the scans.

Basic procedures

To get the most from scanning, it is a good idea to follow some commonsense procedures designed to help streamline your working methods.
• Plan ahead—collect all your originals together before starting.
• If you have a lot of scans to make from a variety of different types of original, sort them out first. If, for example, you scan all black and white originals and then all color transparencies you will save a huge amount of time by not having to alter the scanner settings continually.
• Scan landscape-oriented images separately from portrait-oriented ones. This saves you from having to rotate the scans. And you will minimize visits to dialog boxes if you classify originals by the final file size or resolution you want.
• If you are using a flatbed scanner, clean your scanner's glass plate, or platen, before starting.
• Make sure originals are clean. Blow dust off with compressed air or a rubber puffer. Wipe prints carefully to remove fingerprints, dust, and fibers.

Setting up a scanner

Many scanners give excellent results with practically no adjustment at all. However, it pays to calibrate your scanner carefully right from the outset.

1 Obtain a standard target, such as that illustrated opposite. The IT 8.7/1 is intended for use with color transparency film, and the IT 8.7/2 is for color prints. These targets may be supplied with your scanner; if not, a camera store may be able to order them. Alternatively, choose an original for scanning that is correctly exposed and contains a good range of colors and subject detail.

2 Make an initial scan using the machine's default settings—those set at the factory.

3 Check the image produced by the scan against the original. If necessary, make changes using the scanner driver's controls so that the scan matches the original. Some scanners require you to make these changes in the preview window. However, be aware that on some scanners, the preview image is not really an accurate representation of the final scan. You need to experiment with your particular equipment. For the best results, you also need to calibrate your monitor (*see pp. 92–3*).

4 Once you have a scan you are happy with, save or note down the settings. Call it by the name of the film used—such as "Kodak Elite 100" or "Fuji Provia."

5 Repeat these steps with all the various types of film you scan—color negatives and transparencies use different scanner settings.

6 Then, for all subsequent scans, load the relevant saved settings as your starting point.

Scanners compared
Two high-quality scanners—a Nikon LS-2000 (*top*) and a Microtek 4000t (*above*)—can produce very different results from an identical standard target image. This demonstrates just how important it is to set up your scanner controls carefully.

- Align originals on the scanner as carefully as you can: realigning afterward may blur fine detail.
- Scan images to the lowest resolution you need. This gives you the smallest practicable file size, which, in turn, makes image manipulation faster, takes up less space on the hard disk or other storage media, and gives quicker screen handling.
- Use file names that are readily understood. A file name you choose today may seem obscure in a few months.
- When scanning, crop as much extraneous image detail as is sensible in order to keep file sizes small, but allow yourself room to maneuver in case you decide to crop further at some later stage.
- You may need to make your output image very slightly larger (say, an extra 5 percent all around) than the final size. This may be essential if, for example, you want your image to "bleed," or extend to the very edge of the paper so that no white border is visible.

Preview window
All scanners show a representation of the image in a preview window (*above*) prior to the final scan (*top*). This gives you a chance to make improvements before committing to a final scan. While it will save you time and effort later if you make the preview image as good as you can, bear in mind that it is only a general indication of the final scan. With some scanners, the preview may actually be rather inaccurate: if yours is one of these, you may need to experiment in order to learn how to compensate for its quirks.

Using flatbed scanners

Flatbed scanners are intended primarily for two-dimensional artwork and printed material, but you can also use them with small, solid objects. For scanning small-format film, such as 35 mm, it is best to use a special film scanner: only the larger, costlier flatbed scanners are suitable for these miniature formats. You can satisfactorily scan medium-format and larger films on flatbed scanners, which makes them very versatile pieces of equipment.

Getting the best from your scanner

One way of thinking of what a scanner does is to regard it as a type of camera. Just as being careful when capturing an image via a camera increases your chances of a high-quality image, so careful scanning ensures that you have a good-quality digital image to manipulate—and it also cuts out unnecessary correction time on the computer.

• Keep the scanner's glass bed spotless. If you have a transparency adapter, make sure that is also clean. Lint-free microfiber cloths are available from camera stores or opticians to clean the glass without the risk of scratching it.

• Check that the colors you have seen on the prescan match those of the final scan.

• Be systematic about your filing and the names you give your images.

• Allow the scanner to warm up for at least five minutes before making your best-quality scans.

• If you are scanning, say, a large book, don't damage the hinge of the scanner lid by forcing it down. Use a heavy weight, such as another book, to hold down and flatten the original against the scanner's glass.

• Save your scanned images to the file format that is easiest for your software to access and use. It is a waste of your time to change file formats more than is absolutely necessary.

• Line up any rectangular originals as carefully as you can on the scanner glass. Rotating the image after scanning in order to square it up (to correct a sloping horizon, for example) can significantly degrade image quality—especially of line art, such as black and white artwork.

Scanning photographic prints

There may be times when you get better results by first making a print in the darkroom from a negative, and then scanning the print, rather than scanning the negative directly and working on that in the computer. Certain manipulations, such as the local contrast controls known as burning-in and dodging (*see pp. 104–5*), are often far easier to achieve in the darkroom than by manipulating a scanned image.

If the print intended for scanning has a glossy surface, take care to clean it carefully—every speck of dust, fiber, or loose hair will show up sharply on the resulting scan.

Scanning printed material

There is a wealth of printed material in general circulation, in books, magazines, posters, album covers, and so on, that appears ideal for scanning. But the likelihood is that most of it is protected by copyright restrictions, and you are likely to be in breach of these restrictions if you scan such material without the copyright holder's written consent (*see pp. 196–7*).

However, in general, if you scan for the sole purpose of study or research, or you intend to make no commercial use of the material, then your actions will probably be exempted.

Scanning stamps and coins

Flatbed scanners are ideal pieces of equipment for making records of valuable items, such as stamp collections (*see opposite*) and coins. The main advantage that a scanner has over a conventional camera is that the scanner is capable of making very accurate records of objects with very little distortion. In addition, a scanner will record the real size of items extremely precisely, and this could be a crucially important consideration for some collectors.

Another factor you might want to consider is that the relatively low light-levels needed for scanning are less likely to harm the delicate coloring of, say, stamps than photographic tungsten lamps, which burn very bright and hot.

Hobbyists
Scanners are perfect for many hobbies, including stamp and coin collecting and autograph hunting, as well as for studies such as graphology. Scanners not only make precise 1:1 (life-size) copies, they also make excellent enlargements of, for example, the slight imperfections that can be so important to some collectors. The magnified view of these stamps (*left*) shows the enlarged "L" that distinguishes this batch.

Starting from a print
Sunlight reflecting off these nurses' white uniforms created a contrasty negative. Working digitally, by scanning the original negative, would have meant losing the attractive graininess of the image. In this example, the negative was first printed conventionally, and the resulting print scanned. The digital equivalent was then worked on—principally by slightly warming up the image tones.

Optical character recognition

If you scan text documents, such as letters or pages from a book, to create image files, you can edit them only as images. However, by using optical character recognition (OCR) software, which is often bundled with scanners, you can scan text documents to create word-processor files. This gives you the option of editing the text directly. For documents that are clearly printed, such as those from a laser printer, inexpensive OCR software is adequate. You will need a small piece of software to bridge the OCR with your scanner, which is usually available free from the scanner manufacturer's website. Once it is installed, operation is normally very simple, and you may be able to fax, print out, or save documents directly from the OCR application.

Quick fix Scan resolution

Often, one of the most important decisions you have to make when it comes to scanning an image is determining the most appropriate resolution to set.

Problem

When scanning, you may be tempted to set a low resolution in an attempt to keep file sizes as small as possible—especially if your computer has inadequate RAM or hard-disk space is tight. If, however, you set too low a resolution figure, then the resulting image will look unsharp, image detail will be missing, or the image will appear pixelated.

Setting a higher resolution holds out the promise of higher-quality digital output, but if file sizes become too large, then there is a price to pay—images will take longer to scan, the resulting files will need more storage space, they will take longer to load or transmit, and they will need more memory to manipulate on screen. And files can grow very large, very quickly, when you start to work with multiple layers. Yet higher resolutions do not even guarantee better-quality results.

Analysis

Two approaches are possible. First, you could scan every image at the highest resolution you are ever likely to need, producing files of, say, 25–30 MB in size. You can then make copies, adapting image resolution to each task while copying. This saves you from having to scan an image each time you want to use it for a different job. This way of working uses a lot of data capacity, but it is a good solution for, say, a busy studio.

Alternatively, you scan specifically for the task in hand, and if a new use of the image calls for a higher or lower resolution, then you need to make a new scan. This is the most economical method of working if throughput is not particularly great.

Solution

Check image size The simplest method is to work by the size of the image file: use the table here (see opposite) as a guide for color images. For black and white images, use files a third of the size—instead of 1.9 MB for a 3 x 5 in (7.5 x 12.5 cm) print, use 0.6 MB. When you

make the prescan and crop to the part of the scan that you want (see pp. 80–1), tell the scanner driver the size of the printout required. The driver will then tell you the size of file you will obtain after scanning. If it is not right, simply change the resolution settings until you obtain the approximate file size suggested by the table.

Bear in mind that when you calculate the file size of an image, the size of the original is irrelevant. Whether you reduce a poster to fill a monitor screen or enlarge a postage stamp to fill the same area, the correct file size is exactly the same.

Calculate resolution The more rigorous approach is based on the fact that the number of pixels needed to be input from the scanner equals the total number of pixels needed for output. The calculation is as follows:

input resolution = (size of output x output resolution)/size of original

Ensure that the size of output and size of original are in the same units—both inches or centimeters—then the input and output resolutions will be the same. Another formula giving the same result is the following:

input resolution = percentage increase in size x output resolution

You may take the size of the output and the size of the original as one dimension—say, length. Suppose your original is 2 in long and the print you want is 10 in. If you need an output resolution of 300 lpi (lines per inch), then you need 300 x 10 pixels—a total of 3,000 pixels—for output. The input resolution must, therefore, be 3,000 divided by 2 in (the size of the original), which gives the required scanner resolution of 1,500 ppi (points per inch).

The key is to determine the correct output resolution.

- For inkjets, use anything between 80 and 200 lpi, depending on paper quality.
- For screen-based work, use 72 dpi or 96 dpi.
- For reproduction in print, first determine the screen frequency—it is commonly 166 lpi for good-quality magazines and books but can vary from 96 to 300 lpi. Then multiply the screen frequency by a "quality factor" of 1.5. For example, if the screen frequency used is 150 lpi, the output resolution required is 1.5 x 150 = 225 ppi.

Here are some examples to illustrate these principles. Note that although the final settings are in lines, pixels, or dots per inch, you can work the early parts of the

Screen shot: film scanner

A dialog box for a film scanner may ask for output sizes: the proportion of length to width is often set by cropping the image, or it may be typed in. The resolution setting can also be entered by hand or by setting the scale and letting the software calculate resolution. A useful check is file size: high resolution (2,500 ppi) and a 7 MB file size suggest the image is black and white.

Screen shot: flatbed scanner

Complicated-looking dialog boxes, such as the one here for a flatbed scanner, are usually not that difficult to use. Here, you must set an output ruling (166 lpi in this example) and the scaling is set to "Factor," which is indicated at 100 percent. From the dimensions of the frame for the cropping, the scanner calculates the rest, including the resolution—given here as 400 dpi. The expected file size is shown at the top of the box.

calculations using metric measurements if you wish:

1 Your original image is 35 mm long, and you want to make a print that is 250 mm long, and the assumption is that you are using an inkjet printer with an output resolution of 120 lpi.

Input resolution = (120 x 250)/35

$= 30,000/35$

$= 857$ pixels per inch

Since the original is 35 mm (1.4 in) long, there will be a total of 857 x 1.4 = 1,200 pixels on its long side.

2 Your original is 35 mm long and you want a scan of sufficient quality to be suitable for magazine reproduction up to 250 mm long. Working on the assumption that the magazine prints to a 150 lpi line screen, and with a quality factor of 1.5, the output resolution needed, therefore, is

150 x 1.5 = 225 lpi.

Input resolution = (225 x 250)/35

$= 56,250/35$

$= 1,607$ pixels per inch or, say, 1,600 ppi

Since the original is 35 mm (1.4 in) long, there will be a total of 1,600 x 1.4 = 2,240 pixels on the long side of the image.

Determining file size

Look up the file size for the output you desire, then make sure the scanned file is about the same size by adjusting the dpi or resolution in the scanner driver.

Inkjet print	3 x 5 in (7.5 x 12.5 cm)	1.9 MB
	4 x 6 in (10 x 15 cm)	2.7 MB
	8 x 10 in (20 x 25.5 cm)	5 MB
	Letter (A4)	6.9 MB
	Tabloid (A3)	12.6 MB
Image for webpage	480 x 320 pixels	0.45 MB
	600 x 400 pixels	0.7 MB
	768 x 512 pixels	1.12 MB
	960 x 640 pixels	1.75 MB
Book/ magazine printing	Letter (A4)	18.6 MB
	8 x 10 in (20 x 25.5 cm)	13.6 MB
	5 x 8 in (A5)	9.3 MB
	5 x 7 in (12.5 x 17.5 cm)	6.7 MB

How to avoid the problem

Experiment with using the lowest resolutions you can manage that do not compromise the quality of the image. The exercise is most valuable when you are using an inkjet printer. Working with the smallest possible files will help to save you both time and money. Your work is likely to fall into a pattern after a while: keep a note of the settings that produce satisfactory results and reapply them to your new work. If you are outputting using commercial printers, ask them for their recommendations.

File formats: A summary

Most types of data files are produced by application software to be used specifically by that software, so there is only limited potential for interchange with other programs. However, image files are different, since they can be accessed and used by a range of programs. This is achieved by building them in widely recognized data-structures, or formats. The following are commonly supported.

TIFF

(Tag Image File Format) A method of storing image data, the best choice for images used in print reproduction, and a de facto standard. A bitmapped or raster image file format supporting 24-bit color per pixel, with such data as dimensions and color lookup tables stored as a "tag" and added to the header of the data file. A variety of tag specifications give rise to many types of TIFFs, leading to compatibility problems. The format can be compressed without loss (or losslessly) using LZW compression. This reduces file size by about half on average, but slightly slows down file opening. It is always safe to compress TIFF files, although some print bureaus may specify uncompressed files. The Windows suffix is .tif.

JPEG

(Joint Photographic Expert Group and pronounced "jay-peg") A format based on a data-compression technique that can reduce file sizes to as little as 10 percent of the original with only a slight loss of quality. This is the best choice for photographs intended for use on the Internet. When files are saved as JPEGs you will be offered different levels of quality. For general use, a middle setting (5 or 6) is sufficient, since it gives very good reductions in file size without noticeable loss in image quality. A high setting of 9 or 10 is the level you should choose for high-quality work—the file size is still smaller than that possible with LZW compression and loss of quality is all but invisible. The Windows suffix is .jpg.

Photoshop

This is an application-native format that has become so widespread that it is now almost a standard. Photoshop supports color management, 48-bit color, and Photoshop layers. Many scanners will save directly to the Photoshop format, and the format used on other types of scanners may, in fact, be Photoshop, albeit under a different name. The Windows suffix is .psd.

GIF

(Graphic Interchange Format) A compressed file format designed for use over the Internet, comprising a standard set of 216 colors. It is best for images with graphics—those with larger areas of even color—but not for photographic images that have smooth tone transitions. It can be compressed losslessly using LZW algorithms. The Windows suffix is .gif.

PDF

(Portable Document Format) A file format native to Adobe Acrobat based on PostScript. It preserves the document text, typography, graphics, images,

"Save as" screen shot
Whenever you save a digital picture file you need to make a decision about which format to save it in. The safest choice is TIFF, which is very commonly recognized, but specific picture needs, perhaps for publication on a website for example, may demand that you use another type of format. You can use this dialogue box to change from one format to another. To preserve the original, save your new file under another name when choosing a different format.

and layout. There is no need to embed fonts. It can be read, but not edited, by Acrobat Reader. The Windows suffix is .pdf.

PICT

(Macintosh Picture) This is a graphics format for Mac OS. It contains raster and vector information but is nominally limited to 72 dpi, being designed for screen images. PICT2 supports color to 24-bit depth, and it can be opened by very simple programs, such as SimpleText.

PNG

(Portable Network Graphics) A file format for losslessly compressed web images. It supports indexed-color, grayscale, and true-color images (up to 48 bits per pixel), plus one alpha channel,

with sample bit depth of up to 16 bits. It is intended as a replacement for GIF and may well also replace TIFF on the Web.

Raw format

Many digital cameras produce files in what is called, variously, the RAW, Raw, or raw format. There is no single raw format because each camera model produces files organized in different ways. Raw files save data directly from the analog-to-digital converter at the camera sensor, so the data has not received any processing for color, contrast, sharpness, and so on. Raw files are favored for quality and flexibility, but their variety and patchy documentation raise doubts for the long term. The DNG (Digital Negative) format has been proposed as an open standard for raw files.

JPEGs in detail

JPEG compression is efficient due to the fact that several distinct techniques are all brought to bear on the image file at the same time. Although it sounds complicated, thankfully, modern computers and digital cameras have no problem handling the calculations. The technique, known as "jay-pegging," consists of three steps.

1 The Discrete Cosine Transform (DCT) orders data in blocks measuring 8 x 8 pixels, which creates the characteristic "blocky" structure you can see in close-up (*see right*). Blocks are converted from the "spatial domain" to the "frequency domain," which is analogous to presenting a graph of, say, a continuous curve as histograms that plot the frequency of occurrence of each value. This step compresses data, loses no detail, and identifies data that may be removed.

2 Matrix multiplication reorders the data for "quantization." It is here that you choose the quality setting of an image, balancing, on the one hand, your desire for small-sized files against, on the other, the loss of image quality.

3 In the final stage of jay-pegging, the results of the last manipulation are finally coded, using yet more lossless compression techniques.

JPEG artifacts

This close-up view of a JPEG-compressed image shows the blocks of 64 pixels that are created by the compression feature. This can create false textures and obscure detail, but on areas of even tone, or where image detail is small and patterned, such artifacts are not normally visible—even with very high levels of compression. Note how the pixels within a block are more similar to each other than to those of an adjacent block.

The effect of these compressions is that JPEG files can be reduced by 70 percent (or, reduced to just 30 percent of their original size) with nearly invisible image degradation; you still have a usable image even with a reduction of 90 percent. However, this is not enough for some applications, and so a new technology, known as JPEG2000, based on another way of coding data, offers greater file compression with even less loss of detail.

Quick fix Problems with scans

Scanning puts your film-based work into digital form, which you can work with on your computer. The quality of the digitization is crucial to the quality of everything you subsequently do with your images, so you can see that it is important to take considerable care at this stage of the process. You do not want to work at an image for days only to discover it was scanned at too low a resolution or that it has defects that are too deep to remove without undoing all your work.

Problem: File size is too small

The most common error is working on a file size that is too small for the intended task (*see pp. 84–5 for details on how to calculate the optimum file size*). Always check your image's file size before you do any work on it: you want it to be neither too large (as it will slow your work down unnecessarily) nor too small (as output quality will then be too low).

Solution

If you discover that the file size you are working on is too small for what you want to do with it, then you have no option other than rescanning and starting again. The sooner you come to this decision, the less of your work you will have to redo.

Image size screen shot
The settings on this dialog box are something you should never see in reality. They show that a small image of 3.2 MB in size is about to be enlarged to a normal page-size print. For the resolution required, however, the resulting file size will grow to more than 16 MB (shown in the top line)—five times larger than the original. With this level of interpolation enlargement, the result will show broken-up detail. In this case it would be better to rescan the image to the required 16 MB.

Problem: Newton's rings

When you place a film strip directly on the glass surface of your flatbed scanner, although you may not realize it you are also trapping a thin layer of air beneath the film. This layer of air acts like an oil film—of the type you often see on a road surface—that causes the light to split into rainbow-colored patterns, known as "Newton's rings." These colored distortions are extremely troublesome to remove from the image and it is best to prevent them from occurring in the first place.

Solution

Avoid placing film strips directly on the scanner's glass surface. Most scanner manufacturers provide special holders for film strips or individual frames. If this is not the case with your machine, then make certain that the scanner is well warmed up before starting—hot, dry air seems to reduce the incidence of Newton's rings.

Newton's rings
This film (only a portion of which is seen here) was scanned on a flatbed scanner because, having been produced by a panoramic camera, it was too long to fit into a normal film scanner. When held down by the scanner's lid, the trapped air created these tree-ring-like patterns (which have been slightly exaggerated for reproduction purposes). They are extremely difficult to remove as they cover a large area and are also colored.

Problem: Jitter and other artifacts

Before starting work on an image, examine it closely for signs of any features that are not part of the original. Even the most expensive scanners can introduce artifacts, or imperfections, such as tiny black dots in light areas. These may be so small that they are invisible at normal size; some other errors, however, such as jitter, or the uneven movement of the scanner head, cause defects that are obvious at normal print sizes (*see right*)— although they may be invisible at screen resolution. Defects may result from movement of the original during scanning—for example, if your book slips slightly, the image will appear slightly stretched or smeared.

Solution

Rescanning on the same or on a better-quality scanner will solve the problem, unless the defect is due to the movement of the original.

Scanner jitter
A scan from an inexpensive scanner produced these streaks, which are due to the uneven movement of the scan head. The streaks have been exaggerated for reproduction purposes, but would be visible anyway when printed. Small areas could be improved by cloning, but essentially a better scanner is required.

Problem: Moiré from printed material

This problem arises when there is a clash between the regular pattern of the dots on the printed page of a book or magazine, say, and the regular raster pattern of the scanner. This conflict can cause a new pattern— known as a moiré pattern—to be superimposed over the image, usually with unsightly results.

Solution

There are several methods of dealing with moiré. You can rescan the original using a slightly different resolution setting, or you could try aligning the page slightly differently on the scanner's platen—just a small change of angle may be enough to do the trick. Some scanner software offers filters designed to remove, more or less successfully, such moiré patterns, but this is often at the cost of critically sharp image detail. Bear in mind that using sharpening filters (*see pp. 106–9*) may bring out

Moiré patterns
Just a small area of a photograph of a heron printed in a book was scanned for this example. You can readily see that the resulting image has picked up the array of half-tone dots that make up the printed original. The pattern of these dots has clashed with the regular array of pixels, resulting in the creation of another pattern. Seen here, it gives the impression of looking at the scene through an intervening fence of chicken wire.

uick fix Problems with scans continued

roblem: Noisy shadows

ge "noise," or pixels with random values, are
ountered in scanned images most frequently in the
dow regions of the image. In the example shown
e (see below), the dark areas should be black with
ooth transitions to the lighter areas, but the speckled
earance shows a very noisy scan, which was
duced by an inexpensive scanner.

olution

is may be improved by increasing the overall brightness
ne image, but that may be at the cost of losing
light detail. If the shadows are of very high density—
example, those in high-definition transparency film—
may need to scan on a better-quality machine.

Problem: Underexposure

You may have set the brightness level too low—this
often occurs as a result of compensating for a previous
original that was too bright. You may also have assessed
the prescan with the monitor screen incorrectly adjusted
The result is a scan with all the data skewed toward the
shadow regions. An underexposed scan can, of course,
also result from an underexposed camera original.

Solution

Make a new scan. If the original is underexposed,
improve it as far as possible at this stage rather than
in post-scanner processing. It may help to scan at the
highest bit-depth available (say, 36- or 48-bit), make the
tonal corrections, and then convert to normal 24-bit.

Levels screen shot
The numerous gaps between the columns seen here
indicate lack of data, while the way they are interspersed

Levels screen shot
The Levels histogram seen here (above) confirms the
underexposure seen in the image (top)—subject data is

Quick fix Inaccurate printer colors

The basic problem of color reproduction is that monitors produce colors in a very different way from printers. Bearing this in mind will help you avoid harboring unrealistic expectations. You can see from any diagram comparing the color spaces enclosed by printers compared with the color space of monitors (*see p. 67*) that the deeper blues, greens, and reds seen on a monitor cannot be reproduced in print. These colors are the typical hues that are "out-of-gamut" for printers—in other words, cannot be printed.

Problem: Screen/printer colors don't match

If image colors look correct on the screen but not when they are printed, there is a failure of communication between your software, monitor, or printer. Assuming that your monitor, software, and printer are correctly set up, you may need to alter the printer's advanced settings or options. You can usually change color balance by dragging the sliders provided: change these by small increments, note the settings ("capture," or save, them if the facility is available), and then reprint. Repeat this procedure until you obtain the results you want.

Problem: Bright colors merge

You have oversaturated colors. Although they appear distinct on screen, they are out-of-gamut on the printer. As a result, what were different colors blend into one hue. Try to reduce saturation overall by, say, 10 percent at a time until you start to see the separation of colors in the print. If this makes the other colors in the print too dull, try selecting the most vivid colors using, for example, Photoshop's Replace Color function, and then reduce the saturation of a limited range of colors. Color gamut of printers is usually largest if you use the best quality of glossy paper and the manufacturer's own inks. Change the paper if you are not using the best quality.

Problem: Weak colors with patterns

You have chosen a regular dither pattern. "Dithering" is a method of simulating a wide range of colors from a limited choice. For photographic images, you need a random dither pattern, while a regular one is better for business graphics (and it prints much faster, too). Choose random, or diffuse, dither in your printer driver options.

Equivalent printed image

On-screen image

Print brilliance
These images simulate the change you could see when printing out a highly saturated screen image on paper. The loss of depth and richness of color is dramatic when you compare them side by side in this fashion. Fortunately, most people looking at your prints will never see the screen image for comparison—as a result, they would accept the print on its own terms.

Dither patterns
What should be a smooth transition from pale blue to violet here appears banded and patterned. This is not because a small number of colors was used to simulate what really required hundreds of colors for accurate reproduction, but because the colors were ordered into regular patterns. If distribution were more random, the gradient would look much smoother.

Basic color management

One of the final frontiers of technology is how to get hundreds of different monitors, printers, inks, and papers, as well as cameras and scanners, to work together to produce results with reliable color. The goal is simply stated: we need colors to be reliably accurate. But this is a slippery and elusive process. The reason for color management is to ensure that the color information for different devices is used in a consistent and reproducible way. It is based on a common set of colors, called the profile connection space—essentially, all the colors that a normal human eye can see.

First steps

Your monitor is central to color management. Not only do you view and manipulate your images there, but the monitor is also easily adjusted to meet a standard. That is the process of calibrating.

Your computer operating system will allow you, through a control panel or system preferences, to calibrate the screen using simple visual controls (see your system's Help section). Essentially, the correct settings are those that give you reliable results on your printer. Try these settings: set the brightness to maximum, or a little less if it is uncomfortable; for the Gamma (or Target Gamma), set 1.8 or "Native"; for White Point, set D65 (or 6500 K) or higher—for example, 7000 K.

Calibration methods based on on-screen controls are inexpensive but unreliable. The most objective, but relatively costly, method is hardware calibration, in which a color sensor is attached to the monitor. It reads the different colors in order to calibrate and characterize the monitor's color.

Precautions

Whichever calibration method you use, observe the following precautions. If you use a CRT monitor, let it warm up for at least 30 minutes before attempting calibration. Remove any devices that may cause magnetic interference, such as a hard disk drive or speakers. Calibrate the monitor in the light you normally work in—ideally, low enough to make it difficult to read a newspaper. Do not allow desk lamps to shine on the screen (*see also pp. 32–3*). Recalibrate CRT monitors monthly (more often if used heavily) and if the monitor is moved. The slightest change in magnetic field can affect color performance.

Color profiles

The way one device handles color is defined by the differences between its own set of colors and that of the profile connection space. This information, called the color profile, is embedded in the image and includes other data about the white point and

Calibration frequency

Professional users, whose work relies on consistency from day to day, should calibrate their monitors about once a week, or at least every month. Monitors should be recalibrated if moved (even a small distance), if new electrical equipment is installed nearby (due to the effect of magnetic fields), or following any changes to screen resolution or color depth. It follows that frequent changes to screen resolution are not recommended. Other equipment should be calibrated following any major change, such as when ink supplies are changed, a new type of paper is used, the printer is transported any distance from its normal position, or if the printer drivers are updated.

Native gamma

On-screen procedures for calibrating a monitor will offer prompts such as this one, which asks the user to alter a setting while watching a target disappear into the background. This can be fairly accurate, but procedures that ask you to decide when a color looks neutral are decidedly unreliable.

how to handle out-of-gamut colors. When an image carries a color profile, a piece of equipment receiving the file will "know" how to interpret the colors and adjust them, if necessary, for reproduction. There are different types of profiles according to the device being used, but the key to color management is that every image you use should carry an appropriate profile. Adobe RGB (1998) is widely used for digital images.

Soft-proofing

Once you have calibrated your monitor, you can use it to check how your images will look when printed; this is called soft-proofing. For this, you need the output profile for the combination of printer and paper that you will use. This profile can be set as the output space or applied to the image directly. It may make the image look duller than normal but should more closely match the print.

Profile connection space

This diagram demonstrates how color characteristics of different devices can be translated to each other, using color profiles and a common color space.

Source profiles are seldom used because the majority of files are processed visually and are only of value with digital images in highly controlled environments, such as studios.

An image file may be embedded with a color profile so that it can be accurately reproduced when it enters a different working color space.

Working color space is your starting point. The RGB color space is widely used for digital cameras and gives acceptable results. Another standard is Adobe RGB (1998), which gives better results for professional use.

Inkjet profiles are perhaps the most troublesome for avid photographers. But produced accurately and used correctly, they can help maintain reliable, consistent results.

Monitor profiles are important because they help the computer system control the monitor, ensuring that colors are produced accurately.

CMYK output profiles are important for professional users and publishers of magazines and books, but they need not concern the majority of photographers.

Gamma settings

The gamma of a screen measures the way the image is projected on screen: for Apple computers and the print industry, the standard is 1.8, giving an image that is brighter in the midtones. The 2.2 gamma setting gives richer, darker midtone colors. Use the setting that gives you reliable printing results.

Target white point

The D50, or 5000 K, white point is a standard widely used in the printing industry. However, it appears too yellow and may make it difficult to obtain a true black. A white point of 9300 K, as used in domestic TV sets, is too blue. A good compromise is 6500 K, or D65, which is similar to midday sun.

All about image manipulation

4

First steps

The usual way to open a file is to double-click on it; you place the cursor over the icon for the file and quickly click the mouse twice. The computer's operating system then checks to see what type of file it is and launches a suitable software application. This, though, is not the best way, as the wrong software application may start up. The computer may also display a warning saying the file could not be opened (*see below right*). A better method is to start the application first and then open the file from within it. This often succeeds when files have lost their association with an application and cannot be opened with a simple double-click.

Image sources

Images from certain sources, such as PhotoCDs and images taken with professional Kodak cameras, should be opened from within the application recommended by the manufacturer. This is because the files may need to be uncompressed or otherwise processed to extract the best image quality before they are used.

Internet downloads

Images from an Internet site are usually in JPEG format (*see pp. 86–7*). If you expect to work on an image and then save it for extra treatment later on, it is good practice to perform a Save As on the file into a different format—for example, Photoshop or TIFF. Each time you save and close an image in JPEG, it is taken through the compression regimen—the file size may not reduce greatly, but quality progressively degrades.

Copyright and watermarks

Images from picture-agency CDs, the Web, or those on CDs given away with magazines may show a "watermark"—the company's or photographer's name—printed across the image. This prevents piracy and asserts the copyright-holder's rights. Images may also be invisibly marked—although there is no printing overlaying the images, they resist all but the most destructive changes to the files and suitable software can readily detect the invisible identification watermark.

Image degradation
This original portrait (*top left*) was saved several times with maximum JPEG compression (*top right*). Used small like this, the image is acceptable but, in fact, the original is far better, with smoother tones and more accurate color.

A close-up look at the original image (*above left*) shows continuous tones and unbroken lines, while the damage to the compressed version (*above right*) is obvious. A large print made from the JPEG image would simply not be acceptable.

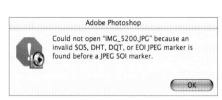

"Could not open" warning
If you see this warning box on your screen, or one like it, do not worry. You should be able to open the file concerned from within an application. To do this, launch the application first and then try to open the file using the menu options provided.

Color mode

Automatic Levels can lead to various results, depending on color mode. The initial RGB scan of this picture was dark and too warm in color (*above left*). Still in RGB (*p. 117*), the first correction was too bright (*above right*). This is because invoking Automatic Levels indiscriminately spreads values evenly in each channel. But after turning the image into LAB mode (*p. 127*), automatic correction produced a very accurate outcome (*right*).

⚠ Could not find the application program that created the document named "microtk settngs".

To open the document, select an alternate program, with or without translation:

☐ Photoshop® 6.0
☐ Adobe GoLive 5.0 with QuickTime translation
☐ Adobe Illustrator® 9.0
☐ Appearance
☐ Apple DVD Player with QuickTime translation
☐ CanoScan Toolbox

☑ Show only recommended choices

[Cancel] [**Open**]

"Could not find" warning

If you see this warning, or one like it, just look for the appropriate application on the list and click on it. If your application does not appear, do not panic: it is still in the computer. Start the application first, then try to open the file from within it.

Checking the image

• Check color mode. Some scanners produce LAB files or may have been incorrectly set. Most image-manipulation software works in 24-bit RGB color, and if the image is not in the correct mode, many adjustments are unavailable or give odd results.

• Assess image sharpness. Are the colors clear and accurate? If not, you may have scanned it incorrectly or opened up a low-resolution version.

• Check that there is no excess border to the image

caused by inaccurate cropping during scanning (*see pp. 98–9*). If there is, remove it with the Crop tool. Unwanted black or white regions will distort tonal calculations.

• Check the file size. It should be adequate for your purposes but not much larger. If it is too small, you could work on it for hours only to discover that it is not suitable for the output size desired. If it is too large, you will waste time, since all manipulations take longer than necessary to complete.

Cropping and rotation

Always check that scanned images are correctly oriented—in other words, that left-to-right in the original is still left-to-right after scanning. This is seldom a problem with images taken with digital cameras, but when scanning a film original it is easy to place the negative or transparency the wrong way around—emulsion side either up or down, depending on your scanner—so that the scanned results become "flipped." Getting this right is especially important if there is any writing or numbering in the image to prevent it reversing, as in a mirror image.

Image cropping

The creative importance of cropping, to remove extraneous subject detail, is as crucial in digital photography as it is when working with film. But there is a vital difference, for not only does digital cropping reduce picture content, it also reduces file size. Bear in mind, however, that you should not crop to a specific resolution until the final stages of image processing, as "interpolation" may then be required. This reduces picture quality, usually by causing a slight softening of detail. Image cropping without a change of resolution does not require interpolation.

In general, though, at the very least you will want to remove the border caused by, for example, inaccurate cropping when making the scan. This area of white or black not only takes up valuable machine memory, it can also greatly distort tonal calculations, such as Levels (*see pp. 102–3*). If a border to the image is needed, you can always add it at a later stage using a range of different applications (*see p. 112*).

Image rotation

The horizon in an image is normally expected to run parallel with the top and bottom edges of the image. Any slight mistakes in aiming the camera, which is not an uncommon error when you are working quickly or your concentration slips, can be corrected by rotating the image before printing. With film-based photography, this correction is carried out in the darkroom during the printing stage. But since it is a strictly manual process, you should not expect this type of correction to be an option available from the fully automatic printers found in minilabs.

In digital photography, however, rotation is a straightforward transformation, and in some software applications you can carry out the correction as part of the image-cropping process.

Note that any rotation that is not 90°, or a multiple of 90°, will need interpolation. Repeated rotation may cause image detail to blur, so it is best to decide exactly how much rotation is required, and then perform it all in a single step.

Fixed-size cropping

Some manipulation software, such as Photoshop, allows you to crop to a specific image size and to a specific output resolution—for example, 5 x 7 in (13 x 18 cm) at 225 dpi. This is useful since it combines two operations in one and is very convenient if you know the exact size of image needed— perhaps a picture for a newsletter. If so, enter the details in the boxes, together with the resolution. The crop area will then have the correct proportions, allowing you to adjust the overall size and position of the image for the crop you require. Cropping to a fixed size is useful for working rapidly through a batch of scans.

Crop Options screen shot
By clicking on "Fixed Target Size" you can crop to a specific size and resolution. This is a convenient way to change not only the image size but also to change the resolution of your image.

Image size and memory

Reducing the size of an image by half reduces its file size by three-quarters. In this series, the size of the third-largest image is half that of the largest, but its file size is a quarter. The smallest image here has a file size a full 16 times smaller than the size of the original. This is why even a small crop can cause a significant saving in machine memory.

File size: .25 MB   File size: 1 MB   File size: 2 MB   File size: 4 MB

Sloping horizon

A snatched shot taken with a wide-angle lens left the horizon with a slight but noticeable tilt, disturbing the serenity of the image. But by rotating a crop it is possible to correct the horizon, although, as you can see from the masked-off area (*above left*), you do have to sacrifice the marginal areas of the image. Some software allows you to give a precise figure for the rotation; others require you to do it by eye. Some scanner software gives you the facility to rotate the image while scanning.

Saving as you go

Adopt the habit of saving your working file as you proceed: press Control + S (PC) or Command + S (Mac) at regular intervals. It is easy to forget in the heat of the creative moment that the image on the monitor is only virtual—it exists just as long as the computer is on and functioning properly. If your file is large and what you are doing is complicated, the risks that the copmuter will crash are increased (and the resulting loss of the work more grievous). A good rule to remember is that if your file is so large that making frequent saves is an inconvenient interruption, then you definitely should be doing it, inconvenient or not.

Quick fix Poor subject detail

Although in most picture-taking situations the aim is to produce the sharpest possible image, there are situations where blur is desirable.

Problem

Images lack overall "bite" and sharpness and subject detail is soft or low in contrast overall.

Analysis

Unsharp subject detail and low contrast can have many causes: a poor-quality lens; inaccurate focusing; subject movement; camera movement; dust or scratches on the lens; an intervening surface, such as a window; and overmagnification of the image.

Solution

One of the great advantages digital photography has over film-based photography is that unsharpness can, to varying extents, be reduced using image-processing techniques. The main one is unsharp masking (USM). This can be found on nearly all image-manipulation software: in Photoshop it is a filter; it is provided by plug-in software such as Extensis Intellihance; and the software drivers for many scanners also provide it. Some digital cameras also apply USM to images as they are being recorded (see pp. 106–9).

However, while USM can improve the appearance of an image, there are limits to how much subject information it can retrieve. In particular, unsharpness caused by movement usually shows little or no improvement with USM. At times, a simple increase in image contrast and color saturation can help to improve the appearance of image sharpness.

Turning the tables
Blurred, low-contrast images are not necessarily failures. This portrait was taken through a dusty, smeary window. The diffusion has not only softened all image contours, it has also reduced contrast and introduced some flare into the shadow areas. These are usually fatal image flaws, but if they appear in association with the right subject they can add a degree of character and atmosphere, rather than detract from picture content.

How to avoid the problem

● Keep the front surface of your lens and any lens filters clean. Replace scratched filters if necessary.

● Focus as precisely and carefully as possible.

● Release the shutter smoothly, in a single action. For longer handheld exposures, take the picture as you breathe out, just before you start to breathe in.

● For long exposures, use a tripod or support the camera on some sort of informal, stable support, such as a table, window ledge, wall, or a pile of books, to prevent camera movement.

● Experiment with your lens—some produce unsharp results when they are used very close-up, or at the extreme telephoto end of the zoom range

Quick fix Poor subject color

If, despite your best efforts, subject color is disappointing, there is still a range of image-manipulation options to improve results.

Problem
Digital images are low in contrast, lack color brilliance, or are too dark. Problems most often occur in pictures taken in overcast or dull lighting conditions.

Analysis
Just like film-based cameras, digital cameras can get the exposure wrong. Digital "film" is, if anything, more difficult to expose correctly, and any slight error leads to poor subject color. Furthermore, high digital sensitivities are gained at the expense of poor color saturation; so, if the camera's sensitivity is increased to cope with low light levels, color results are, again, likely to be poor.

Overcast light tends to have a high blue content, and the resulting bluish color cast can give dull, cold images.

Solution
An easy solution is to open the image in your image-manipulation software and apply Auto Levels (see pp. 102–3). This ensures that your image uses the full range of color values available and makes some corrections to color casts. Although quick, this can overbrighten an image or make it too contrasty.

Some software, such as Digital Darkroom and Extensis Intellihance, will analyze an image and apply automatic enhancement to, for example, concentrate on increasing the color content or correcting a color cast.

The handiest single control is the universally available Saturation (see pp. 110–11 and 114–17).

Problem...

...solution

Manipulation options
The original scan (*top*) is not only dull, it is also not an accurate representation of the original scene. However, Auto Levels has generally brightened up the image (*above*). Color saturation was increased using the Hue and Saturation control, and, finally, the USM filter was applied to help improve the definition of subject detail.

How to avoid the problem

● In bright, contrasty lighting conditions it may help to underexpose by a small amount: set the camera override to -½ of a stop or -⅓ of a stop, depending on what the controls permit.

● Avoid taking pictures in dull and dark conditions. However, bright but partly overcast days usually provide the best color saturation. On overcast days, consider using a warm-up filter (a very light orange or pink color) over the camera lens.

● Avoid setting the camera to very high sensitivities—for example, film-speed equivalents of ISO 800 or above. And avoid using high-speed color film of any type in a conventional camera if color accuracy is crucial.

Levels

The Levels control shows a representation, in the form of a histogram, of the distribution of tone values of an image. Levels offers several powerful options for changing global tone distribution. The easiest thing to do is to click on the Auto Level button. This, however, works effectively in very few cases. What it does is take the darkest pixel to maximum black and the brightest pixel to maximum white, and spreads everything else evenly between them. This, however, may change the overall density of the image.

Another control that may be available is Output Level. This sets the maximum black or white points that can be produced by, say, a printer. Generally, by setting the white point to at least 5 less than the maximum (in other words, to about 250) you prevent the highlight areas in your output image from appearing totally blank. Setting the black point to at least 5 more than the minimum (in other words, to about 5) you will help to avoid the shadow areas looking overly heavy in your output image.

Auto Level

An underexposed image contains dark tones with few high-value ones (*far left*), confirmed in the Levels display (*bottom far left*). The gap on the right of the histogram indicates an absence of values lighter than three-quarter tone, with peak values falling in deep shadow. Applying Auto Level (*left*) spreads all available pixel values across the whole dynamic range. The new Levels display (*bottom left*) has a characteristic comblike structure, showing gaps in the color data. Auto Level not only brightens colors and increases contrast, it also causes a slight overall color shift.

How to read Levels

The Levels histogram gives an instant check on image quality—perhaps warning of a need to rescan.
- If all values across the range are filled with gentle peaks, the image is well exposed or well scanned.
- If the histogram shows mostly low values (weighted to the left), the image is overall low-key or dark; if values are mostly high (weighted to the right), the image is high-key or bright. These results are not necessarily undesirable.

- If you have a sharp peak toward one or other extreme, with few other values, you probably have an image that is over- or underexposed.
- If the histogram has several narrow vertical bars, the image is very deficient in color data or it is an indexed color file. Corrections may lead to unpredictable results.
- A comblike histogram indicates a poor image with many missing values and too many pixels of the same value. Such an image looks posterized.

Well-distributed tones

As you can see from this Levels histogram, a bright, well-exposed image fills all the available range of pixels, with no gaps. Since the image contains many light tones, there are more pixels lighter than midtone, so the peak of the histogram lies to the right of center. This image would tolerate a lot of manipulation thanks to the richness of color data it contains.

Deficient color data

An image with only a limited color range, such as this still-life composition, can be turned into a very small file by saving it as an indexed color file (p. 123). In fact, just 55 colors were sufficient to represent this scene with hardly any loss of subject information. However, the comblike Levels histogram associated with it indicates just how sparse the available color data was. Any work on the image to alter its colors or tonality, or the application of filter effects that alter its color data, would certainly show up artifacts and produce unpredictable results.

Histogram display

The histogram for this image shows midtones dominated by yellow and blue with large amounts of red in mid- to light tones, consistent with the strong orange color of the shirt. This display is from the FotoStation application, which displays histograms for each RGB separation in the corresponding color.

Burning-in and dodging

Two techniques used in film-based and digital photography for manipulating the local density of an image are known as burning-in and dodging.

Controlling density

Burning-in increases the density in the area of the image being worked on, while dodging reduces it. Both techniques have the effect of changing the tonal reproduction of the original either to correct errors in the initial exposure or to create a visual effect. For example, the highlights and shadows of both film and digital images are low in contrast, and to counteract this you can burn in and dodge

to bring out what shadow and highlight detail does exist by increasing local image contrast.

The same techniques can be used in order to reduce contrast—to darken highlight areas, for example—to bring them tonally closer to image midtones. An often-used application of this in conventional photography is burning in areas of sky when printing to darken them. Increasing the exposure of the sky (while shading, or dodging, the rest of the print) not only helps differentiate sky and cloud tonally, it also helps to match the sky tones to those of the foreground.

Digital techniques

In digital photography, burning-in and dodging are easily achieved using the tools available in all image-manipulation software. Working digitally, you can be as precise as you like—down to the individual pixel, if necessary. And the area treated can be between 1 and 100 percent of the image area, nominated by the Marquee or Lasso tool.

A drawback of working digitally, however, is that when manipulating large areas, results are often patchy and uneven, while working on large areas in the darkroom is easy.

Working digitally, some applications allow you to set the tool for the shadows, midtones, or highlights alone. Carefully choosing the tonal range to be manipulated helps avoid telltale signs of clumsy burning-in and dodging. Corresponding techniques, available in Photoshop and some other professional software packages, are known as Color Dodge and Color Burn painting modes.

Color Dodge is not only able to brighten up the image, but also pushes up image contrast as you apply the "paint." In addition, if you set a color other than white, you simultaneously tint the areas being brightened. Color Burn has similar effects—darkening and increasing image contrast.

Correcting exposure
Taken on a bright winter afternoon, the camera's meter was fooled by the sudden appearance of the sun within the picture area, causing it to underexpose the scene (*above left*). This situation can be rescued using the Dodging tool set to work on the highlights areas alone. However, to produce the corrected image shown here (*above right*), the Paintbrush tool was chosen and set to Color Dodge. By using the brush in this mode, set to a mid-gray color and with lowered opacity (for example, 50 percent), you will obtain more rapid results with less tendency to burn out subject details. As an optional way of working, paint onto a new layer set to Color Dodge mode.

Correcting color balance
Looking at the original image (*above left*), the temptation to burn in the foreground and some of the background in order to "bring out" the sheep is irresistible. Brief applications of the Burn tool on the foreground (set to mid-tone at 10 percent) and background hills, plus the Dodge tool on the sheep (set to highlight at 5 percent) produced an image (*left*) that was very similar to the scene as it appeared at the actual time of shooting.

HINTS AND TIPS

● Apply dodging and burning-in techniques with a light touch. Start off by using a light pressure or a low strength of effect—say, 10 percent or less—and then build up to the strength the image requires.

● When burning in image highlights or bright areas, set the tool to burn in the shadows or midtones. Do not set it to burn in the highlights.

● When burning in midtones or shadows, set the tool at a very light pressure to burn in the highlights or midtones. Do not set it to burn in the shadows.

● When dodging midtones, set the tool at very light pressure to dodge the highlights or midtones. Do not set it to dodge the shadows.

● When dodging shadows, set the tool to dodge the highlights. Do not set it to dodge the shadows.

● Use soft-edged or feathered Brush tools to achieve more realistic tonal results.

Sharpening

The ease with which modern image-manipulation software can make a soft image appear sharp is almost magical. Although software cannot add to the amount of information contained in an image, it can put whatever information is there to the best possible use. Edges, for example, can be given more clarity and definition by improving local contrast.

Digitally, sharpen effects are true filters, since they hold back some components and selectively let others through. A Sharpen filter is, in reality, a "high-pass" filter—it allows high-frequency image information to pass while holding back low-frequency information.

Unsharp Masking

The most versatile method of image sharpening is Unsharp Masking (USM). This takes a grid of pixels and increases edge definition without introducing too many artifacts. Unsharp Mask has three settings. In Photoshop, they are called Amount, Radius, and Threshold. Amount defines how much sharpening to apply; Radius defines the distance around each pixel to evaluate for a change; Threshold dictates how much change must occur to be acceptable and not be masked.

It is possible to overdo sharpening. In general, assess image sharpness at the actual pixel level, so that each pixel corresponds to a pixel on the monitor. Any other view is interpolated and edges are softened, or antialiased, making sharpness impossible to assess properly.

As a guide, for images intended for print, the screen image should look very slightly oversharpened, so artifacts (such as halos or bright fringes) are just visible. For on-screen use, sharpen images only until they look right on the screen.

Sharpening makes deep image changes that cannot easily be undone, so it is generally best to leave sharpening to last in any sequence of image manipulations, except for combining different layers. However, if you are working on a scan with many dust specks and other similar types of faults, you should expect the final sharpening to reveal more fine defects, so be prepared for another round of dust removal using cloning.

Undersharpening
In images containing large amounts of fine detail, such as this scene taken in Uzbekistan, applying a modest strength of USM filtering (55) and a large radius (22), with a threshold set at 11, does little for the image. There is a modest uplift in sharpness, but this is due more to an overall increase in contrast than to any other effect.

Oversharpening

The maximum strength setting used for this version results in over-sharpening—it is still usable and is arguably a good setting if you intend to print on poor-quality paper. The same setting applied to the Kashgar image (*pp. 108–9*) would simply bring out all the film grain—a technique for increasing noise in the image.

Ideal setting

The best settings for images with fine detail is high strength with a small radius and a very low threshold: here, strength was 222, the radius was 2, and the threshold was kept at 0. Details are all well defined, and if large-size prints are wanted, details are crisper than those obtained with sharpening using a larger radius setting.

Sharpening continued

Original image
This photograph of the main town square in Kashgar, Xinjiang, China, has large areas of smooth tone with little fine detail, and it would clearly benefit from the effects of image sharpening.

Using an advanced Photoshop technique for image sharpening, first mask off areas (such as a face) to be protected from oversharpening and any associated increase in defects. Next, produce a duplicate layer of the background and set it to Soft Light mode. This increases contrast overall. Then apply the High-Pass filter (found under the Filter menu in Other > High Pass). Increasing the radius strengthens the effect (passes higher frequencies, or more detail). You can now enter Quick Mask mode or add a layer mask to control which areas of the image will be sharpened by the High-Pass filter. This method is also effective for sharpening an image overall and can be controlled by direct settings and by opacity. However, the preview window in the dialog box does not give an accurate view because it samples only the top layer.

Oversharpening
If you increase the sharpening effect (222 in this version) and reduce the threshold (0), but reduce the radius to 2, virtually everything in the image increases in sharpness. The result is that film grain and fine detail are sharpened to an undesirable extent. Compare the result of these settings with that of an image that contains a mass of fine detail (p. 106).

Sharpening areas of tone

A moderate amount of sharpening (55) and a relatively wide radius for the filter to act on (22) improve sharpness where there is subject detail, without bringing out film grain or unwanted information, such as in the subject's skin tones. A threshold setting of 11 prevents the filter from breaking up smooth tonal transitions, as the sharpening effect operates only on pixels differing in brightness by more than 11 units.

Extreme settings

This version results from maximum amount and radius settings. The effect is extreme, but a threshold of 32 controls coloration. Even so, the image has highly saturated colors and brilliant contrast. In addition, film grain is emphasized. The random appearance of film grain gives more attractive results than the regular structure of a digital image, so if you want to use this effect, introduce image noise first.

Quick fix Image distractions

Unless there is a fundamental problem with your image, most minor distractions can be removed, or at least be minimized, using digital techniques.

Problem

While concentrating on your subject, it is easy not to notice distracting objects in the picture area. This could be something minor, such as a discarded food wrapper, but out-of-focus highlights can also be a problem.

Analysis

The small viewfinders of many cameras make it difficult to see much subject detail. Furthermore, though something is distant and looks out of focus, it may still be within the depth of field of your lens. At other times, you simply cannot avoid including, say, telephone lines in the background of a scene.

Solution

You may not need to remove a distraction completely—simply reducing the difference between it and adjacent areas may be enough. The usual way to achieve this is with cloning—duplicating part of an image and placing it into another part (see pp. 164–9). For example, blue sky can be easily cloned onto wires crossing it, as long as you are careful to use areas that match in brightness and hue. If you clone from as close to the distraction as possible, this should not be too much of a problem.

You could also try desaturating the background: select the main subject and invert the selection; or select the background and lower saturation using Color Saturation. You could also paint over the background using the Saturation or Sponge tool set to desaturate.

Another method is to blur the background. Select the main subject and invert the selection, or select the background directly, and apply a Blur filter. Select a narrow feather edge to retain sharpness in the subject's outline. Choose carefully or, when Blur is applied, the selected region will be left with a distinct margin. Try different settings, keeping in mind the image's output size—small images need more blur than large ones.

How to avoid the problem

Check the viewfinder image carefully before shooting. This is easier with an SLR camera, which is why most professionals use them. Long focal length lenses (or zoom settings) reduce depth of field and tend to blur backgrounds. And, if appropriate to the subject, use a lower viewpoint and look upward to increase the amount of non-distracting sky.

Problem...

...solution

Foreground distraction
An old man photographed in Greece shows me a picture of his sons. As he leans over the balcony, the clothespins in front of his chin prove impossible to avoid.

Cloning
Luckily, in this example there was enough of the man's skin tone visible to give a convincing reconstruction. To do this, the skin part of the image was used to clone areas of color over the

Problem...   ...solution

Background distractions
In the chaos of a young child's room, it is neither possible nor desirable to remove all the distractions, but toning them down would help to emphasize the main subject.

Desaturated background
Applying Desaturate to the background, turning all the colors into gray, has helped separate the girl from the numerous objects surrounding her. A large, soft-edged Brush tool was chosen and the printing mode was set to desaturation at 100 percent.

Problem...   ...solution

Selective blur
Despite using a large aperture, a wide-angle lens setting still produced more depth of field than I wanted in this example (*above left*). To reduce the intrusive sharpness of the trees, I used the Gaussian Blur filter set to a radius of 9 pixels (*right*). First, I selected the figure with a feathering of 5 and then inverted this selection in order to apply the Gaussian Blur to the background alone (*above right*).

Gaussian Blur

OK

Reset

☑ Preview

⊟ 100% ⊞

Radius: 9 pixels

Quick fix Image framing

Don't allow your images to become unnecessarily constrained by the sides of the camera viewfinder or the regular borders of your printing paper. There are creative options available to you.

Problem

The precise and clear-cut rectangular outlines around images can not only become boring, but sometimes they are simply not appropriate—for example, on a website where the rest of the design is informal. What is needed is some sort of controlled way of introducing some variety to the way you frame your images.

Analysis

In the majority of situations, producing images with clean borders is the most appropriate method of presentation. But with the less-formal space of a webpage, a looser, vignetted frame might be a better option. On occasion, a picture frame can also be used to crop an image without actually losing any crucial subject matter.

Solution

Scan textures and shapes that you would like to use as frames and simply drop them onto the margins of your images. Many software applications offer simple frame types, which you can easily apply to any image and at any size. Special plug-ins, such as Extensis Photoframe, simplify the process of applying frames and provide you with numerous, customizable framing options.

How to avoid the problem

The need to create picture frames usually arises from the desire to improve an image that has not been ideally composed. Nobody thinks about picture frames when looking at a truly arresting photograph. Inspect your pictures carefully, checking the image right to the edges. Tilting the camera when shooting creates a different style of framing, or simply crop off image elements you don't need.

Framing option 1

The first option applies a geometric frame in which it partially reverses the underlying tones of the image. It is effective in hiding unwanted details in the top left of the image, but its outline is perhaps too hard in contrast with the soft lines of the subject's body.

Framing option 2

The simplest frame is often the best— here it is like looking through a cleared area of fogged glass. The color of the frame should be chosen to tone in with the image. However, you should also consider the background color: on this black page, the contrast is too high, whereas against a white page or an on-screen background, the nude figure

Framing option 3

Here, a painterly effect is combined with a frame that reverses both hue and tone (a Difference mode). By carefully adjusting the opacity of the frame, the colors were toned down to match that of the main image. Finally, the frame was rotated so that the main axis nude figure runs across the diagonal, leading the eye from the thigh to her just-revealed breast.

Quick fix Converging parallels

While the brain largely compensates for visual distortions—so, in effect, you see what you expect to see—the camera faithfully records them all.

Problem

Images showing subjects with prominent straight lines, such as the sides of a building, appear uncomfortable when printed or viewed on screen because the lines appear to converge. Regular shapes may also appear sheared or squashed (*see also p. 62*).

Analysis

The change in size of different parts of the image is due to changes of magnification—different parts of the recorded scene are being reproduced at different scales. This occurs because of changes in distance between the camera and various parts of the subject. For example, when you look through the viewfinder at a building from street level, its top is farther away than its base—a fact that is emphasized by pointing the camera upward to include the whole structure. As a result, the more distant parts appear to be smaller than the closer parts.

Solution

Select the whole image and, using the Distortion or Transformation tool, pull the image into shape. If there are changes in magnification in two planes, both will converge, and so you will need to compensate for both.

How to avoid the problem

• Choose your shooting position with care and try to compose the image in order to keep any lines that are centrally positioned as vertical as possible. In addition, look to maintain symmetry on either side of the middle of the picture.

• Rather than pointing the camera upward, to include the upper parts of a building or some other tall structure, look for an elevated shooting position. This way, you may be able to keep the camera parallel with the subject and so minimize differences in scale between various parts of the subject as they are recorded by the camera.

1 Verticals converge
Shooting from ground level with the camera angled upward caused the scene to appear to tilt backward.

2 Image manipulation
Stretching the lower left-hand corner of the image using the Distortion tool is the solution to this problem.

3 Verticals corrected
The corrected image looks better and corresponds more closely to the way the scene looked in reality.

Color balancing

All image-manipulation software allows you to adjust the overall color of an image. Most also offers Levels and Curves control. In powerful software such as Photoshop, you have separate tools for controlling an image's hue and saturation, as well as others for replacing specified colors.

Color Balance control

This control makes global changes to the standard primary or secondary hues in an image. In some software, you can restrict the changes to shadows, highlights, or midtones. This control is useful for making quick changes to an image that has, for example, been affected by an overall color cast.

Levels control

This can be used to alter color balance of an image by adjusting separately the Level in each color channel. It is similar to the Color Balance facility,

but it provides you with greater control over brightness. The great advantage of Levels is that, in most software, settings can be saved and reapplied to other images.

Curves control

This controls the tonal reproduction of image brightness values, represented by a curve running from the lightest to darkest values. It can do everything the Levels control can, but with more precise location of where changes in tonal value occur. By carefully manipulating the curves in separate color channels, you can change the color balance to counteract irregularities in color reproduction in both film-based and digital originals. For example, you can decrease the blue content of shadows, to remove cold-looking tones, while leaving the rest of the image's color balance untouched (*for more details, see pp. 118–22*).

Warm white point
The original picture of a simple still-life (*above left*) has reproduced with the strong orange cast that is characteristic of images lit by domestic incandescent lamps. The corrected image (*above right*), was produced using Color Balance. It is still warm in tone because a fully corrected image would look cold and unnatural.

White point

A quick method of working when you wish to color-correct an image is to decide which part of the picture you want to be the white point—that part you want to be seen as pure white. You then use the Highlight Dropper tool, which is commonly available in image-manipulation software as well as part of scanner drivers, to select that area. If the white point needs to be corrected, the whole image will change in tonality (it is said to be mapped to the new white point) to reflect the fact that your selected area is now the "official" pure white point. This, like all color-correction methods, works only if the image has no strong color cast. If it has, then more drastic measures may be needed.

Color adjustments

With some types of software, you can control the hue and saturation levels of a picture file globally and by waveband. In Photoshop, for example, the Hue control shifts all colors or a band of colors (for example, reds or cyans) around the color wheel (*see p. 65*). You can also select colors directly from the image. The Saturation control increases color purity by decreasing its gray/white content.

The Lightness control is useful for improving poor scans and digital pictures (*see also see pp. 84–5 and 127*).

Original image
This original image has not been corrected in any way, and it accurately reproduces the flat illumination of a solidly cloudy sky.

Replace Color control
This replaces one hue, within a "fuzziness" setting or waveband, with another. Select the colors in the image you wish to change by sampling the image with the Dropper tool, and then transform that part via the Hue and Saturation dialog box (*see p. 117*). By setting a small fuzziness factor—the top slider in the dialog box—you select only those pixels very similar in color to the original; a large fuzziness setting selects relatively dissimilar pixels. It is best to accumulate small changes by repeatedly applying this control. Replace Color is good for strengthening colors that printers have trouble with (yellows and purples), or toning down colors they overdo (reds, for example). Film, monitors, or prints reproduce less than a third of the colors perceived by our eyes. But although we can distinguish very slight errors in reproduction when comparing samples side by

Color Balance control
Strong changes brought about via the Color Balance control, mainly by increasing yellow in the midtones—

which is the lowest slider in the dialog box here—make the scene look as if it has been lit by an early evening sun.

Levels control
A golden tone has been introduced to the image here by forcefully lowering the blue channel in the Levels control—the middle slider beneath the

histogram—thus allowing red and green to figure more strongly. Red and green additively produce yellow, and this color now dominates the highlights of the image.

Color adjustments continued

side, we cannot remember colors with anything like the same degree of precision. In addition, we remember some colors better than others.

Color balancing in photography is, therefore, usually not about achieving perfect reproduction but about controlling the process so that the output is not only accurate, given the limitations and characteristics of the medium used, but also pleasing to the eye.

What is color balance?

In the context of color, "balance" refers not to harmony or equality, but to neutrality. A scene that is color balanced is one in which the illuminating light offers all hues in equal proportion: in other words, the illumination is white and not tinted with color. Thus, a scene can be full of blues or greens yet still be color balanced, while another scene with a well-judged combination of secondary colors may look harmonious, but may not be color balanced at all.

The aim of color balancing is to produce an image that appears as if it were illuminated by white light, achieved by adjusting the white point

(*see p. 114*). However, there are different standards for white light, and so there are different white points. For example, it would not look natural to correct an indoor scene lit by domestic lamps in order to make it look like daylight; rather, a warm-toned white point is called for instead. However, in a scene containing brilliant colors, a cool-toned white point is more acceptable (giving colors like that from a bright Mediterranean sky). A color balance that is slightly warmer than neutral is generally preferred by most viewers.

Curves control
A simple inversion of color and tone leaves dark shadows looking empty and blank. Manipulating tonal reproduction via the Curves dialog box, however, gives you more control, allowing you to put color into these otherwise empty deep shadows (the bright areas after inversion). In the

dialog box here you can see how the curve runs top left to bottom right—the reverse of usual—and the other adjustments that were made to improve density in the image's midtones.

Color temperature

The color temperature of light has, in fact, nothing to do with temperature as we traditionally think of it; rather, color temperature is measured by correlating it to the color changes undergone by an object as it is heated. Experience tells us that cooler objects, such as candles or domestic lights, produce a reddish light, whereas hotter objects, such as tungsten lamps, produce more of a blue/white light.

The color temperature of light is measured in Kelvins, and a white that is relatively yellow in coloration might be around 6,000 K, while a white that is more blue in content might be, say, 9,500 K.

While color slide film must be balanced to a specific white point, digital cameras can vary their white point dynamically, according to changing needs of the situation.

Working in RGB

The most intuitive color mode to work in is RGB. It is easy to understand that any color is a mixture of different amounts of red, green, or blue, and that areas of an image where full amounts of all three colors are present give you white. The other modes, such as LAB and CMYK, have their uses, but it is best to avoid using them unless you have a specific effect in mind you want to achieve. When you are producing

image files to be printed out on paper, you may think you should supply your images as CMYK, since this is how they will be printed. However, unless you have the specific data or separation tables supplied by the processors, it is preferable to allow the printers to make the conversions themselves. In addition, CMYK files are larger than their RGB equivalents and thus are far less convenient to handle.

Hue/Saturation control

In this dialog box you can see that image hue has been changed to an extreme value, and this change has been supported by improvements in saturation and lightness in order to produce good tonal balance. Smaller changes in image hue may be effective

for adjusting color balance. Bear in mind that colors such as purples look brighter and deeper on a monitor than in print because of limitations in the printer's color gamut (pp. 67 and 176–9).

Replace Color control

Four passes of the Replace Color control were made to create an image that is now very different from that originally captured (p. 115). The dialog box here shows the location of the colors selected in the small preview window, and the controls are

the same as those found in the Hue and Saturation dialog box (above left), which allow you to bring about powerful changes of color. However, for Hue and Saturation to have an effect, the selected values must indeed have color. If they are gray, then only the lightness control makes any difference.

Curves

The Curves control found in image-manipulation software may remind some photographers of the characteristic curves published for films. This is a graph that shows the density of sensitized material that will result from being exposed to specific intensities of light. In fact, there are similarities, but equally important are the differences. Both are effectively transfer functions: they describe how one variable (the input either of color value or of the amount of light) produces another variable (the output or density of silver in the image).

The principal difference is that when it comes to image-manipulation software, the curve is always a 45° line at the beginning. This shows that the output is exactly the same as the input. However, unlike the film curve, you can manipulate this directly by clicking on and dragging the curve or by redrawing the curve yourself. In this way, you force light tones to become dark, midtones to become light, and with all the other variations in between. In addition, you may change the curve of each color channel separately.

Original image and curve
Since the original negative was slightly underexposed, the image from the scan is tonally rather lifeless. You cannot tell anything about exposure by looking at the curve in the screen shot (*above*) because it describes how one tone is output as another. As nothing has been changed, when it first appears the line is a straight 45°, mapping black to black, midtone to midtone, and white to white. It is not like a film characteristic curve, which actually describes how film is responding to light and its processing.

Boosting the midtones
The bow-shaped curve displayed here subtly boosts the midtone range of the image, as you can see in the resulting image (*top*). But the price paid is evident in the quarter-tones, where details in the shadows and the details in the highlights are both slightly darkened. The result is an image with, overall, more tonal liveliness; note, too, that the outline of the subject's face has been clarified. With some image-manipulation software, you have the option of nudging the position of the curve by clicking on the section you want to move and then pressing the arrow keys up or down to alter its shape.

What the Curves control does

The Curves control is a very powerful tool indeed and can produce visual results that are impossible to achieve in any other way. By employing less extreme curves, you can improve tones in, for example, the shadow areas while leaving the midtones and highlights as they were originally recorded. And by altering curves separately by color channel, you have unprecedented control over an image's color balance. More importantly, the color changes brought about via the Curves

control can be so smooth that the new colors blend seamlessly with those of the original.

In general, the subjects that react best to the application of extreme Curve settings are those with simple outlines and large, obvious features. You can try endless experiments with Curves, particularly if you start using different curve shapes in each channel. The following examples (*see pp. 120–2*) show the scope of applying simpler modifications to the master curve, thereby changing all channels at the same time.

Emphasizing the highlights

The scan's flat, dynamic range suggests that it could make an effective high-key image by changing the curve to remove the black tones (the left-hand end of the curve in the screen shot is not on black but is raised to dark gray) and mapping many highlight tones to white (the top of the curve is level with

the maximum for nearly a third of the tonal range). The result is that the input midtone is set to give highlights with detail. Very small changes to the curve can have a large effect on the image, so if you want to adjust overall brightness, it is easier to commit to the curve and then use Levels to adjust brightness (*pp. 102–3*).

Emphasizing the shadows

The versatility of the original image is evident here, as now it can be seen working as an effective low-key picture. The mood of the picture is heavier and a little brooding, and it has lost its fashion-conscious atmosphere in favor of more filmic overtones. The curve shown in the screen shot has been adjusted not simply to

darken the image overall (the right-hand end has been lowered to the midtone so that the brightest part of the picture is no brighter than normal midtone). In addition, the slight increase in the slope of the curve improves contrast at the lower midtone level to preserve some shadow detail. This is crucial, as too many blank areas would look unattractive.

Curves continued

Original image

The image you select for manipulating Curves does not have to be of the highest quality, but it should offer a simple shape or outline, such as this church. In addition, the range of colors can be limited—as you can see below, dramatic colors will be created when you apply Curves with unusual or extreme shapes.

Reversing dark tones

A U-shaped curve reverses all tones darker than midtone and forces rapid changes to occur—an increase in image contrast, for example. The deep shadows in the church become light areas, giving a negative type of effect, but the clouds have darkened and greatly increased in color content. The effect of using this shape curve is similar to the darkroom Sabattier effect, when exposed film or paper is briefly reexposed to white light during development.

Reversing light tones

An arc-shaped curve reverses the original's lighter tones, giving the effect shown here. Although it looks unusual, it is not as strange as reversing dark tones (*left*). Note that the curve's peak does not reach the top of the range— the height of the arc was reduced to avoid creating overbright white areas. The color of the building changes as the red-green color in the normal image was removed by the reversal, allowing the blue range to make its mark.

Tone/color reversal

Applying an M-shaped curve plays havoc with our normal understanding of what a color image should look like. Not only are the tones reversed as a result, but areas with dominant color whose tones have been reversed will also take on a color that is complementary to their own. And since parts of the tonal range are reversed and others are not, the result is a variegated spread of colors.

Using small files

When working on smaller image files, the results on the image of applying extreme curves become increasingly unpredictable due to gaps in the color data the software has to work with. When a W-shaped curve is applied, the picture becomes rather garish, an effect emphasized by the theatricality of the black sky. You can also see how some picture areas have sharply defined colors while others have smooth transitions, due to variations in the pixel structure of JPEGs (*pp. 86–7*).

Curves continued

Posterized effects

By applying a shape of curve that exhibits more peaks, such as that here, less of the image is reversed to dark tones. Although, as you can see in the resulting image, this produces a much brighter image overall, the many steep parts of the curve cause an effect something like that of posterization—the posterlike separation of colors into clearly segregated bands without the usual color transitions. This in large part contributes to the broken-up texture of the picture. If you wished to refine this style of image to a greater degree, then it might be best, after applying the Curve control, to bring the Dodge, Burn, and Saturation tools to bear in order to tidy up small areas of the picture. Such an area in the example shown here might be the distracting appearance of the black cloud looming ominously behind the church tower.

Keyboard shortcut

When you are experimenting with the Curves control to discover the range of possible effects offered by your particular software, you may not have to start from scratch each time. In many image-manipulation applications, including Photoshop, if you press a key, such as Alt or Option, while accessing the tool, it will open with the last used settings in place. With extreme Curves invoked, very small changes can have a marked effect on the image. Experiments such as these are all part of the fun.

Bit-depth and color

The bit-depth of a color file tells you how finely a piece of equipment can recognize or reproduce colors. It is a measure of resolution. Modern film scanners work to 24-bit RGB depth, or better (8 bits x 3 channels gives 24 bits). This means, in theory, that each channel is divided up into 256 equally spaced steps, which is the minimum requirement for good-quality reproduction. The total number of colors, if all combinations could be realized, is in the region of 16.8 million.

Higher resolution

Increasingly, we are finding that 24-bit does not measure up to our expectations—tones are not smooth enough and there is insufficient data to allow for dramatic changes in tones or colors. This is why, when applying curves with very steep slopes, the image breaks up into separate blocks of color. Better-quality scanners can work in 36-bit depth or more—even when images are down-sampled back to 24-bit, results are better than if the scanner had worked in 24-bit. Some scanners even provide 48-bit RGB files, but there are very few image-manipulation software packages that can use them. Even the professional application Photoshop is limited in its ability to manipulate 48-bit files. But results are worth the extra effort, as images exhibit far smoother tones and fewer problems when Levels or Curves tools are used.

File size

Once the image is ready for use, you may find that very few colors are needed to reproduce it. A picture of a lion among sun-dried grass stems on a dusty plain will have very few colors, for example. Because of this, you may be able to use a small palette of colors and greatly reduce file size.

Some software allows images to be stored as "index color." This allows image colors to be mapped onto a limited palette of colors—the advantage being that the change from full 24-bit RGB to an index reduces the file size by two-thirds. Reducing the color palette or bit-depth should be the last change to the image, since the information you lose is irrecoverable.

Color bit-depth and image quality
When seen in full color (*top*), this image of colored pens is vibrant and rich, but is the next image (*middle*), which contains a mere 100 colors, significantly poorer in quality? Yet this index color image is only a third of the size of the full-color original. As the color palette is reduced still further, to just 20 colors (*above*), the image is dramatically inferior. However, since this change does not reduce file size any further, there is no point in limiting the color palette beyond what is necessary.

Color into black and white

Creating a black and white picture from a color original allows you to change the shot's emphasis. For example, a portrait may be marred by strongly colored objects in view, or your subjects may be wearing clashing colored clothing. Seen in black and white, the emphasis in these pictures is skewed more toward shape and form.

The translation process

A black and white image is not a direct translation of colors into grayscale (a range of neutral tones ranging from white to black) in which all colors are accurately represented—many films favor blues, for example, and record them as being lighter than greens.

When a digital camera or image-manipulation software translates a color image, it refers to a built-in table for the conversion. Professional software assumes you want to print the result and so makes the conversion according to a regimen appropriate for certain types of printing presses and papers. Other software simply turns the three color channels into gray values before combining them—generally giving dull, murky results.

There are, however, better ways of converting to black and white, depending on the software you

have. But before you start experimenting, make sure you make a copy of your file and work on that rather than the original. Bear in mind that conversions to black and white loses color data that is impossible to reconstruct.

Before you print

After you have desaturated the image (*see box below*), and despite its gray appearance, it is still a color picture. So, unless it is to be printed on a four-color press, you should now convert it to grayscale to reduce its file size. If, however, the image is to be printed in a magazine or book, remember to reconvert it to color—either RGB or CMYK. Otherwise it will be printed solely with black ink, giving very poor reproduction.

Four-color black

In color reproduction, if all four inks (cyan, magenta, yellow, and black) are used, the result is a rich, deep black. It is not necessary to lay down full amounts of each ink to achieve this, but a mixture of all four inks (called four-color black) gives excellent results when reproducing photographs on the printed page. Varying the ratio of colors enables subtle shifts of image tone.

Desaturation

All image-manipulation software has a command that increases or decreases color saturation, or intensity. If you completely desaturate a color image, you remove the color data to give just a grayscale. However, despite appearances, it is still a color image and looks gray only because every pixel has its red, green, and blue information in balance. Because of this, the information is self-canceling and the color disappears. If, though, you select different colors to desaturate, you can change the balance of tones. Converting the image to grayscale at this point gives you a different result from a straight conversion, since the colors that you first desaturate become lighter than they otherwise would have been.

Saturation screen shot
With the color image open, you can access the Saturation control and drag the slider to minimum color. This gives a

gray image with full color information. In some software you can desaturate the image using keystrokes instead (such as Shift+Option+U in Photoshop, for example).

Color saturation

While the original color image is full of light and life, the colors could be seen as detracting from the core of the image—the contrasts of the textures of the water, sand, and stones. This is purely a subjective interpretation, as is often the case when making judgments about images.

Color desaturation

By removing all the colors using the Saturation control to give an image composed of grays, the essentials of the image emerge. The Burn and Dodge tools (*pp. 104–5*) were used to bring out tonal contrasts—darkening the lower portion of the picture with the Burn tool, while bringing out the sparkling water with the Dodge tool.

Overcoming distracting color

The strong reds and blues (*above left*) distract from the friendly faces of these young monks in Gangtok, Sikkim. However, a straight desaturation of the image gives us a tonally unbalanced result. Attempts to desaturate selectively by hue will founder because the faces are a pale version of the red habits. We need to compensate for the tonally unattractive product of desaturation (*middle*) by redistributing the tones to bring attention to the boys' faces. This involves reducing the white point to control the sunlit area in the foreground, plus a little burning-in to darken the light areas of the habit and the hand of the monk behind. Then, to bring some light into the faces (*right*), we use the Dodging tool set to Highlights.

Levels screen shot

With the desaturated image open, move the white point slider in the Levels dialog box to force the brightest pixels to be about a fifth less bright: in other words, to have a value no greater than 200.

Color into black and white continued

Channel extraction

Since a color image consists of three grayscale channels, the easiest way to convert the color to grayscale is to choose, or extract, one of these and abandon the others. This process is known as "channel extraction," but it is available only as part of more professional software packages.

When you view the image normally on the monitor, all three color channels are super-imposed on each other. However, if you look at them one channel at a time, your software may display the image as being all one color—perhaps as reds of different brightnesses, or as a range of gray tones, according to the software preferences you have set. If your software gives you the option, choose to view the channels as gray (by selecting this from the preferences or options menu). Then, simply by viewing each channel, you can choose

the one you like best. Now, when you convert to grayscale, the software should act on the selected channel alone, converting it to gray.

Some software may allow you to select two channels to convert to gray, thus allowing you a great deal of experimentation with the image's appearance. In general, the channels that convert best are the green, especially from digital cameras, because the green channel is effectively the luminance channel, and the red, which often gives bright, eye-catching results.

Another method, available in Photoshop, is to use Split Channels to produce three separate images. With this, you save the image you like and abandon the others. Note, however, that this operation cannot be undone—the extracted file is a true grayscale, and is just a third the size of the original file.

Red-channel extraction
While the colors of the original image are sumptuous (*above left*), black and white seemed to offer more promise (*above right*). It is clear that the sky should be dark against the mane and cradling hand, so the green and blue channels (*right*) were of no help. Neither was the lightness channel (*opposite*), since it distributes tonal information too evenly. The red channel, however, presented the blues as dark and the brown of the horse as light. So, with the red channel extracted, no extra work was needed.

Channels screen shot
If your software allows, select color channels one at a time to preview the effects of extraction. Turn off the color if the software shows channels in their corresponding colors.

Blue channel

Red channel

Green channel

Lab (with Lightness channel extracted)

Comparing channels

The three grayscale images that make up the original color image (*top left*), photographed in Kenya, can be seen in the Channels screen shot (*above*). An image from the blue channel alone is very dark because there is little blue in the image. In contrast, the red channel is too light and seems to make the girl's face look insubstantial, while the dress is nearly white because of its high red content. The green channel is, overall, the best balanced since it carries much of the detail information. As a final experiment, the color image was converted from RGB to Lab mode and the Lightness channel extracted (*right*)—the other two carry hardly any detail information. The advantage of this approach is that, given a well-balanced original, it needs no further manipulation.

Lab mode

When you convert a color image image to LAB, or Lab mode, the L channel carries the lightness information, which contains the main tonal details about the image. Using software such as Photoshop, you can select the L channel and manipulate it with Levels or Curves. With the L channel selected, you can now convert to grayscale and the software will use only the data in that channel. If your software gives you this option, you will come to appreciate the control you have over an image's final appearance, and results are also likely to be sharper than if you had extracted another of the channels to work on. The extracted file is a true grayscale, so it is only a third the size of the original color file.

Color into black and white continued

Original image
A simple conversion of this image could make colors look lifeless—a problem avoided by using the Channel Mixer control (*below*).

Working in RGB mode
In RGB, the blue channel was reduced, making the sky dark, and the red was increased to compensate. Results of using these settings are contrasty and dramatic, but the foreground is too bright.

Working in CMYK mode
With the original image translated into CMYK mode, results are noticeably softer than those achieved via the Channel Mixer in RGB mode.

Channel Mixer control

A colored filter used in black and white photography looks a certain color because it transmits only its own color waveband of light. Thus, a yellow filter looks yellow because it blocks non-yellow light. If you then use this filter to take a picture (making the appropriate exposure compensation), yellows in the resulting image are white and the other colors look relatively dark.

Lens filters are limited by the waveband transmissions built into each piece of glass, irrespective of the needs of the subject. But using the Channel Mixer tool you can, in effect, choose from an infinite range of filters until you find the ideal one for each subject.

Using this tool, you can now decide how to convert a color image to grayscale—making greens brighter in preference to reds, for example, or making blues dark relative to greens. Depending on your image software, you may also be able to work in RGB or CMYK (*see above*), the two methods producing different results.

Channel Mixer screen shot
With the control set to monochrome, the result is gray. If one channel is set to 100 percent, and the others at 0, you are effectively extracting that channel. This is more powerful than channel extraction (*pp. 126–7*).

If you set the control to Preview, you can see the image change as you alter the settings. For landscapes, increase the green channel by a large margin and correct overall density by decreasing the red and blue channels. Channel mixing is useful for ensuring that reds, which are dominant in color images, are rendered brighter than greens.

Separating tones

Starting with this color image (*top left*), a standard grayscale conversion gives acceptable results (*middle left*), but channel mixing separates out the tones more effectively, particular in shadow areas (*bottom left*). The settings required were complicated, and arrived at by trial and error (*screen shot above*). The work done reduces the need for further processing of the image, but if you wish to refine the results further, a channel-mixed image makes such techniques as burning-in and dodging (*pp. 104–5*) easier to apply, since, as you can see, the shadows on the shirts are far more open and susceptible to local density control.

To help learn how to isolate colors using the tools available in your software, start by selecting a bright, multicolored image—perhaps a collection of fruit, a flower stand, or something similar. Working on a copy of the image, now decide which color you wish to emphasize by making it light after conversion to grayscale. Use Color Balance, Replace Color, Hue and Saturation, or Channel Mixer tools to obtain the required result. If your first try does not work, return to the image and try a series of new settings. When you have a result you are happy with, note the settings. Use this information to replace another color in the image, and see if you can get to the desired result more quickly than the first time.

When color just won't do
The original image of this Chinese girl was brilliantly colored. However, by converting it to black and white, all distractions are removed and attention is focused into the girl's eyes.

Duotones

Much of the art of traditional black and white printing lies in making the most of the limited tonal range inherent in printing paper. A common tactic is to imply a wider tonal range than really exists by making the print contrasty. This suggests that shadows are really deep, while highlights are truly bright. The success of this depends on the subtleties of tonal gradation between these extremes. A further technique is to tone the print, adding color to the neutral gray image areas.

Modern digital printers have opened up the possibilities for toning well beyond that possible in the darkroom. The range of hues is virtually unlimited—you can simulate all those that can be created with the four-color (or more) process.

Creating a duotone

Starting with an image, even a color one, first turn the file into a grayscale (*see pp. 124–9*) using, in Photoshop, the Image > Mode menu. This permanently deletes color information, so you need to work on a copy file. Similar results can be obtained in the Sepia Tone effect, a menu option in almost all image-manipulation applications.

Now that you have a grayscale image, you can enter the Duotone mode, where you have a choice of going it alone or loading one of the preset duotones. If you are not familiar with the process, use the Duotone Presets (usually found in the "Presets" folder of Photoshop). Double-click on any one to see the result.

Simple duotones
This view of Prague (*left*) has been rendered in tones reminiscent of a bygone era. After turning the image to grayscale, two inks were used for the duotone, neither of them black. This gave a light, low-contrast image characteristic of an old postcard.

Duotone Options screen shot
The curve for the blue ink (*above*) was lifted in the highlights in order to put a light bluish tone into the bright parts of the image and also to help increase the density of the shadow areas.

Clicking on the colored square in the dialog box (*see opposite*) changes the color of the second "ink." Bright red could give an effect of gold toning; dark brown, a sepia tone. This is a powerful feature—in an instant, you can vary the toning effects on any image without any of the mess and expense of mixing chemicals associated with the darkroom equivalent.

If you click on the lower of the graph symbols, a curve appears that tells you how the second ink is being used, and by manipulating the curve you can change its effect. You could, for example, choose to place a lot of the second ink in the highlights, in which case all the upper tones will be tinted. Or you may decide to create a wavy

curve, in which case the result will be an image that looks somewhat posterized.

In Photoshop, you are able to choose to see Previews. This updates the image without changing the file, thereby allowing you to see and evaluate the effects in advance.

You need to bear in mind that a duotone is likely to be saved in the native file format (the software's own format). This means that to print it, you may first have to convert it into a standard RGB or CMYK TIFF file, so that the combination of black and colored inks you specified for the duotone can be simulated by the colored inks of the printer. This is the case whether you output on an inkjet printer or a four-color press.

Retaining subject detail

In this original image (*above*), there was so much atmosphere, it was a shame to lose the color. But the resulting duotone, with a green second ink, has its own charms (*above right*).

To reduce overall contrast and allow the green ink (chosen via the Color Picker dialog box, *below*) to come through, it was necessary to reduce the black ink considerably—as shown by the Duotone Curve dialog box (*right*).

Duotone Curve screen shot

The low position of the end of the curve in the dialog box (*above*) indicates a low density of black, but the kinks in the curve were introduced to increase shadow contrast and

retain subject detail. The lifted end of the curve shows that there are no real whites: the lightest part still retains nearly 14 percent of ink, as shown in the top box labeled "0:" in the Duotone Curve dialog box.

Tritones and quadtones

The addition of one or more inks to a duotone (*see pp. 132–3*) adds extra layers of subtlety to an image. Using most image-manipulation software, you will have tritone or quadtone boxes offering additional inks and curves for you to apply.

Bear in mind that with the extra inks offered, you can produce tinted highlights, or you can hint at colors in the shadows that are not present in the midtones, and in this way create more tonal separation. But there is no substitute for experimenting by applying different curves and colors, since this is the best way to learn how to use this powerful control. As a starting point, try using color contrasts by applying third and fourth inks in small amounts. Or, if you want a graphic-arts effect, try curves with sharp peaks.

One technical reason for using a quadtone is to help ensure accurate color reproduction. While not guaranteeing results, the chances of an accurate four-color black are greatly increased by specifying a quadtone in which the colors used are the standard cyan, magenta, yellow, and black of the printing process.

You can save curves and sets of colors and apply them to other grayscale images. When you find a combination that appeals to you, save it for future use in a library of your favorite settings.

Original image
Starting with this view of the city of Granada, in southern Spain (*above*), I first made a copy file of the original to work on. Then, using the copy file, I removed all the color information to make a grayscale, before deciding on which inks to apply.

Quadtone
For this image, black has been assigned to the dark, featureless shadows, green to those shadows that still retain details, and blue to the lower and midtones. This is shown by the peaks in the graphs next to each color ink in the Duotone Options dialog box (*above right*). Adjusting the heights of the peaks changes the strength of the colors.

Tritone
Assigning different-colored inks to specific tonal densities in the image produces visual effects that are very difficult to achieve in any other way. In this tritone version of the scene, the fourth (blue) color has been switched off, and the result is a brighter, lighter image compared with the quadtone (*left*).

Sepia tones

With digital technology, you can bring about image changes with more control than is possible in a darkroom. A prime example of this is the digital equivalent of sepia toning—the low-contrast, nineteenth-century technique that gives warm, brown tones with no blacks or whites.

Old prints lack contrast due to the film's recording properties and the makeup of the print's emulsion. The softness is likely due to the lens, while the brown tone is down to the print's being treated with a thiocarbamide compound.

Many digital cameras produce "sepia-toning," if correctly set, and most image-manipulation applications will also give these effects with just a single command, though with little control. For

greater control, first convert your grayscale image to RGB color mode. Once in RGB, desaturate the image. Use the Levels command (*see pp. 102–3*) to make the image lighter and grayer, and then remove the blacks and whites.

Now you can add color. The easiest way to do this is by using Color Balance (*see p. 114*) to increase the red and yellow. Or use the Variations command (if available) to add red, yellow, and possibly a little blue to produce a brown that you find suits the content of your image.

Another option is to work with a grayscale image in Duotone mode to add a brown or dark orange as the second ink. Using Photoshop, this provides the most subtle effects.

Using Variations
There are several ways to add overall color to the type of interior view shown here. Although subject content is strong, the black and white version (*top left*) lacks atmosphere. The multi-image Variations dialog box (*right*), an option available in most image-manipulation software packages, presents several versions of the toned original from which to choose. By clicking on one (*shown outlined in the dialog box above*), you turn it into the image of choice, and you can then compare it against the original. To arrive at the final sepia-toned image (*bottom far left*), the Levels control was used to reduce shadow density and so produce a flatter contrast.

Split toning

Toning is a traditional darkroom technique—or workroom technique, as darkness is not essential for the process. Here, the image-forming silver in the processed print is replaced by other metals or compounds to produce a new image tone.

The exact tone resulting from this process depends, in part, on the chemical or metal used and, in part, on the size of the particles produced

by the process. Some so-called toners simply divide up the silver particles into tinier fragments in order to produce their effect. Where there is variation in the size of particles, the image takes on variations in tone—from red to brown, for example, or from black to silvery gray. This variation in tone is known as split toning and is caused by the toning process proceeding at

Using the Color Balance control

Images with well-separated tones, such as this misty mountain view, respond best to split toning. To add blue to the blank, white highlights of the mist, an adjustment layer for Color Balance was created. The Highlight Ratio button was clicked and a lot of blue then added. Another adjustment layer was then created, but this time the tone balance was limited to

the shadows. The Preserve Luminosity check-box was left unchecked in order to weaken the strong corrections given: the screen shot (*above*) shows that maximum yellow and red were set. Further refinement is possible in software packages such as Photoshop (*see right*).

Blending Options

This is part of the Blending Options box from Photoshop. The color bars show which pixels from the lower and which from the upper layer will show in the final image. With the sliders set as here, there is partial showthrough— allowing a smooth transition

between the blended and unblended image areas. For this layer, the underlying area shows through the dark blue pixels. In addition, a wide partial blend was indicated for all channels, allowing much of the light blue to show over the dark, reddish tones.

different rates. These rates are dependent on the density of silver in the original image.

This, perhaps, gives you a clue about how the effect can be simulated digitally in the computer—by manipulating duotone or tritone curves (*see pp. 132–4*) you can lay two or more colors on the image, the effects of which will be taken up according to image density.

Another method is to use Color Balance (*see p. 114*), which is available in all image-manipulation software. This is easiest to effect in software that allows you to adjust the Color Balance control independently for highlights, midtones, and shadows. If your software does not allow this, you can achieve a similar effect with Curves, working in each color channel separately (*see pp. 118–22*).

Using Tritone
The Tritone part of the Options dialog box for the final image shows a normal curve for the first, orange-brown, color. The second, blue, color is boosted to darken the midtones, while the third color, another blue, supports the first blue. Without the addition of this third color, the midtones would look a little too weak and lack visual impact.

Using Color Balance
The aim here was to highlight the similarity in shape between the tree reflected in the store window and the lamps within in the original image (*top left*). At first, two colors—brown and blue—were used, but it was hard to create sufficient contrast between the dark and light areas. To help overcome this problem, another blue was added to boost the dark areas, as shown in the Duotone Options dialog box (*above left*)—the blue plus brown giving deep purple. Color Balance (*above right*) was shifted to help shadow saturation, and the lamps were also dodged a little, to prevent them from being rendered too dark.

Hand-tinting

Ever since the early days of photography, the hand coloring of black and white prints has been considered an art form, with its own palette of "permitted" tones. And because of the undeniable skill required by practitioners, the process tends not to be for the faint-hearted—the slightest mishap could cost you the entire print.

Working digitally

However, hand coloring in the digital domain is very different. It allows risk-free experimentation, no commitment to interim results, and, of course, it is an entirely mess-free process.

This said, there are still some points you need to consider. Many photographers make the mistake of painting directly onto their image with the Brush tool set to Normal. This never works well because you are switching the pixel values of your image directly into the Brush color. You may then try painting into a layer, but this does not help much either. Even if you change the opacity percentage in an attempt to make the effect more subtle, it still appears as if the color has replaced the image. What you need to do instead is add the color values, still using the Brush tool but to the grayscale values of the image, without changing

Color combinations
To suit the strong shapes of the original (*top*), equally strong colors were called for. You can work with any combination of colors, and it is worth experimenting—not only will some combinations look better, but some will also print more effectively than others. Bear in mind that

a blank area will not accept color if the Color or Blending mode is set to Colorize. To give white areas density, go to the Levels control and drag the white pointer to eliminate pure white pixels. Once the pixels have some density, they have the ability to pick up color. To give black areas color, reduce the amount of black,

again via Levels control. Although the "paint" is applied liberally (*above left*), note in the finished print (*above*) that color does not show up in the totally black areas.

the luminance value of the pixels. That is the job of the Color or Colorize mode.

There are two ways of proceeding. The method that most closely imitates painting is to use the Brush set to Color. The second method is to create a new layer set to Color above the image, and paint into this. This makes it possible to erase errors without damaging the underlying image. If you find it easier, add strong colors to see what you are doing and then reduce the opacity afterward.

Pastel shades are often out-of-gamut with color printers and monitors (*see p. 67*), so you may need to work with barely visible subtleties for the

printed result to look soft enough. As yet, the porcelain-like textured finish of a good-quality, hand-colored print is beyond the ability of inkjet printers. The careful use of papers with tinted bases can help the effect, since the paper's tints will narrow the dynamic range and soften contrast.

Painted layer
When tinting an image, you can apply the paint quite freely—as you can see in this image of the painted layer that lies above the base image. However, for a realistic final effect you need to use a range of colors to give variety. Unlike using real paints on a print, you can easily erase any unwanted mistakes and repaint the layer as often as you wish.

Reduced opacity
The springtime foliage deep within an old woods (*above*) was emphasized by a great deal of detailed dodging (*pp. 104–5*) to lighten individual leaves. In order to introduce some color into the scene, a new layer was created and its Blending mode was set to Color—this means that only areas with density are able to pick up color (*above right*). The paint was then applied to this layer. Finally, the opacity of the layer was reduced to 40 percent for the final image (*right*) to allow the quality of the foliage to show through the color overlay.

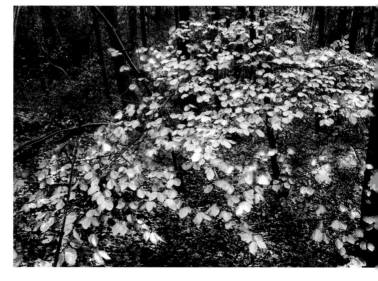

Cross-processing

Of the numerous unorthodox ways to process color film, perhaps the most popular are developing transparencies in chemicals designed for color negatives and processing color negatives in chemicals designed for color transparency film.

Cross-processing techniques make fundamental and irreversible changes to the film, so there is much to be said for simulating the effects using digital image-manipulation techniques. There is a further advantage to working digitally. Color negative film is overlaid with an orange-colored mask whose job it is to correct inherent deficiencies in the color separation or filtering process during exposure. Before the final print can be made, this mask has to be replaced or neutralized.

Color negative film to transparencies

Results from this type of cross-processing have flat tones and muted colors due to the fact that color negative film is low in contrast and transparency processing chemicals compress highlights. Color is also unpredictable, resulting in color balance in the highlights being different from that in the lower midtones and shadows.

Digitally, the Curves control is the best way to simulate this effect, though don't be alarmed if

Processing negatives as transparencies

The flattening-out of image contrast and the semblance of color toning that results from processing color negative film in chemicals intended for transparencies can create an interesting portraiture effect. By applying different curves to each color channel (*above*), the color balance was shifted away from the red (*above left*) toward the yellow-green coloration that is typical

of this form of cross-processing (*left*). Note the posterization beginning to become apparent in the shadow areas around the subject's eyes. This is due to the original image being shot on high-speed film. The curves that are given here are for your guidance only: you can start with these, but you are likely to want to adjust them, particularly the master RGB curve, to suit the particular images you are working on.

your image becomes too dark or light—you can adjust overall brightness later. Another possible image outcome is posterization. If you find this effect unattractive, then the quality of the scan may not be good enough. If that is the case, your only option is to rescan the original image, possibly to a higher bit-depth (*see p. 123*).

From transparencies to color negatives

Results from processing transparencies as color negatives are often contrasty, with color shifts toward cyan. They also have an open tonality, often with highlights reproducing as featureless white. This occurs because of the need to print inherently high-contrast transparencies on paper meant for the lower contrast of color negatives.

The best way to create this effect digitally is to manipulate the separate channels in the Curves control. When you have a set of curves that work, you can save and reapply them to any image.

If you find it hard to concentrate on the overall lightness of the image while juggling different channels, leave overall density to the end and work just on the colors and contrast. Once you are satisfied with these, call up the Levels control (*see pp. 102–3*) to adjust overall brightness.

Processing transparencies as negatives

The high-contrast effect that results from cross-processing color transparency film in color negative chemicals works with subjects that have strong outlines and punchy colors (*above left*). By applying the set of curves shown here (*right*), the result is brilliant color and the type of washed-out highlights typical of this form of cross-processing (*above right*). Since the highlight areas are tonally balanced by the full shadows and strong colors, they are more acceptable than in an image with a normal tonal range. The curves are given here are for your guidance only: you can start with these, but you are likely to want to adjust them, particularly the master RGB curve, to suit your particular images.

Filter effects

One of the alluring features of working digitally is being able to create, at the touch of a button, fantastic visual effects. These range from the dazzling to the ridiculous. However, while filter effects can impress, they are often solutions looking for visual problems. Experienced digital workers use filters only when they have a definite objective in mind.

Special filter effects are most useful when judiciously used with standard operations, where they lift an image into the extraordinary. However, not all filters give strange or even obvious results: some, such as Unsharp Masking, are essential tools.

The variety of different filter effects can be bewildering at first glance, so it may be helpful to classify them into broad categories.

Sharpness and Blur filters These affect the image, or selected areas, uniformly (*see pp. 106–9*). They work at the edges of image detail to increase differences at these boundaries (sharpening) or decrease differences (softening or blurring).

Distortion filters These change the shape of the image—either overall or small portions of it. These can be very tricky to control and need to be used with care (*see pp. 54 and 144*).

Art Materials and Brushstroke filters These filters aim to simulate such effects as charcoal drawing or painting brushstrokes by using image information and combining it with effects based on mimicking real artists' materials. With these may be grouped filters that are designed

Distortion filters
This extreme shape distortion was created using the Liquify filter in Photoshop. The effects can be extreme and cartoon-

like in appearance. However, delicate distortions are also possible—putting a smile on a person's face, for example.

Art Materials filter
Filters designed to imitate artists' techniques are readily available, and can be effective when applied to appropriate

imagery. Adjustments to tone, color, and sharpness after application of the filter often determine whether the effect is a success or failure.

to break up the image into blocks or add "noise" (*see p. 147*).

Stylizing filters These use geometric shapes to build up the image, or else they base the new image on features, such as edges, of the original (*see p. 149*).

Texturizing filters These filters (*see p. 143*) are similar to Rendering filters in 3-D modeling programs. For example, lighting effects simulate a light shining on the image, and by altering the "surface" of the image, the light appears to give the image a texture. These filters make heavy demands on the computer, and you may find that large files cannot be processed if the machine does not have enough RAM.

Using filters

- Practice on small files when experimenting with filter effects.
- Try the same filter on different styles of images to discover which filters work best on particular types of imagery.
- Filters often work best if applied to selected areas.
- Repeated applications of a filter can lead to unpredictable results.
- You usually need to adjust contrast and brightness after applying a filter.
- Reduce the image to its final size on screen to check the effect of filters.

Stylizing filters
These filters take their cue from geometric shapes, applying them to images to create mosaic-like effects. Dramatic, three-dimensional effects, such as Extrude, are also possible. They usually need to work on images that feature clear shapes and strong colors.

Texturizing filters
Texturizing filters, or the very similar Rendering filters, provide a range of challenging effects for digital photographers. The computer, too, is likely to be challenged by them, since they all soak up a great deal of computing power.

Filter effects continued

Distortion filters

In essence, Distortion filters work by changing the position of a pixel in an image by moving its value onto another pixel while leaving the original color and brightness information intact. The key point here is that the distance the pixel value is moved depends on its original position.

The effects of the filters can be applied over small, repeated grids, such as in the Glass Distortion, or globally, as in the Pinch filter effect. These filters change the inherent shape of objects in ways that are simply impossible to imitate using any type of conventional treatments, such as the special effects filters used on the camera lens or in a traditional darkroom.

ZigZag (ripples)

This Distortion filter makes an image look as if it is a reflection in a pond. With any Distortion filter, it is vital to be able to control the degree of the effect (*above*). For an animation, you can increase the effect progressively, adding more ridges and saving separate images (later to be the animation "frames") for each step.

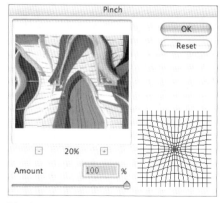

Pinch

This filter acts as if the image is on a rubber mat being squeezed or stretched. It compresses the "mat" toward the center, with most effect away from the diagonals. When lightly applied to a limited area, the filter is useful for subtle shape changes of small features. You can also experiment with rotating the whole canvas before applying the filter. Try rotating the image a little and applying the filter; then repeat with another small rotation. If any distortion is not enough, reapply the effect to strengthen it.

RAM problems

Rendering and Distortion filters use large amounts of RAM. If you run low, try distorting the image one channel at a time. However, if the image is not full of information, or suffers from noise, the effects of this method may not be the same as a single, simultaneous application. If you run out of RAM with other operations, try reducing the image file size a little at a time until you can perform the operation. Rendered images seldom need the resolution of an unblemished one, so you can resize images without worrying about loss of detail.

Glass
Looking at an object through a refracting medium, such as glass, causes distortion. This filter imitates different types of glass, which you can nominate, as well as the size and strength of the effect. One way of using this filter is to duplicate the image on another layer, apply the effect, and then merge it with the original.

Polar Coordinates
This filter performs some very complicated mathematics in order to show how an image might look if it were projected onto a sphere. Notice how the vertical lines in the church have been mapped into circular lines, as though the original image (p. 142) had been a two-dimensional map of a three-dimensional globe, and the filter has returned the image to its original shape. However, since the original image was not corrected for projection distortions, the filtered image appears strongly distorted.

Filter effects continued

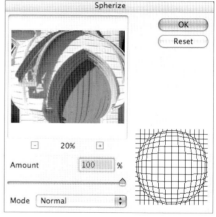

Smart Blur
With this filter you can specify a radius that sets how far the filter searches for dissimilar pixels to blur. In addition, you can set a threshold that determines how different the pixels' values should be before they are blended. In short, the filter can be set to leave the edges but blur lower-contrast detail. You can also set a mode for the entire selection or for the edges of color transitions. Where there is significant contrast, Edge Only gives black and white edges; Overlay Edge gives white.

Spherize
This filter produces a simple distortion, making the image look as if seen through a water droplet. With high settings (*above*) the effect is not obviously useful, but when applied with a light touch it can be used for correcting lens distortions, such as those introduced by lens attachments. Try applying the filter to small sections of the image at a time— the effects on images that have clear lines can be visually very intriguing.

TRY THIS

The best way to learn about digital filters is to work systematically through them, using a variety of images each time. Start by selecting three different color images. One should have a single, strong shape, such as a leaf or a silhouette of a church. Another should have masses of detail—perhaps a landscape full of trees. The

third test image should feature strong colors arranged in a pattern, which could be abstract. Resize the images to about 1 MB and save them with a new file name. Now try the different filters you have available on each one and make notes of which types of filters work best with each type of image.

Art Materials filters

Filters that imitate the effects of artists' materials can be very rewarding. Different software packages approach this class of filter with varying degrees of success—ultimately, a filter that applies its effects in an indiscriminate manner across an image is not as versatile as building up effects by hand. However, they provide quick solutions: the trick is in selecting the right type of image to work on. Choose those with simple outlines and clear shapes that do not rely on intricate details.

Crosshatch

This filter is often more effective when it is applied to black and white images, since it mimics the strokes used by artists to cover an area in tone. You need to experiment with different settings for length of stroke and other features (*above*). You have a choice of applying another filter to improve the Art Materials filter's appearance or to change the image to black and white. Another option with an image such as the one here is to print it onto highly textured paper. If you select the right paper stock, the interaction of the crosshatched strokes and the texture of the paper can create a very realistic impression of an artist's work.

Plastic Wrap

Filters can produce a metallic effect by creating neutral highlight areas accompanied by shadow regions. This is called Plastic Wrap in Photoshop, and by varying (in particular) Highlight Strength (*above*) with Detail set to follow the image outlines, the resulting image looks as if it has been printed and embossed onto a metal plate. If the shininess is too hard, however, image noise can increase as a result.

Filter effects continued

Spatter

The Spatter filter imitates an oil painting in which color has been applied with a broad-bristle brush. Starting with an image that has very clear outlines is essential. To improve the simulation of the work of a real artist, you can increase the saturation of colors, and add a little unexpected color to uniform areas. Since an artist is unlikely to leave any canvas bare, you may need to clone some strokes into any white, empty areas.

Cutout

This filter uses areas of flat color to produce an effect similar to a woodcut. It reduces an image to its bare essentials and is useful when quick, graphics-like effects are called for. "No. of Levels" in the dialog box refers to the number of different grayscale steps per channel. If you choose a high figure, there are more colors, and this reduces the effect of the graphic simplification of detail.

High Pass

This filter, in the Corel Painter application, produces a very surprising result when it is applied. The original image was too dark and also lacked color saturation, but with a little extra work, the final result (*left*) has certain attractive, painterly qualities. The lesson to be learned here is that even if you know, or think you know, what a filter will do to an image, it is still worth taking the time to experiment—sometimes you will be surprised. "High Pass" is a technical term describing a filter that passes subject detail, or high-frequency information.

Stylizing filters

This class of filter uses image color data from the original to build up blocks of color, or the location of image edges, as the basis for producing graphics-style effects. It is always best to check the appearance of the image at the final size it will be viewed—some effects may look eye-catching when they are seen at large screen magnifications, but they are subsequently lost when printed out at their final size. Beware of options such as Find Edges. These have alluring effects that seem to improve any image to which they are applied, but are popular to the point of being a cliché.

Mosaic

The filter produces pixelated-style images. It creates a representation of what an image would look like if you were to reduce its resolution considerably, and then enlarge it back up to the required size. In fact, it makes a lot of sense to work in just this way, since the resulting image will then be just a tiny fraction of its original file size. However, when using the filter, you can preview the results more easily. To improve further the effect of a low-quality image, you can posterize the colors, thus reducing the number of colors used in the image.

Crystallize

This simple filter averages out the color under irregular, polygonal areas and gives each polygon a uniform hue. The size of polygons can be varied to match the output size (*above*). Some applications may call this filter effect Mosaic or Tessellation: the idea is that there are no gaps between blocks of color, which fully cover the image. With filters of this type, you may need to reduce the density of black areas of the image if they predominate. Not only can you work with very low-resolution images, you may in fact achieve better results if you do. One experiment worth trying is to compare the effects of the filter on the same image at both high and low resolutions.

Filter effects continued

Glowing Edges

The Glowing Edges filter builds on the Find Edges filter by adding a solarization effect. This partially reverses image tones and produces a neonlike glow around image borders. As a result, images are always dark and benefit from being lightened after the filter has been applied. "Edge Width" in the dialog box (*above*) preserves the original image outlines if it is kept to low figures.

Emboss

This filter emphasizes image outlines while leaving all other details a neutral gray. The outlines are then shown as if they are an embossed surface lit from the side. If you wish to obtain the best from this filter, experiment with the controls offered, which adjust not only the strength of the effect but also the direction from which the light appears to come.

Working with filters

● When trying filters, use small files. Those 1 MB or smaller speed up all operations. Larger files of the same image, however, may give slightly different results.
● Make a careful note of any filter settings you try that produce effects you like.
● Avoid running other applications or performing tasks such as printing or Internet operations while using filters, since these slow down your machine.

● A filter, once used, is likely to run faster the next time (on modern computers it will have been stored in the RAM cache), so it may be easier to keep a few small images open and apply the same filter to each to try it out, rather than try a different filter each time.
● Incorporate the figures of settings you like to use by including them in the file name ("tree glow 2 6 5", for example).

Texturizing or plug-in filters

Filters that work on original image data and change its color values and pixel position can sometimes have weird and wonderful effects. These are said to be Rendering filters, since they apply a combination of surface texture and lighting properties—rather like the rendering processes in 3-D modeling programs that create computer-game backgrounds.

Many filters designed to work within software applications, such as Photoshop or Painter, fall into the same category. They plug into these existing, larger applications, and it can take many hours of trial and error to learn how to use them effectively. Plug-in effects are readily available as Web downloads; in addition, they are frequently offered on a free trial basis with digital photography and computing magazines (*see also pp. 214–15 and 218–19 for further information*).

Lens Flare
This filter imitates the effect of a bright light source flaring into the camera lens. Plug-in collections that give a full range of effects are available, though software such as Photoshop has only basic controls. The dialog box here shows just three types of effects, corresponding to different lenses, and a flare-strength control. You can also change the position of the "light source." Although it appears to be a simple filter, it makes considerable demands on the computer, so you need ample RAM.

Stained Glass
This filter combines the effects of an Art Materials filter with Texture and Lighting filters. You need to choose the color of the borders with care: an inappropriate one will ruin the effect of the changes. Since this and similar filters, such as Mosaic, greatly simplify color data as well as reduce detail, you can save images as very small JPEG files without worrying about loss of quality.

Filter effects continued

Clouds (via Levels)

The Clouds filter reverses color values in a non-uniform way. The result of applying this filter is difficult to predict, but on images with plain, clear outlines, it can be dramatic. If you apply the filter, then reduce its opacity over the original image, you can produce a very passable imitation of a badly faded color print. In addition, you can apply the filter twice (*top*) and darken with Levels (*top and above*) to elaborate the effect—or even more times to explore stranger and stranger effects (*below*).

PhotoGroove

The PhotoGroove is a plug-in filter from the Extensis Phototools set, and it is useful for giving images a highly customizable border—as if they were wrapped over a frame, for example. Not only can you vary the width and height of the border, but the profile of the border's shape can also be precisely drawn (*above*). The border design here suggests that the image has been printed onto a metallic box (*top*).

Multiple clouds

Applying filters more than once can give rise to unpredictable results. Here, the colors are far removed from those of the original, while the sharpening effect on image contours was unexpected.

Fractal Explorer

This filter, part of the range of KPT plug-in filters, delivers a bewildering array of options that operate together to produce millions of visually stunning combinations.

Terrazzo

The Terrazzo plug-in filter from Xaos Tools is a very efficient shortcut to some striking graphics effects. Quick and easy to use, it is able to turn the most mundane of images into stunning patterns. It works rather like a kaleidoscope, in which you can control, to a fine degree, the number and placement of mirrors. The filter acts on a nominated part of the image—here, the boy in the tree—and the resulting render, or tile, is repeated until the whole image area is filled.

Lighting Effects

The dialog box for this filter looks complicated (*above*), but it is worth persevering with. The filter allows you to apply different shapes and qualities of light, varying its color and position, and applying simple textures. The filter takes some time to work, due to the calculations needed, but the preview image is accurate and you can try different settings before you commit to one. It is easy to get lost, so make notes of setting combinations you like before moving on to a new one. For this effect (*top*), the settings have increased contrast and made the image look as if it is printed on a textured, metallic surface with a strong light from the lower left.

Behind the scenes

Image filters are groups of repeated mathematical operations. Some work by operating on small parts of an image at a time; others need to "see" the entire image at once. For example, the USM filter looks at blocks of up to 200 pixels square at a time, while Rendering loads the entire image into memory. A simple filter effect to understand is Mosaic. The filter takes a group of pixels, according to the size you set, and calculates their average value by adding them all and dividing by the number of pixels. It then gives all the pixels in the group the same value, so the pixels appear greatly enlarged. The filter then moves to the next set of pixels and repeats the operation. Most Mosaic filters can work on small image segments at a time, but some need to operate on the entire image for each calculation. These latter types require a great deal of computer memory and calculating power. Add all of these operations together and you obtain the pixelated effect of the Mosaic filter.

Selecting pixels

There are two ways of limiting the action of an image-manipulation effect: using a tool that applies the effect locally (a Dodge tool or Brush, for example); or selecting an image area and applying the effect just to those pixels.

Making a selection

One method is to select every pixel contained within an area defined using, say, the Lasso or Marquee tool: these pixels can be of any value or color. In this case, the pixels are said to be contiguous. Or you can select pixels from across the image that are the same as or similar to a color you specify, using a tool often called the Magic Wand. Since there may be gaps between these areas, this selection is said to be noncontiguous.

A crucial aspect of selection is that you can partially select a pixel near the edge of a selection in order to "feather" the effect. This creates a gradual transition across the boundary from pixels that are fully selected through those that are partially selected to those that are unselected, thus smoothing out the image-manipulation changes.

The effect of selecting a local, defined set of pixels for the changes to work on has an effect similar to that of masking (*see pp. 158–9*). But there are important differences. First, a selection is a temporary mask—it disappears as soon as you click outside a selected area. Second, in software with Layers, the selection applies only to the layer that is active or chosen. Third, with some software, you can copy and move selected pixels—something that cannot be done with a mask.

Some advanced software provides two different types of image data—bitmap and vector. With these, you need to use different tools to make selections. When you select pixels, you can also create selections using the Pen or Shape tools to give precise outlines called paths. A path is a vector shape that contains no pixels.

Original image
This cropped view of a church in New Zealand shows the original, unmanipulated image. The change I wanted to make here was to the windows, which looked too dark in contrast to the color of the boarded exterior.

Making a selection
Using Photoshop's Lasso, with a feathering width set to 11 pixels, I selected the dark glass within the window frames. To start a new area to be selected, hold down the the Control key (for PCs) or Command key (for Macs)—the selected area is defined by moving dashes, known as "marching ants." When the Levels command is invoked, settings are applied only to the selections.

Final effect
In some circumstances, the somewhat uneven result of using the Lasso selection can produce more realism than a perfectly clean selection would give. The dark areas remaining toward the bottom of the right-hand windows correspond to the area omitted from the selection in the previous image (*above left*).

● Learn about the different ways of making a selection. Some are obvious, such as the Lasso or Marquee tool, but your software may have other less-obvious methods, such as Color Range in Photoshop, which selects a band of colors according to the sample you choose.

● Use feathered selections unless you are confident you do not need to blur the boundaries. A moderate width of around 10 pixels is a good start for most images. But adjust the feathering to suit the task—for a vignetted effect, use very wide feathering, but if you are trying to separate an object from its background, then very little feathering produces the cleanest results. Set the feathering before making a selection.

● Note that the feathering of a selection tends to smooth out the outline: sudden changes in the direction of the boundary are rounded off. For example, a wide feathering setting to a rectangular selection will give it radiused corners.

● The selected area is marked by a graphic device called "marching ants"—a broken line that looks like a column of ants trekking across your monitor screen: it can be very distracting. On many applications you can turn this off or hide it without losing the selection: it is worth learning how to hide the "ants."

● In most software, after you have made an initial selection, you can add to or subtract from it by using the selection tool and holding down an appropriate key. Learning the method provided by your software will save you the time and effort of having to start the selection process all over again every time you want to make a change.

● Examine your selection at high magnification for any fragments left with unnatural-looking edges. Clean these up using an Eraser or Blur tool.

● Making selections is easier to control with a graphics tablet (see p. 30) than with a mouse.

Original image
The brilliant red leaves of this Japanese maple seem to invite being separated out from their background. However, any selection methods based on outlining with a tool would obviously demand a maddening amount of painstaking effort. You could use the Magic Wand tool, but a control such as the Color Range (right) is far more powerful and adaptable.

Color Range screen shot
In its implementation in Photoshop, you can add to the colors selected via the Eyedropper tool by using the plus sign; or by clicking the Eyedropper tool with a minus sign (beneath the "Save" button), however, you can refine the colors selected. The Fuzziness slider also controls the range of colors selected: a medium-high setting, such as that shown, ensures that you take in pixels at the edge of the leaves, which will not be fully red.

Manipulated image
Having set the parameters in the Color Range dialog box (above left), clicking "OK" selects the colors—in this case, just the red leaves. By inverting the selection, you then erase all but the red leaves, leaving you with a result like that shown here. Such an image can be stored in your library to be composited into another image or used as a lively background in another composition.

Quick fix Removing backgrounds

One of the most common image-manipulation tasks is to eliminate a background. There are two main methods: one is to remove the background directly by erasing it (time-consuming); the other is to hide it under a mask.

Problem

The main problem is how to separate a foreground object from its background while retaining fine edge detail, such as hair, or maintain the transparency of a wine glass and retain shadows and blurred edges.

Analysis

Almost all edges in images are slightly soft or fuzzy—it is more the transitions in color and brightness that define edges. If a transition is more sudden and more obvious than other transitions in the locality, it is seen as an edge. If you select the foreground in such a way as to make all its edges sharp and well defined, it will appear artificial and "cut out." However, much depends on the final size of the foreground: if it is to be used small and hidden by a lot of other detail, you can afford a little inaccuracy in the selection. If not, you must work more carefully.

Solution

Make selections with edge transitions that are appropriate to the subject being extracted. The usual selection methods—Lasso or Magic Wand—are sufficient most of the time, but complicated subjects will need special tools, such as Corel KnockOut, Extensis Mask Professional, or the Extract Image command in Photoshop.

How to avoid the problem

With objects you expect to separate out, it is best to work with a plain backdrop. However, while a white or black background is preferable to a varied one, even better is a colored ground. The aim is to choose a color that does not appear anywhere on the subject—if your subject is blond, has tanned skin, and is wearing yellow, a blue backdrop is perfect. Also, avoid using rimlighting, since this imparts a light-colored fringe to the subject. In addition, avoid subject-movement blur and try to keep an extended depth of field so that any detail, such as hair behind the subject's head, is not soft or fuzzy.

Low tolerance
With simple tasks, such as removing the sky from this image, the Magic Wand or similar tool, which selects pixels according to their color and is available in almost all image-manipulation software, is quick to use. It has just one control—the tolerance—which allows you to set the range of colors to be selected. If you set too low a tolerance (here the setting was 22) you obtain a result in which only a part of the sky is selected, seen by the "marching ants" occupying just the right-hand portion of the sky and small, isolated groups.

Removing the sky
Adjusting the tolerance setting in small, incremental steps allows you to see when you have captured just the right area to be removed. Then, pressing "OK" removes your selection. The edges of the selection may be hard to see in a small image, but are clearly visible on a large monitor screen.

High tolerance
If you set too high a tolerance, you will capture parts of the building where it meets the sky. Here, notice the result of setting a large feathering (111 pixels) to the selection—pixels a long way to either side of a target pixel are chosen. As a result, the selection is smoothed out and the boundary is very fuzzy.

riginal image

his original image of a young Afghan girl, who is also
xpert carpet weaver, shows her taking to the floor to
e. Unfortunately, the distracting background does
dd to the image as a whole.

2 Defining fore- and background

Using Corel KnockOut, I first drew inside the girl's
outline to define the foreground and then outside her
outline to define the background. The region between the
two outlines comprises the transition area that allows
soft boundaries to be smoothly masked.

Making the mask

Using the information from the previous step, a mask
eated. The mask outlines the foreground while hiding
background: the black shows the hidden area and the
e where the image will be allowed to show through.

4 Knocking out the background

Now, while the mask hides part of the image on
its own layer, it does not affect images on another layer
(*below left*). Therefore, if you place an image behind the
mask, you will see that image appear.

Layers screen shot

The Layers dialog box shows the little girl and
ssociated mask lying over the introduced image.
use the mask was produced by extracting the girl,
riginal background is gone, waiting for a new
round image to be introduced

6 Masked combination

The background was lightened to tone in with the
colors of the girl. The mask has preserved the softness of
the girl's outline, and now she appears to be dancing in
front of the wall-hanging. An extra refinement would be
to soften the background so that it appears less sharp

Masks

Masks allow you to isolate areas of an image from color changes or filter effects applied to the rest of the image. Unlike real-life masks, digital types are very versatile: you can, for example, alter a mask's opacity so that its effects taper off, allowing you to see more or less clearly through it. Using image-manipulation software, you can alter a mask until you are satisfied with it and then save it for reuse. When you do so, you create what are known as "alpha channels," which can be converted back to selections. Technically, masks are 8-bit grayscale channels—just like the channels representing the colors—so you can edit them using the usual array of painting and editing tools.

If your software does not offer masks, don't worry—it is possible to carry out a good deal of work by the use of selections. But remember that selections are inclusive—they show what will be included in a change; masks work the opposite way, by excluding pixels from an applied effect.

Software takes two approaches to creating masks. First is Photoshop's Quick-mask, which gives direct control and allows you to see the effect of any transitional zones. Or, you can create a selection that is turned into a mask. This is quick, but transitional zones cannot be assessed.

Quick-mask

In Photoshop and Photoshop Elements, you hit the Q key to enter Quick-mask mode. You then paint on the layer and hit Q again to exit, but in the process, you turn the painted area into a selection. You can also invert your selection (select the pixels you did not first select)—sometimes it is easier to select an area such as bright sky behind a silhouette by selecting the silhouette and then inverting the selection. You then turn the selection into a mask by adding a layer mask.

The layer mask makes all the underlying pixels disappear, unless you tell it to leave some alone. When applying a layer mask, you can choose to mask the selected area or mask all but the selected area. The advantage of Quick-mask is that it is often easier to judge the effect of the painted area than it is to make many selections. It also means that an accidental click of the mouse outside a selection does not cancel your work—it simply adds to the mask. Use Quick-masking when you have many elements to mask out at once.

Turning selections into masks

Some methods of selecting pixels have already been discussed (*see pp. 154–5*). If you need a

Using Quick-mask

Bottom layer

Quick-mask, or any method where you "paint" the mask, is best when you are not attempting to enclose a clearly defined shape, such as a person's silhouette. It is best first to place the image that will be revealed under the mask—in this example, it is an Islamic painting.

Creating the mask

Next, the mask is applied to the main leaves in this negative image. The red color shows where the freehand masking will be created. When it is turned into a mask, this is the area that will allow the base image to show through.

sharp-edged selection whose scale you can change without losing crispness of line, then you need to create a clipping path.

Although almost anything you can do with masks can be done with selections, it is convenient to turn a selection into a mask, since it is then easier to store and reuse—even for other images. It is good practice to turn any selection you make into a mask (just in case you wish to reuse it), particularly if it took a long time to create.

Alpha channels

Alpha channels are selections stored as masks in the form of grayscale images. The convention is that fully selected areas appear white, nonselected areas are shown black, while partially selected areas appear as proportionate shades of gray. In effect, an alpha channel is just like a color channel, but instead of providing color, it hides some pixels and allows others to be visible. An alpha channel can be turned into a selection by "loading" the selection for that channel. The term "alpha" refers to a variable in an equation defining the blending of one layer with another.

Limiting filter effects
Here (*top*), the mask has been applied to "protect" the child's face from the effect of the Stylize/Extrude filter. Note that when you turn the painted area into the selection, the mask would be applied only to that selection, so you have to invert the selection to take in everything but the face. When the filter was applied (*above*), it worked only on the pixels that were not protected.

Quick-mask Layers screen shot
This dialog box shows that the painting forms the bottom layer (but not the background, since masks cannot be applied to the background). The top layer consists of the grass and, to the right, the mask is also shown.

Final effect
You can move the underlying image around until you are happy with the results—in other words, when the most effective areas are showing through within the areas defined by the masking.

Grayscale and color

The usual way to obtain grayscale images—those with no color information—is by making a scan of existing artwork. Even if the artwork contains color, you can still scan into grayscale, which, incidentally, will usually speed up scanning. Or you can scan in full color and then drop the color data to make a grayscale (*see pp. 124–9*).

If the artwork consists of sharp black and white lines, you will need to take extra care with the scanning if you hope to maintain the crispness of the contours, and you will also need a high resolution setting on your scanner. Should you wish to scan into bitmap (an image in only black or white), then you should set the highest possible resolution. This is because you lose the anti-aliasing effect provided by the intermediate tones and, therefore, need the highest possible resolution to avoid stair-stepping or jagged-edged artifacts ("jaggies"). This applies particularly to originals with subtleties of shape and form. Unfortunately, when you use the highest resolution required to capture the fine details, you will also pick up all the defects in the paper that we normally ignore. Do not be tempted to remove them by raising the contrast of the image—you will destroy detail in the scan. Instead, use cloning tools to remove the defects (*see pp. 164–9*).

● Remove dust specks and other defects carefully before combining a grayscale with other images. These defects can be hard to spot, but they can become very evident in certain layer blend modes.

● You can control the effect of certain blends by changing the opacity of either top (blending) or bottom (source) layers—not just the uppermost layer.

● For best results, avoid increasing the size of a component image by a large amount once it is layered with another image. Rescan if necessary—otherwise the mix of sharp and unsharp images that results will look unprofessional.

Output densities
If your image has large, completely black areas, you need to take special care when printing or the paper may become saturated with ink. Reduce the output levels in the Levels control, or equivalent, in your software.

Choosing the color component
When I was considering which color picture to combine with the grayscale image (*above right*), I looked for a subject that was soft in contrast and contained lots of texture. In order to combine the two images, the grayscale component must be turned to full-color.

The grayscale component
I scanned the original graphite drawing as a grayscale image with the background kept gray rather than white. This was essential because I intended to add color to the whole image, and pure white would not be colored.

A change of mood
Simply by using a different image to add color to the grayscale, as done here, you can very quickly achieve a totally different feel and atmosphere. Since the donor image was pastel in tone, it was placed at 100 percent.

Colored drawing
By laying the colored image over the grayscale and setting the Layer mode to Color, you effectively add color to the drawing without overriding the underlying tones. You will need to adjust both the opacity of the top layer and the tonal quality of both layers to obtain exactly the right effect. If the receiving (lower) layer is darker, it takes on more color; if the donor (top) layer is of higher opacity, it places more color into the lower layer. Here, the opacity was reduced to 85 percent in order to soften the colors.

Difference mode
For a totally different type of toning effect for grayscale images, try applying the top layer in Difference mode. This mode, as always, produces dramatic effects. By reducing the opacity, or strength, of the mode in the Layers dialog box to just 35 percent (*above right*), an intriguingly rich texture has been added to the drawing (*above left*). The image in the color layer was moved sideways to ensure that any distracting details were not located on the face.

Text effects

Typefaces, also known as letter-forms or fonts, can be treated in many unique ways using image-manipulation software. Letters can be made to burn up, for example, dissolve into clouds, recede and blur into the distance, or appear transparent over another image—the possibilities are truly unlimited. All image-manipulation applications offer at least a basic range of effects, but if they also accept Photoshop-compliant plug-ins, you can greatly extend your repertoire.

Note, however, that text can sit uncomfortably with image pixels. The reason is that type is best digitally encoded as "vector graphics," whereas photographic images are best encoded as "bitmap graphics" (*see below*). Nearly always, the text would have to be turned from vector into a set of bit-mapped pixels, resulting in a loss of clarity and sharpness. As a consequence, as you increase the size of an image that incorporates text, the letter-forms quickly start to look ragged, with poorly defined outlines. More than anywhere else in image manipulation, if you work with text, always work at the full output size; and avoid altering the image size after applying text to the image.

Bitmap and vector graphics

There are two classes of graphic image. Digital cameras all produce a bitmap type of image, also called a raster image, which is based on a grid of data (the colored pixels). Each pixel is placed in a specific location and given a color value. Image manipulation is all about altering pixels, and so such images are resolution-dependent—that is, they start with a fixed number of pixels and thus a change in image size alters the amount of detail that is available.

Vector graphics, also known as object-oriented images, are described according to their geometrical basics—lines, circles, and so on—with their location, together with operations such as stroke (to draw a line) or fill (to cover an enclosed area with color). Vector graphics are said to be resolution-independent—that is, they can be scaled to any size and printed at any resolution without losing sharpness, and so can always use the output device's highest resolution.

Vectors are best for describing text as well as graphics such as company logos, and are created by graphics software such as Macromedia FreeHand, Corel Draw, or Adobe Illustrator. You may discover that the more complicated letter-forms, such as those with scrolls or long loops, may not print properly in your printer: if so, you may need to install special software to interpret the vector information, called a PostScript RIP (Raster Image Processor).

Display type
If you wish to add effects to a typeface, it is advisable to start with a chunky display type such as Postino Italic, shown here, with its vertical scale increased to stretch its height. With a color chosen to contrast with the rest of the image, the effect is unattractive and garish, but it is easy to read at any size.

Drop shadow
By asking the image-manipulation software to create a drop shadow, you make the letters appear as if they are floating above the image. The overall effect is of a poster. The color of the type was toned down to that of a tint of white: any light tint of white is likely to be an effective and safe choice of color for type.

It is always best to check the typeface at full size by printing it out. Check again if you change the face: even at the same point size, different typefaces vary widely in legibility. Consider, too, the following points:

● Use typefaces with narrow lines where they contrast well with the background; those with broad shapes should be used where the contrast is less obvious.

● You can use typefaces with narrow outlines if you create effects that separate the text from the underlying image, such as drop shadows.

● Use typefaces with broad lines if you want to use them for masking or to allow images to show through.

● Avoid faces with narrow serifs—the little extensions to the end of a stroke in a letter—since these are easily lost into the underlying image. In addition, avoid letter-forms with hollow strokes or those made up of double strokes for the same reason.

● Use only small amounts of text when combining it with images—at best a heading and at most a short block of text; but avoid using more than 50 words.

Inner shadow
Here, an inner shadow in pink has been applied with a high level of noise, so creating the appearance of rough texture. Drop shadows have been retained, but note that the "light" can be made to come from different directions.

Text warp
Distortion of text can be effective for drawing the viewer's attention. Here, the text has been warped as if it is a waving flag. In addition, various stroke and inner glow effects were applied to make the type look metallic.

Graduated overlay
Another way of making the type lively is to make the color appear graduated. Here, colors move between yellow and orange. The gradient chosen was sloped so that it runs across the type at an angle. With these effects you can produce comic-book effects that once had to be laboriously hand-painted.

Eye Candy's Fire
Plug-in software can bring very powerful effects to type. Here, with the type area of the image selected, Eye Candy's Fire filter was applied to make the words look as if they are going up in flames. You can adjust all the important parameters of the effect—such as the size of the flames, their angle, and their colors.

Cloning techniques

Cloning is the process of copying, repeating, or duplicating pixels from one part of an image, or taking pixels from another image, and placing them on another part of the image. First, you sample, or select, an area that is to be the source of the clone; second, you apply that selected area where it is needed. This is a basic tool in image manipulation, and you will find yourself constantly turning to it whenever you need, say, to

replace a dust speck in the sky of an image with an adjacent bit of sky, or remove stray hairs from a face by cloning nearby skin texture over them.

This is only the start, however. Such cloning makes an exact copy of the pixels, but you can go much farther. Some applications, such as Corel Painter, allow you to invert, distort, and otherwise transform the cloned image compared with the source you took it from.

Original image
An unsightly tarred area of road left by repairs marred this street scene in Prague. All it will take is a little cloning to bring about a transformation.

History palette
The screen shot of the History palette shows the individual cloning steps that were necessary to bring about the required transformation.

Manipulated image
The result is not perfect—it has none of the careful radial pattern of the original—but it is far preferable to the original image. It was finished off by applying an Unsharp Masking filter plus a few tonal adjustments.

HINTS AND TIPS

The following points may help you avoid some of the more obvious cloning pitfalls:

● Clone with the tool set to maximum (100 percent). Less than this will produce a soft-looking clone.

● In areas with even tones, use a soft-edged or feathered Brush as the cloning tool; in areas of fine detail, use a sharp-edged Brush.

● Work systematically, perhaps from left to right, from a cleaned area into areas with specks—or else you may be cloning dust specks themselves.

● If your cloning produces an unnaturally smooth-looking area, you may need to introduce some noise to

make it look more natural: select the area to be worked on and then apply the Noise filter.

● You can reduce the tendency of cloning to produce smooth areas by reducing the spacing setting. Most digital Brushes are set so that they apply "paint" in overlapping dabs—typically, each dab is separated by a quarter of the diameter of the brush. Your software may allow you to change settings to that of zero spacing.

● If you expect to apply extreme tonal changes to an image using, say, Curves settings, apply the Curves before cloning. Extreme tonalities can reveal cloning by showing boundaries between cloned and uncloned areas.

Original image

Suppose you wished to remove the lamp on the far left of this image to show an uninterrupted area of sky. You could use the cloning tool to do this, but it would be a lot of work and there would be a danger of leaving the sky's tones unnaturally smoothed-out in appearance.

1 Marquee tool

The Marquee tool was set to a feather of 10 pixels (to blur its border) and placed near the lamp to be removed to ensure a smooth transition in sky tones.

2 Removing the lamp

By applying the Marquee tool, you can see here how the cloned area of sky is replacing the lamp. Further cloning of sky was needed in order to smooth out differences in tone and make the new sky area look completely natural.

3 Looking at details

The final removal of the lamp was done with a smaller Marquee area, with its feather set to zero (as sharp as possible). Finally, the lamp behind the one removed was restored by carefully cloning from visible parts of the lamp.

4 Cleaned-up result

As a finishing touch, a small area of cloud was cloned over the top of the lamp and its lid was darkened to match the others left on the pier.

Cloning techniques continued

Special cloning

In addition to the corrective type of cloning seen on pp. 164–5, it is possible to take the process further and use it creatively.

In most software, there are two main ways of applying a clone. The basic method is what is now known as nonaligned, or normal: the first area you sample is inserted to each new spot the Brush tool is applied to. The other cloning method keeps a constant spatial relationship between the point sampled and the first place the sample is applied to—in other words, an offset is maintained so that the clone is aligned to the source point.

However, software such as Corel Painter offers as many as nine other ways of aligning the clone to the source. You can distort, shear, rotate, mirror, scale up or down, and so on. The procedure is more complicated than with normal cloning because you need to define the original scale and position prior to applying the clone. You first set the reference points in the source image, then set the transformation points; this can be either in the original image or in a new document. It is this latter feature that gives Painter's cloning tools tremendous power.

One interesting feature is that as your cloned image is being built up, it can itself become the source material for more cloning.

The examples below illustrate just how far it is possible to move away from the source material, as well as how diverse the results can be. Remember, though: with all cloning experiments, you should work on a copy of the original image.

Original images
Both of these originals (*left*) were taken in New Zealand. Note that images do not have to be the same size or shape for cloning to take place, but look for originals with strong, simple shapes. Sharpness and color were improved prior to the cloning: increasing sharpness after cloning can exaggerate the patches of cloned material.

Manipulated images
The originals were first cloned into a new file, but with added textures and overlaid with several layers. The first image (*below*) is intended to give a modern feel to the Chinese character "good fortune"; the other (*right*) has been given a distressed look.

Original image
Any original image can be cloned onto itself to make complexes of line and form. Starting with an image with clear-cut lines and simple colors, such as this, special cloning techniques can make images that are difficult to produce in any other way.

Original image
Very interesting results can be achieved by cloning an ordinary, everyday object, such as this brightly colored shirt (above), into a new document.

Rotation and scale
Cloning with rotation and scale calls for two points to be set to define the source, and a corresponding two points to determine the clone. By experimenting with different positions of the source and clone points, you can create a wide range of effects: here, the boy appears to be spinning into an abyss.

Bilinear transformation
Here, bilinear transformation was used to bring about this dramatic transformation. This technique warps the image according to the relative positions of the reference points set. By experimenting with the positions of the clone points, a totally unexpected shape was produced from a simple original image of a shirt.

Perspective tiling
Here, the boy was cloned with perspective tiling applied twice to different parts of the image. This requires four points to be set as the source, and four for the clone. Switching around the positions of the reference points produces wild perspective distortions that could have come from a science-fiction comic.

Dust removal

PenDuster is a component of the PenTools software, which comes bundled with the Wacom graphics tablet. It is an excellent tool for neatly and effectively removing dust and hairs, and it employs a special type of cloning technique that replaces the dust with pixels from immediately adjacent areas. So useful is this feature for the digital photographer that it alone is worth the purchase price of a small Wacom tablet.

Cloning techniques continued

Natural media cloning

Many image-manipulation filter effects (*see pp. 142–53*) take photographs into the realm of painting and the textures of fine art materials. Filters operate on the whole image simultaneously, with overall control possible only over the strength of effect, and no local control at all. Very different effects result, however, if you lay down the strokes yourself using cloning that imitates natural, or art, media.

Don't be afraid if you think you are not artistic: the beauty of working digitally is that if you are not happy with the results, you can step backward to undo the work and start again. Experiment for as long as you like until the result is to your satisfaction. And don't think you are being

"amateurish" if it takes hours: some professionals will confess that it can take them days before they achieve results they are content with.

All digital image-manipulation software offers art material effects as special "paints" with which Brushes may be loaded. The difference is that instead of simply loading a Brush with color, it is loaded with instructions: to vary color or intensity as the stroke progresses, to add texture to it or "dilute" the color as if you were mixing water in, and so on. The Brush color can be based on the colors of an underlying or source image, so offering you a shortcut to a radical modification of the original. You can turn a sharp digital image into a soft watercolor, or a colorful abstraction

Jerusalem 1
Once I had settled on an image I wanted to use, I started to experiment with the Curves setting to see what would happen if I set a very distorted value (*pp. 118–22*). The result that seemed to have the most potential turned the image into a metallic rendering, something like a weathered painting. The trick to this mode of working is knowing

when to stop: you can work endlessly trying out different effects. Remember to save promising-looking images as you go so that you can assess them in the cold light of day.

Jerusalem 2
Only those images that have clear outlines and distinct features will survive the detail-destroying aspects caused by applying brushstrokes. Here, Impressionist-like strokes were applied. Taking their color from the original picture, the strokes build up a new image by cloning, or copying, picture information from one image into another. At the same time, the strokes were set to respond to the underlying texture of the paper. You can experiment with different settings and directions of "painting" as often as you like.

into a vibrant "oil painting" with strong strokes of color and the texture of a bristly brush.

The reason for working with a low-resolution file is that it is smaller and the effects you apply will, therefore, appear on screen much faster than with a large file. It makes the whole system much more responsive to your Brush. You will obliterate any fine detail anyway, so it is not necessary to keep all the image data. Reduce the source file resolution to at least half that normal for the output you envision. But when you are happy with your work, change resolution back to normal, in order to avoid pixelation (*see pp. 180–1*).

Many people prefer using a graphics tablet instead of a mouse for this way of working. The graphics tablet and pen responds to many levels of pressure, speed of stroke, and even to the angle of the pen, thus making for livelier, more natural-looking and varied strokes (*see p. 30*).

HINTS AND TIPS

For the most effective results when cloning, you will find it easiest to work when the source image:
- offers clear outlines and strong shapes—fine details, such as those of grass or hair or facial features, are generally lost;
- has areas of strong color;
- does not have extensive areas of either black or white;
- is relatively low-resolution.

Applying art effects
Powerful software, such as Painter, offers a bewildering choice of effects to experiment with, but you will probably find that you regularly use only a fraction of the range available. The transformation from the original image of a chest of drawers seen in the screen shot panel (*upper left*) to that rendered in Natural Media (*lower right*) took less than an hour to achieve, yet suggested many other possible treatments on the way.

Image before and after
The shadows in the original (*top*) were replaced by textures from a drawing on rough-textured paper, which were applied using a Brush tool. Parts of the image were cloned into other areas and tonally adjusted to balance.

Photomosaics

Since digital pictures are composed of an array of individual pixels, it is only a short step to making up an image from an array of individual pictures. This is the principle behind photomosaics: you can replace an image's pixels with tiny individual images, like the tiles of a traditional mosaic.

Preparation

As with an image hose, you need to prepare images with which to create the mosaic. The small "mosaic pieces" may be tiny versions of the larger one or different images. Photomosaic software treats individual pictures as if they are pixels,

looking for best matches between the density and color of the small images to the pixel of the larger image that is to be replaced.

Specialty stand-alone photomosaic software usually provides libraries of mosaic pieces for you to work with, but it is more fun to create your own. However, the large numbers of images needed mean that this can be a long process. Advanced users can create batch processing sets to automate the process of rendering files into the specific pixel dimensions needed for the mosaic pieces. Other sources are the thumbnails (small files) found in some collections of royalty-free CDs.

Composite photomosaic
The original image was relatively complicated, but its clear lines and shapes, as well as the repeated elements it contained, made it a suitable candidate for photomosaic techniques. By selecting a small size for the mosaic "tiles" the resulting image still, overall, retains many details, but with an added richness of texture that invites closer inspection. The close-up view of the photomosaic (*below*) shows an intriguing mixture of images. Varying the component images is one way to produce an entirely different feeling to the image, while still retaining the outlines of the originals.

HINTS AND TIPS

If you are thinking of producing a photomosaic, bear the following points in mind.

● Provide a wide range of images from which to make up the mosaic pieces.

● Remember that smaller mosaic pieces produce finer, more detailed photomosaics.

● Use subjects with very clear or recognizable outlines;

avoid complicated subjects lacking clear outlines, since the process destroys all but the largest details.

● Bear in mind that if you create images in which a high level of detail is replaced with large mosaics, the resulting files will be very large.

● The rendering process that creates the photomosaic can take some time for your machine to carry out.

High-key photomosaic
The large, even spread of tones presents a challenge to photomosaic software, as identical images next to each other must be avoided, or else false patterns are created. However, the photomosaic has superimposed an attractive texture over this image. The close-up view (*below*) is richly rewarding.

Image stitching

Panoramic views can be created by "stitching," or overlaying, images side by side. Essentially, a sequence of images is taken from one side of the scene to the other (or from the top to the bottom). The individual images are then overlapped to create a seamless composite.

You do not need special software to achieve panoramas if the original shots are taken with care. You simply create a long canvas and drop the images in, overlapping them. However, small errors in framing can make this a slow process, since you must blend the overlaps to hide seams.

Appropriate software

Special panoramic software makes connecting component shots far easier, especially if they were taken without a tripod. Different software packages offer various approaches. Some try to match overlaps automatically and blend shots together by blurring the overlaps. Results look crude but are effective for low-resolution use. Other software applications recognize if the overlaps do not match and try to accommodate the problem—some by distorting the image, others by trying to correct perspective. Many digital cameras are supplied with panorama-creation software.

For more unusual effects, experiment with placing incongruous images together, or deliberately distort the perspective or overlaps so that the components clash instead of blend. There is a great deal of interesting work still to be done.

Photographs © Louise Ang

- Beware that a panorama resulting from, say, six average-size images will be a very large file: reduce the size of the component images first to avoid overstretching your computer's capacity.
- If you want to create a panorama that covers half the horizon or more, it may be better to stitch it in stages: three or four images at a time, then stitch the resulting panoramas. Keep an eye on the image size.
- Place all the component images together into one folder: some software will not be able to access images if they are in different folders.

Assembly

To start the assembly (*left*), move the component images into a single folder where the software can access them. With some software, you will be able to move images around to change their order, while in others you will have to open the images in the correct order. To merge the images, the software may need extra instructions, such as the equivalent focal length of the lens used.

Final version

The component images show very generous overlaps, which make it easier for the software to create smooth blends. Once the component images are all combined on one canvas, you can use the facilities offered by the particular software to blend and disguise the overlaps to create a seamless, single image (*below*). Once you are happy with your work, save the file as a TIFF, not as a JPEG, for best-quality results.

The output
adventure

5

Proofing and printing

It is an exciting moment. You have worked for hours at your computer, using all your know-how to create an image that looks just the way you want it, and now you are ready to print. You take a deep breath and press the button to send the file to the printer. If, then, the printer produces satisfactory results for most images, without any intervention on your part or setting up, you are lucky (make sure you note the settings in the printer driver for future reference). Unfortunately, the experience for many digital photographers is that the results of printing will be disappointing.

An important point is that mismatch between the monitor image and the printer is not, in the first instance, caused by any malfunctioning of your printer or monitor. The basic problem is that the monitor produces colors by emitting a mix of red, green, and blue light, while a print reflects a mix of light to produce the colors you perceive. These fundamentally different ways of producing color lead to a difference in gamut, which is the range of colors which can be produced by a device (*see p. 67*).

There are two main approaches open to you. You can adjust the image to compensate for the differences between what you see on screen and the resulting print, then print again and again, repeating the process until the print is satisfactory. This is not only unscientific, but the adjustments apply only to one image. The best way is to use software, such as Photoshop, that offers color-management facilities.

Printing with color management
To use color management for printing, you must first calibrate your monitor (*see pp. 92–3*). Note, too, that for the highest reliability, settings will apply only for the paper and inks with which you make the test. The basic idea is that you will first specify the source color space containing the colors you want to send to your printer—those that typically relate to your monitor. Second, you specify the color space of the printer, usually tied to the material being used. This gives the software the information it needs in order to make the necessary conversions.

A typical task is to proof an image currently in the monitor RGB space as it will appear on an offset printer (a commercial machine). The source color space uses the soft-proof profile, while your printer profile is the printer space. The following description details the steps to follow in Photoshop.

First choose File > Print Options and select "Show More Options," then "Color Management." For Source Space, select "Document" to reproduce colors as interpreted by the profile currently assigned to the image. Select "Proof" to reproduce document colors as interpreted by the current proof profile. Under Print Space, choose the profile that matches the color space of your

Color settings
The dialog box controlling color settings looks complex, and careful attention is needed to make full sense of it. However, there are many guides—such as those provided in printer and software manuals—that should help you master it. The crucial point to keep in mind is that, unless you are producing work to be printed by a commercial press for a mass market, you need not worry about these settings. You can get by without touching them: however, if you can control them, it will be far easier to obtain reliably good prints from your desktop printer.

Source Space
- ● Document: Colorperfexion RGB
- ○ Proof Setup: Offset B

Print Space
- Profile: | EPSON Stylus Photo EX Photo Paper 1440 ▸ |
- Intent: | ✓ Perceptual ▸ |
  - Saturation
  - Relative Colorimetric
  - Absolute Colorimetric

Printer settings

A driver that complies with the ColorSync protocol for color management will offer a dialog such as that shown here. The Source Space is the color space or profile for the image: here, I have specified a commercially defined standard, which defines an RGB space in a way that is optimized for print. The Print Space is not only that of the printer but of the paper and print quality being set. "Perceptual" has been chosen for the Intent, or preference for color conversions of colors that fall out of gamut, since that is most likely to give a photographically acceptable print.

What is PostScript?

This is the most important of a range of programming languages that describe text and graphics on a page. PostScript breaks the most complex text and graphics into elementary components, such as lines or dots, and into basic operations, such as "stroke" (to draw a line) or "translate" (to turn a component). When a printer receives a PostScript file, it has to interpret it in order to turn these commands into the correct output on the page. This can be done with software in the computer's operating system or through special PostScript RIPs (Raster Image Processors). Using a PostScript RIP is the best way of making sure that complicated graphics and text are properly printed out on the page.

Fantasy colours

When you produce highly manipulated images, even a large error in colour accuracy is unlikely to damage the effectiveness of the image, since most viewers will not ever know what the right colours were supposed to be. Of course, for the sake of artistic integrity, you will strive to produce the exact colour you have in your mind's eye, but the impact of images such as that shown here, with its artificial colours and fantasy content, does not depend on precise colour reproduction.

Proofing and printing continued

printer to print using that printer space or else select "Same As Source" to print using the original source profile.

If you have an inkjet printer, select "Printer Color Management" to send all the color data that is needed for the printer's driver to manage the colors. (Those using a PostScript printer should follow the instructions that are supplied with their PostScript RIP software.) Finally, under "Print Space," choose a suitable "rendering intent" (*see below*).

You are now ready to print, but before proceeding any further, make sure that:

● You are using the same type of paper as that intended for the final output.
● You are using the correct side of the paper.
● There is a good supply of ink (check the level using the printer's controls).
● Your image has been sized to the correct output dimensions.

Previewing

The key to efficient printing practice is to employ soft-proofing as much as possible—that is, checking and confirming everything you can on

Textile color
For accurate records of valuable artifacts, such as this piece of textile (*above*), precise color control is essential. Reds are visually very important, but deep reds can vary considerably between monitor image and paper output. The subtle variations in deep tone are easily lost if a printout is too dark.

What are rendering intents?

Converting from one color space to another involves an adjustment to accommodate the gamut of the destination color space. The rendering intent determines the rules for adjusting source colors to destination gamut: those that fall outside the gamut may be ignored, or they may be adjusted to preserve the original range of visual relationships. Printers that are ColorSync-compliant will offer a choice of rendering intents that determine the way in which the color is reproduced.

● Perceptual (or image or photorealistic) aims to preserve the visual relationship between colors in a way that appears natural to the human eye, although value (in other words, brightness) may change. It is most suitable for photographic images.
● Saturation (or graphics or vivid) aims to create vivid

color at the expense of color accuracy. It preserves relative saturation, so hues may shift. This is suitable for business graphics, where the presence of bright, saturated colors may be important.

● Absolute Colorimetric leaves colors that fall inside the destination gamut unchanged. This intent aims to maintain color accuracy at the expense of preserving relationships between colors (as two colors different in the source space—usually out-of-gamut—may be mapped to the same color in the destination space).
● Relative Colorimetric is similar to Absolute Colorimetric, but it compares the white or black point of the source color space to that of the destination color space in order to shift all colors in proportion. It is suitable for photographic images, provided that you first select "Use Black Point Compensation."

the monitor screen before committing the image to print. If you have implemented the color management suggested in this book (*see pp. 114–7*), the on-screen image should be very similar to the print you obtain. If, though, images are to be printed on a four-color (CMYK) press, set the destination printer or printer profile to that of a standard to which it conforms.

The first check is the output size: most image applications and print drivers will show a preview of the size and/or position of the image on the page before printing it out. If you are not sure of what you are doing, it is best always to invoke print preview to check—the print preview here (*see below*), from Photoshop, shows an image that is too large, while the screen shot (*see bottom*), from an Epson driver, shows an image enlarged 300 percent to make better use of the page. Printer drivers should warn you if the image size is too great to be printed without cropping.

Original image
All digital images are virtual and thus have no dimensions until they are sized for output, with a suitable output resolution. Ideally, there are sufficient pixels in the image for the combination of output resolution and output size, otherwise interpolation is needed to increase resolution.

Photoshop print preview
Some software provides a quick way to check the print size in relation to the paper size set for the printer. Here (*right*) is Photoshop's way of displaying it. The corners of the image fall outside the paper, as can be seen by the diagonals not meeting the corners of the white rectangle, which pops up when you click on a bar at the bottom of the frame: the image is clearly far too large for the paper.

Print Options preview
This screen shot (*left*), taken from a printer driver, shows how a printer expects to produce a given file. The image has been enlarged by 300 percent to make better use of the paper and has been centered (be sure your image has sufficient data to print at this enlargement). Note how the preview shows the image on paper and that it provides you with handy functions, such as being able to position the image, as well as a choice of units of measurement. Modern printers can place an image with great and repeatable precision.

Output to paper

One great advantage of inkjet printers is that they can print on a wide variety of surfaces. In fact, some desktop models will print on anything from fine paper to thin cardboard.

For the digital photographer, there are three main types of paper available. Most papers are a bright white or a near-white base tint, but some art materials may be closer to cream.

Paper types

Office stationery is suitable for letters, notes, or drafts of designs. Quality is low by photographic standards, and the printed images cannot be high in resolution or color saturation. Inkjet paper that is described as 360 dpi or 720 dpi is a good compromise between quality and cost for many purposes.

Near-photographic quality is suitable for final printouts or proofs for mass printing. These papers range from ultra-glossy or smooth to the slightly textured surface of glossy photographic paper. Paper thickness varies from very thin (suitable for pasting in a presentation album) to the thickness of good-quality photographic paper. Image quality can be the best a printer can deliver with excellent sharpness and color saturation. However, paper and ink costs may be high.

Art papers are suitable for presentation prints or for special effects and include materials such as handmade papers, watercolor papers, or papers with burlap or canvaslike surfaces. With these papers, it is not necessary to use high-resolution images or large files that are full of detail.

Paper qualities

If you want to experiment with different papers, just ensure that the paper does not easily shred and damage your machine and clog the nozzles of the inkjet cartridge. If using flimsy papers, it is a good idea to support them on thin cardboard or a more rigid piece of paper of the same size or slightly larger. The main problem with paper not designed for inkjets is that the ink either spreads too much on contact, or pools and fails to dry.

Dye-sublimation printers will print only on specially designed paper—indeed, some printers will even refuse to print at all when offered the wrong type of paper. Laser printers are designed only for office stationery and so there is little point in using other types of paper.

Crucial color
Not only does the blue of this scene test the evenness of printing, it also tests color accuracy. Very slight shifts away from blue will make the image look unbalanced in color and distract the viewer's attention from the relaxed, sun-filled scene. In fact, blue ranks with skin tones as the most important of colors that must be correctly printed, or else the foundation of an image will be seen as unsound.

Dark subjects

The blacker a color image, the more ink will be needed to print it. If your subject is full of very dark areas, such as this scene, the paper could easily be overloaded with ink. The ink may then pool if it is not absorbed and the paper could buckle or become corrugated. To minimize this problem, use the best-quality paper and tone down the maximum of black as much as possible by reducing the black output level in the Levels control.

TRY THIS

To determine the minimum resolution that gives acceptable results on your printer, you need to make a series of test prints with the same image printed to the same size but saved to different resolutions. Start by printing out a good-quality image of about 10 x 8 in (25 x 20 cm) or letter (A4) size at a resolution of 300 dpi—its file size is about 18 MB. Now reduce resolution to 200 dpi (the file size will get smaller but the output size should be the same) and print the file, using the same paper as for the first print. Repeat with resolutions at 100 dpi and 50 dpi. Compare your results and you might be pleasantly surprised: depending on the paper and printer, files with low output resolution can print to virtually the same quality as much higher-resolution files. With low-quality or art materials, you can set very low resolutions and obtain results that are indistinguishable from high-resolution files. In fact, low resolutions can sometimes give better results, especially if you want brighter colors.

Even tones

Subjects with large expanses of even and subtly shifting tone present a challenge to inkjet printers in terms of preventing gaps and unevenness in coverage. However, in this image of a frozen lake in a Kazakh winter, the challenge is not so great because the color is nearly gray, which means that the printer will print from all its ink reservoirs. If there is only one color, most often the blues of skies, you are more likely to see uneven ink coverage.

Quick fix Printer problems

A great deal of computation is needed before your printer can translate the image on screen or captured in a digital camera into a print. Not only must the pixel data be translated to individual dots or sets of dots of color, that translation must ensure that the final print is sized correctly for the page and is the right way around. Everybody has problems with printers; the real surprise is that people do not experience more printer problems than they do.

Troubleshooting

The most common causes of problems with the printer are often the easiest to deal with. As a routine response to problems, check that the power cord and printer cable are securely inserted at both ends, check that your printer has not run out of ink, and make sure that the paper is properly inserted, with nothing jammed inside.

Problem	Cause and solution
Prints show poor quality—dull colors or unsharp results.	If you run the self-check or diagnostic test for the printer and nothing appears to be mechanically at fault, then the cause is a user setting. You may have set an economy or high-speed printing mode. If so, set a high-quality mode. You may be using a low-quality paper or one unsuitable for the printer, or you could be using the wrong side of the paper: change the paper and see what happens. You may be using an uncertified ink cartridge instead of the manufacturer's: use the manufacturer's own brand.
Prints do not match the image seen on the monitor.	Your printer and monitor are not calibrated. Go through the calibration steps (see pp. 92–3). Your image may contain very little color data: check the image using Levels—rescanning may be necessary.
A large file was printed very small.	File size does not alone determine printed size. Change the output dimensions using the Image Size dialog box.
An image does not fully print, with one or more edges missing.	Output size is larger than the printable area of the printer—most printers cannot print to the edge of the paper. Reduce the output or print size of the image in the Image Size dialog box and try again.
The printer works very slowly when it is printing images.	You may have asked the printer to do something complicated. If your graphic has paths, simplify them. If your image has many layers, flatten the image prior to printing. To print landscape-format pictures, rotate the picture in your image-manipulation software prior to printing. If you set the magnification to anything other than 100 percent, the printer must resize the entire image. Change the image size using image-manipulation software before printing.
The print suddenly changes color part of the way through.	Either one of the colors in the ink cartridge has run out or it has become blocked during printing. Clean the nozzles using the driver utilities and try to print again. You may need to repeat the cleaning cycle several times.

Problem	Cause and solution
The printer works slowly even when printing text.	You have set the printer to a high-quality setting, such as high-resolution or fine, or the high-speed or economy mode has been turned off, or you have set the printer to unidirectional or to print on high-quality (photorealistic) paper. Check and reset the printer to high-speed, bidirectional, and reduce the resolution or choose a normal or standard paper.
The printer cannot be found or nothing happens when "OK" is pressed at the printer dialog box.	You may have a conflict—especially if you have just installed a new scanner, mouse, or similar. Reinstall the printer driver software. Make sure you have the latest drivers for the USB ports from the manufacturer's website. Owners of early iMac computers should make sure they have the latest iMac Update.
Prints appear smudged, with colors bleeding into each other.	The paper is damp, you have made settings for the wrong paper type, or there may be ink on the printer's rollers. Store paper in dry conditions inside its original packaging. Check the settings against the paper type. Clean the rolls using a cloth and run the printer cleaner sheets, which are supplied by the manufacturer, through the printer.
The printer produces random lines or crashes the computer.	The system is lacking memory. With Windows, don't try to do anything on the machine while the printer is working; with Mac OS, turn off background printing and restart the printer.
The print is missing lines or there are gaps.	The printer head nozzles have almost certainly become blocked with ink, or the printer head may need to be recalibrated. Clean the nozzles using the driver utilities supplied with the printer and try to print again. You may need to repeat the cleaning cycle several times to solve the problem.
The printer produces garbled text.	You may have connected the printer to the wrong computer port or you may have tried to use the printer port to send a file, fax, or similar. This problem can also occur if you have aborted a print operation some time earlier. If so, turn the printer off, wait a few seconds, turn the printer back on, and try the operation again. With Windows machines, check the spool or print manager for any jobs waiting to be processed—delete them and start again.
The printer produces banded lines in areas of even tone.	The paper transport is not properly synchronized with the print head. This could be a printer fault. If it is not, try changing the weight of the paper used or the thickness setting (usually with a lever on the printer). You could also try adding noise to the image to hide the unevenness of tone.
Details in prints appear blurred and colors dull—despite printing at high resolution and on good paper.	You may be using the wrong side of the paper. Most inkjet papers have a good, receiving side and a support side. Manufacturers often pack their paper with the receiving side facing the back of the pack.

Permanence: Ink and paper

The two main factors governing the permanence of photographic images are the characteristics of the materials used and the storage conditions. Both of the main components of the materials—the ink that makes up the image and the substrate, or supporting layer—are important.

For the ink to be stable, its colors must be fast and not fade in light or when exposed to the normal range of chemicals in the atmosphere. For the paper to be stable, it should be neutral and "buffered" (able to remain neutral when attacked with a small amount of acidic chemicals); it should not depend on volatile chemicals for its color or physical state; and it should not discolor with exposure to light.

When colors fade, one is likely to fade more rapidly than others, which quickly becomes obvious as a color shift. Black and white materials do not suffer from color shift, so appear more stable. Inks based on pigments (materials that are themselves colored) are more permanent than dyes (dissolved pigments that give color to materials).

The substrate may be a source of impermanence: papers fade or become brittle; the layer of plastic used to cover paper may crack and peel apart, taking the image with it; or the plastic itself may discolor.

The careful design of storage conditions can ensure that even highly unstable images are preserved, but these may not be practical. Ideally, images should be stored in chilled conditions—

nearly at freezing point—with low humidity and in total darkness. To ensure the best color stability, exposure to light and chemicals should be kept to a minimum, and storage temperatures and humidity should also be as low as is practicable. In normal room conditions, most materials will last several years, but if you keep pictures in a kitchen or bathroom, you can expect the life expectancy of your prints to be much reduced.

Faded print
With half the print shielded, the exposed half faded after only one week's constant exposure to bright sunlight.

Since some colors are more fast, or resistant to fading, than others, there will be a color shift in addition to an overall loss of density.

Archival storage

Digital photographers have two strategies for the archival storage of images. The first is to store images in the form of prints in the best possible conditions—specifically, in total darkness, low humidity, chilled (to temperatures close to freezing point) with slow air circulation in archivally safe containers. These containers—boxes made from museum board—should emit no chemicals or radiation, be pH-neutral (neither acidic nor alkaline), and, preferably, incorporate a buffer (a substance that helps maintain

chemical neutrality). These conditions are ideal for any silver-based or gelatin-based film or print.

The alternative strategy is to store images as computer files in archivally safe media. The current preferred option is the MO (magneto-optical) disk, but nobody really knows how long they will last. Next down are media such as CDs or DVDs, which are, in turn, more durable than magnetic media such as tapes or hard disks. But you can never be sure: a fungus found in hot, humid conditions has developed a taste for CDs, rendering them useless.

Poster-sized printing

It can be a thrill to see your images enlarged to poster size. The subject of the poster does not have to be unusual—sometimes the simplest image is the most effective—and the digital file from which it is output may not even need to be of the highest resolution. This is because large prints tend to be viewed from a distance, in which case finely rendered detail is not necessarily an issue.

Preparing a print

There are two main approaches to outputting prints larger than tabloid (A3), the maximum that can be comfortably printed on a desktop printer. The first is the simplest: use an oversized inkjet printer. These range from self-standing machines somewhat larger than desktop printers to monsters capable of printing advertisements for the entire side of a bus. These are far too expensive for the average digital photographer to own, so you need to take your file to a bureau. Before you prepare your file, ask the bureau for its preferred format (usually RGB TIFF uncompressed) and which type of media it accepts—all will take a CD-ROM and most will accept Zip disks as well as MO disks. You also need to check the resolution the bureau prefers, and you should adjust the file to the output size you require (although some bureaus do that for you).

There are different printers that produce prints appropriate to different markets. The Iris printer, for example, produces the very highest quality on a variety of papers for art and fine-art exhibition purposes. Inkjet printers, manufactured by, for example, Hewlett-Packard or Epson, generally produce good-quality prints for commercial display and trade exhibitions.

The other approach is a hybrid one, based on the digital manipulation of true photographic materials. Your file is used to control a laser that exposes a roll of photographic paper. This is then processed in normal color-processing chemicals to produce a photographic print. Many offline printing services use the same method to produce small photographic prints from digital image files. The results can be extremely effective and look very much as if they are traditional photographic images from start to finish. Another advantage to this method is that relatively small image files can produce excellent results—20 MB of detail may be sufficient for a print of twice tabloid size (A2). A variant of the hybrid approach is to use the digital file to create a color negative, which is then processed and used to make large color prints. This method is the preferred route if you wish to make many copies of the same image.

Tiling a printout

One way to make prints larger than your printer can print is to output the image in sections, or tiles, which you then join. This is straightforward in desktop publishing applications such as QuarkXPress and InDesign: you simply create a large document size, set up the page for the available paper dimensions, and tell the software to print out each section on the paper supplied. You can then trim the prints to remove the overlaps and butt the edges together to produce a seamless, large-size image. For those occasions when economy is important and critical image quality is not required, tiling is worth considering.

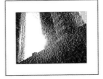

Tiling option
Modern printers work with great precision and consistency, so it is possible to combine tiles almost seamlessly. Use heavier-weight papers, plastic, or filmlike material to help retain shape. Then the overlaps need be only sufficient to allow you to trim off the excess and butt the images together before fixing.

Accurate skin tones
When making prints with brilliant colors,
it is tempting to allow the reds their full
brilliance. But if skin tones are in view,
they must be accurately rendered. The rest
of the print will then fall into place.

Publishing on the Web

The most extensive and wide-ranging part of the wave of digital technologies that has changed the lives of many people on this planet is the Internet and its associated resource, the World Wide Web.

While the exact workings of the Internet and the Web may not be of importance to the typical Internet user, understanding browser software can be useful. Internet browsers, such as Netscape Navigator and Microsoft Internet Explorer, are essentially interpreters of a computer language called HTML, or Hypertext Markup Language. Marking-up is the process of turning simple text documents into formatted text with underlinings, bold lettering, and so on. HTML also tells the browsers where to place any graphic elements and pictures. In short, browsers are similar to any word-processing application that takes a stream of data and converts it into text with headings, bold letters, and other elaborations.

Browsers are easily available; some are free or may be part of the package from your Internet service provider (ISP). But remember to keep your browser software up to date: although earlier versions will work fine, they may not support the latest features incorporated into webpages.

The Internet and compression

When producing pages for the Web, aim to create lively, dynamic, and interesting material that will engage the widest audience possible. To do this, everything reaching the screen should do so quickly and smoothly. The usual practice in this regard is to cater to people with small monitors and less capable computers. The assumption is a screen size of not larger than 15 in (38 cm), which, allowing for the browser, means that full-size images are at best not larger than about 640 x 480 pixels. The other control that reduces the size of the image is file compression—a way of coding the information so that it takes up less room than it would otherwise. You can do this in two ways: you can sacrifice some information in the search for the tiniest file (lossy compression, which gives the highest compression); or you sacrifice no information and, instead, put up with a somewhat larger file (lossless compression). For Internet use, the two most widely used formats are JPEG and GIF. PNG formats can be also used but are not supported by all browsers (see pp. 86–7).

Preparation

There are three main steps in preparing images for use on webpages or sending via the Internet.

Evaluation Assess the image quality and content. If it is photographic, you can convert it to JPEG; if it is a graphic, with few subtle color gradations, you can convert to GIF. Also adjust brightness and color so the image will be acceptable on both Windows and Apple Mac monitors.

Resizing Change the size of copies (not original files) of the images to the viewing size intended, so that the size of files is no larger than necessary. Images may be tiny, perhaps 10 x 10 pixels (for use as buttons), or large, perhaps 360 x 240 pixels (to

Optimizing your pictures on the Internet

You will want those who access your site to receive your images quickly and to have the best experience of your images that the system permits. Here are some tips for optimizing your images on the Internet.

● Use Progressive JPEG if you can. This presents a low-resolution image first and gradually improves it as the file is downloaded. The idea is that it gives the viewer something to watch while waiting for the full-resolution image to appear.

● Use the WIDTH and HEIGHT attributes to force a small image to be shown on screen at a larger size than the actual image size.

● Use lower-resolution color—for example, indexed-color files are much smaller than full-color equivalents. An indexed-color file uses only a limited palette of colors (typically 256 or fewer), and you would be surprised at how acceptable many images look when reproduced even with only 60 or so colors (see p. 123).

Original

JPEG compression

JPEG compression

With minimum JPEG compression, you get maximum quality. In fact, at the highest magnification, it is very hard to see any loss in detail, but at the magnification shown here you can make out, with careful examination, a very slight smoothing of detail in the right-hand image compared with the original on the left. The cost, of course, is that the file is compressed from nearly 7 MB to about half the size, 3.7 MB.

Original

Minimum quality

Quality setting

At the minimum quality setting, the file size is pared down to an impressive 100 K from 7 MB—to just 2 percent of the original size—a reduction of nearly 50 times, and the download time has dropped to an acceptable 16 seconds. The loss of image quality is more evident: notice how the grain in the original (*far left*) has been smoothed out and the girl's arm is altered, with slightly exaggerated borders. But when it is used at its normal size on screen, it is a perfectly acceptable image.

Original

Medium quality

Medium quality

With a medium-quality setting, here showing a different part of the same image, there is a substantial and useful reduction in file size—from nearly 7 MB to just 265 K—some 20 times smaller, or 5 percent of the original file size. The download time is accordingly reduced from over 15 minutes to 50 seconds. This latter figure is still uncomfortably long and the image quality is arguably better than needed for viewing on screen, while being just adequate for printing at postcard size.

Publishing on the Web continued

show off your work). Background images do not have to be large, since the browser will repeat a small tile to fill the screen. In assessing image size, remember: larger images take longer to download.

Conversion Convert images to the correct Web format: image files should be JPEG or GIF, possibly PNG, but not TIFF. In the process, you will have to consider image compression ratios. For most uses, set a compression slightly greater than you would like (the image is degraded just a little more than you would wish). Most visitors to your site will not know your images and will tolerate a slight loss of detail. But they will appreciate not having to wait long for your images to appear. Part of image conversion is to ensure that image files are correctly named, with their appropriate suffix.

Online printing

If you have only the occasional need to print or you wish to make a poster-sized print (see p. 185), you can always consider using an online printing facility. To take advantage of this, you simply send your image file or mail your film to an Internet-based service, together with your credit card details to cover the processing and handling costs. Most of these services allow you to set up your own album or folder in which to keep your images, saving you from having to resend images if you need a repeat printing. Since new services are always being added, and some others may go out of business, it is probably best to use a service that is based in your own country.

Original

GIF 256 colors

GIF 256 colors

This image shows that even when you restrict what looks like a scene with many colors to just 256 colors, you can obtain a very passable reproduction (p. 123). The view shows an enlarged portion of the image—very little quality loss is visible. The file size is about a quarter of the original (far left)—840 K instead of 3.4 MB.

GIF color table

The colors used to reproduce the image are displayed in this table (left)—also known as a color lookup table. Colors here are displayed in order of popularity: the color most used is a near-black followed by four pale blues, and so on.

PNG color table

The color lookup table for PNG (right) shows all the colors that can be reliably reproduced across the Web. Only 136 of the 256 colors available were actually used for the image.

Original

GIF 32 colors

GIF 32 colors

Even when using a mere 32 colors to create the image (*near left*), quality loss is not that apparent, apart from an increase in graininess in the sky. Note that the file size is some 10 percent smaller than the original (*far left*)—a level of compression not equal to that of a JPEG file at the medium-quality setting, yet giving inferior image quality.

Original

GIF 4 colors

GIF 4 colors

By setting the GIF to use only four colors, a graphic image results (*near left*). This is a useful way of creating posterized effects, in which the colors used to reproduce an image are drastically reduced in number.

Original

PNG version

PNG version

The PNG format set to use Web-safe colors— those that can be reliably reproduced, irrespective of browser software— produces inferior results (*near left*). The sky is mottled, yet the file size is only reduced to a quarter of the original (*far left*).

Going further

With the vast quantity of information available, it is relatively easy to find out all you need to know about the many aspects of digital photography: there are videos that guide you step-by-step; CD-ROMs with interactive lessons; and, of course, there are numerous books on the subject. There are also many sources of information on the Internet—although these may vary in both quality and depth, most of them should at least be up to date. The best way to learn from these sources is usually to have a specific task to complete: having a clear direction in mind often greatly speeds up your learning, rather than just picking up on unrelated snippets of information.

Another option to help you go further is to take a course of some description. Many are available, but the best types for most people are those offering intensive or residential tuition. These are often run as summer schools in which you immerse yourself in a completely "digital" environment. Such courses will enable you to concentrate on problem-solving, and being able to ask for help from experts at the immediate time that you need clarification can greatly accelerate the learning process. However, if you do not have the equipment to continue at the same level once you return home, you may quickly forget all you

have learned. To make the most of immersion teaching, you will need to continue using your newly acquired skills. To check if an intensive or residential course is suitable for you, ask these questions when you speak to the administrator or when you read through the prospectus:

● Do the fees include all materials, such as inkjet paper and removable media?
● Will there be printed information to take home and keep?
● Which software will be taught?
● Which computer platform will be used?
● Do students have individual computers to work on or will you have to share?
● What standard is expected at the start; what standard is to be attained by the end?
● What are the qualifications of instructors?

You will gain most from any course if you first thoroughly prepare yourself. Having a project or two in mind to work on prevents your mind from going blank when you are asked what you would like to achieve. And take along some image files or a scrapbook of pictures to use or to scan in. The best way to learn how to use computer software is to have a real task to complete—this might be creating a poster for a community event you are involved in, making a greeting card, or producing a brochure for a company.

Taking a course

To help ensure that you get into the program of your choice, consider the following points.

● Plan ahead: most courses recruit and interview only at certain times of the year.

● Prepare a portfolio – this does not have to comprise professional-quality work. Show the work that you most like, not necessarily the most technically perfect. Be prepared to talk about your work, but don't feel offended if you aren't asked. Inkjet prints are perfectly acceptable. Do not spend a fortune on a large portfolio. Keep it neat and a manageable size – no larger than A3.

● Read up: if the course contains elements you are not familiar with, such as art history, media theory, and so

on, make sure you are interested in them before applying. Further, if you know what the course objectives are, you will then know that what you want to do is in line with what the institution wants to achieve. This is important for you—and it is likely to impress the interviewer.

● Check on any formal requirements, such as minimum educational qualifications. You may need to attend an access or refresher course before entering college.

● Plan your finances: attending classes affects your ability to earn and can itself be a financial drain. Calculate the course fees, then add the materials, equipment, and travel costs to your living expenses to work out how much you need to put aside.

Mounting an exhibition

After spending some time taking photographs and accumulating images, the urge to show your work to people beyond your immediate circle of family and friends may start to grow and gnaw at you. The first thing you must do is banish from your mind any doubts that your work is not good enough to show to the wider public. An exhibition is exactly that: you make an exhibit of yourself. People will not laugh, but they may admire. If you have the drive and the ambition, then you should start planning now—you cannot start this process too early.

Turning a dream into reality

You may feel that you are not ready to mount an exhibition just yet. If so, then perhaps you had better get on with the task of building up a library of suitable images. At some point in the future you will know you have the right material and that the time is right.

Now try to imagine in your mind's eye what the show will look like: visualize how you would light it, how you will position your images for maximum impact, how to sequence photographs to create a particular atmosphere, and create a flow of meaning or narrative. Picture to yourself the size of the prints, how they will glow in the light.

Selling prints

Remember that silver-based prints will continue, for a long time yet, to sell for higher prices than any digitally produced print. Here are some hints for ensuring good, continuing relations with your buyers.

● Don't make unsubstantiated claims about the permanence of printed images.

● Give people advice about how to care for the prints, such as not storing them in humid conditions or where they will be exposed to bright sunlight.

● Never exceed the run when you offer limited-edition prints—produce the specific, guaranteed number, and not one more.

● Print on the best-quality paper you can afford, or that recommended by the printer manufacturer.

This will help to focus your mind and guide your energies as well as act as a spur to your picture- or print-making. Here are some other pointers you might want to consider.

● Choose your venue well in advance, as better-known galleries are under a lot of pressure and have to plan their schedules at least a year ahead. Other galleries may call quarterly or half-yearly committee meetings to decide what to show in the next period. At the other end of the scale, venues such as a local library or a neighborhood community center may be prepared to show work at very short notice. In any event, you will want to give yourself the time necessary for your plans to mature and to give the venue the opportunity to tie something in to the exhibition, such as a concert or lecture (depending on the subject matter of your imagery).

● Choose your venue creatively. Any public space could be a potential exhibition area—indeed, some seemingly improbable spaces may be more suitable for some types of work than a "proper" gallery. Bear in mind that the very presence of your work will transform the space into a "gallery," whether it is on the side of a bus, a shopping mall, or a pedestrian walkway.

● Budget with your brains, not your heart. Put on the best show you can afford, not one that costs more than you can afford. The point of an exhibition is to win a wider audience for your work, not to bankrupt you or to force you to call in financial favors that you might need at some time in the future to further your photographic endeavors.

● Once you have decided on the space you want to use and have received all necessary permissions, produce drawings of the layout of the entire venue. This will also involve you in making little thumbnail sketches of your prints in their correct hanging order: it is much easier to visualize the effectiveness of picture order this way.

Timing

Mounting an exhibition requires very careful planning on many different levels if you want your show to look professional, so don't leave any

Drawing up a budget

When budgeting for the costs of an exhibition, take into account not only your direct photographic expenses but also the range of support services. These include the costs of electricians to light your work, picture-framing, public liability insurance, the building (or renting) of "flats" to break up the exhibition space and provide extra surfaces on which to hang your work. Here are some cost categories to consider.

● Direct photographic costs—including making prints or slide duplication if projected images form part of your show.

● Indirect photographic costs—including retouching, mounting, frame-making, and rental of equipment, such as projectors.

● Gallery costs—including rental fees, deposits against damage or breakages, and paying for flats or similar.

● Publicity—including the cost of producing and mailing out invitations, advertising in trade or local journals or newspapers, as well as the production of an exhibition catalog.

● Insurance—budget for the costs of insuring your work, public liability, and damage to the venue.

● And don't forget—no matter what your final budget figure is, there will always be out-of pocket expenses you cannot identify beforehand. At the last minute, for example, you might decide you want flowers for the opening night. So, as a precaution, add a 15 percent contingency to the final budget figure.

important carpentry, electrical, picture-framing, or similar work to, say, a long weekend or vacation period when you might not be able to gain access to key personnel should something go critically wrong. And you should always count on the fact that something will go wrong.

Looking at sponsorship

One way to offset some of the costs of mounting an exhibition is by sponsorship. The key to success is persuading a potential sponsor that the likely benefits from the relationship will flow both ways. It is obvious that you will benefit from the deal by being offered the use of equipment you might not otherwise be able to afford, perhaps, or complementary or discounted print-making, but what do the other parties get?

The best approach to sponsorship involves persuading potential benefactors that by making equipment or services available to you, they will receive some boost to their business or that their public profile will be somehow enhanced by the association. It could be that, for example, sponsoring individuals, companies, or organizations will receive coverage in trade newspapers or journals as a result of their help.

As a rule, it is always easier to obtain services or products than it is to get cash. Printing materials, exhibition space, scanning, processing, even food and drinks for the opening night are all possible, but cash is unlikely. And remember to make your approach well ahead of time—organizations have budgets to maintain, and once sponsorship allocations have been made, often there may be nothing left until the next financial year.

Finally, even if the answer from a potential sponsor is "no," you can still ask for something that may be even more valuable—information. So ask for suggestions about which other companies or organizations might be interested in helping.

An exhibition is your chance to get your work known by a wider audience, so make full use of the opportunity if it arises by telling everybody you know about it, and encouraging them to spread the word to their contacts.

Finally, mounting a photographic exhibition brings together many different people and skills. They are your sponsors just as much as any commercial contributor, so always take the trouble to acknowledge their invaluable help and contributions, for without them your show might never have gotten off the drawing board.

Copyright concerns

Copyright is a fascinating subject, and one that, due to the rise of digital media and information technology in particular, is becoming even more pertinent. Different traditions of copyright law in different countries lead to varieties not only in the detail but also in the entire approach to this subject. This renders the area of copyright a potential minefield for the unwary, especially since it is so dependent on national boundaries and international relations.

Rather than try to produce the impossible—a brief summary of copyright law and traditions that would be accurate in most places in the world—here are some frequently asked questions and their answers, which have a wide applicability. However, you should always seek professional advice if you are not sure what your rights are or how you should proceed. But you probably will not need to hire a lawyer, since many professional organizations and legal advice centers are willing to provide basic copyright law advice to members of the public who come to them for help. Another source of help is the Internet.

Do I have to register in order to receive copyright protection?

No, you do not. Copyright in works of art—which includes writing, photographs, and digital images—arises as the work is created. In more than 140 countries in the world, no formal registration is needed to receive basic legal protection.

Can I protect copyright of my images once they are on the Web?

Not directly. This is because you cannot control who has access to your website. Make sure you read the small print if you are using free Web space. You may be asked to assign copyright to the Web server or service provider. Do not proceed if you are not happy with this condition.

Can I be prosecuted for any images I place on the Web?

Yes, you can. If your pictures breach local laws—for example, those to do with decency, pornography,

or the incitement of religious or racial hatred, or if they feature illegal organizations—and if you live within the jurisdiction of those laws, you may be liable to prosecution. Alternatively, your Internet service provider (ISP) may be ordered to remove them.

Do I have to declare that I own copyright by stamping a print or signing a form?

In most countries, no. Copyright protection is not usually subject to any formality, such as registration, deposit, or notice. It helps, however, to assert your ownership of copyright clearly—at least placing "© YOUR NAME"—on the back of a print or discreetly within an image on the Web, such as in the lower-right-hand corner.

Is it wrong to scan images from books and magazines?

Technically, yes, you are in the wrong. Copying

Can I prevent my ideas from being stolen?

There is no copyright protection covering ideas to do with picture essays, for example, or magazine features or books. The easiest way to protect your concept is by offering your ideas in strict confidence. That is, your ideas are given to publishers or editors only on the condition that they will not reveal your ideas to any third party without your authorization. Your idea must have the necessary quality of confidentiality—that is, you have not shared the information with more than a few confidants—and the idea is not something that is widely known. The most unambiguous approach to this issue is to require your publisher or the commissioning editor to sign a nondisclosure agreement—a written guarantee. However, this may be an unduly heavy-handed approach. You may preface your discussions with a "this is confidential" statement. If the person does not accept the burden of confidentiality, you should not proceed.

copyright material (images or text) by scanning from published sources does place you in breach of copyright law in most countries. However, in many countries you are allowed certain exceptions; for example, if you do it for the purposes of study or research, for the purposes of criticism or review, or to provide copy for the visually impaired. Bear in mind, though, that these exceptions vary greatly from country to country.

What is a "watermark"?

It is information, such as a copyright notice or your name and address, that is incorporated deep in the data of an image file. The "watermark" is usually visible but may be designed to be invisible. In either case, watermarks are designed so that they cannot be removed without destroying the image itself.

If I sell a print, is the buyer allowed to reproduce the image?

No—you have sold only the physical item, which is the print itself. By selling a print, you grant no rights apart from the basic property right of ownership of the piece of paper—and an implied right to display it for the buyer's personal, private enjoyment. The buyer should not copy, alter, publish, exhibit, broadcast, or otherwise make use of that image without your permission.

What are "royalty-free" images?

These are images that you pay a fee to obtain in the first instance, but then you do not have to pay any extra if you use them—even for commercial purposes. With some companies, however, certain categories of commercial use, such as advertising or packaging, may attract further payments. Royalty-free images usually come on CDs but they may also be downloaded from a website.

How is it possible for images to be issued completely free?

Free images found on the Internet can be an inexpensive way for companies to attract you to visit their site. You can then download these images for your own use, but if you wish to make money from them, you are expected and trusted to make a payment. This fee is usually relatively small, however, so you are encouraged to behave honestly and not exploit the system.

Does somebody own the copyright of an image if that person pays for the film or the rental of the equipment?

In most countries, the answer is no. In some countries, if you are employed as a photographer, it is your employer who retains copyright in any material you produce; in others, however, it is the photographer who retains the copyright. In any circumstance, the basic position can be overridden by a local contract made between the photographer and the other party prior to the work being carried out.

If I manipulate someone else's image, so that it is completely changed and is all my own work, do I then own the copyright in the new image?

No. You need to bear in mind that you were infringing copyright in the first place by making the copy. And then, altering the image is a further breach of copyright. Besides, the new image is not fully all your work: arguably, it is derived from the copy. If you then claim authorship, you could be guilty of yet another breach—this time, of a moral right to ownership.

Surely it is all right to copy just a small part of an image—say, part of the sky area or some other minor detail?

The copyright laws in most countries allow for "incidental" or "accidental" copying. If you take an insignificant part of an image, perhaps nobody will object, but it is arguable that your action in choosing that particular part of an image renders it significant. If this is accepted, then it could be argued that you are in breach. If it makes no real difference where you obtain a bit of sky, then try to take it from a free source (*see p. 216*).

Shopping for equipment

Purchasing all the equipment needed for digital photography can be either bewilderingly off-putting or delightfully full of new things to learn. There is undoubtedly a lot to consider, but if you are not lucky enough to have a knowledgeable friend to help, don't worry. There is a great amount of information available out there—much of it free and not all of it dependent on Internet access.

Where to look for help

Large retailers with a Web presence are the best starting places for information on photographic equipment. Their websites are often superior to the manufacturer's own sites for quality and ease of access to information, and you can easily compare specifications and costs of different models. Many retailers also publish printed catalogs, offering a wide array of information.

There are many websites (essentially magazines) that offer large amounts of information and are constantly updated; they may know more about new products than retailers do. These magazines offer seemingly authoritative reviews, but these days anyone can claim to be a reviewer. Furthermore, there is a tendency for only the more glamorous models to be reviewed in depth. As a result, the quality of information, and the depth of knowledge used to produce it, is variable. Try to obtain a consensus from as many sources as possible.

There are also several specialty magazines, but again, the quality of information is variable, since they may be written by people who are journalists first and photographers second. Added to this, magazines may come under pressure to say good things about a product, so you may have to read between the lines for the criticism.

Buying online

Online purchases can be safe, efficient, time-saving, and economical. The sensible precautions to take for any online transactions apply with equal force for photography. Buy from sites that: guarantee secure transactions; you know about or have been recommended; offer guarantees that cover your purchase, particularly if you are buying from overseas. If possible, use a credit card that protects against fraudulent use. Always print transaction details and keep them safely.

Beware of items that are much cheaper from one source than any others. The importer may not be officially recognized, the guarantee may not cover your region, or the language of the instructions—even on the camera itself—may be foreign to you.

Buying secondhand

The rise of digital photography has helped create a flooded market for secondhand film-based cameras; even professional-grade models can be bought at bargain prices. The rapid development of digital cameras has also created a burgeoning supply of attractively priced equipment. Although the best-known brands are likely to be the most reliable, they also command higher prices. Make sure that digital cameras are sold complete with all original software, chargers, and cables, since some use non-standard items that could be difficult to source.

Renting equipment

Do you ever need expensive equipment but cannot really afford it or would use it only occasionally? You may, for example, need a super-long telephoto lens for a safari trip, a data projector for a talk, a superior-quality scanner, or a replacement computer while yours is under repair. One answer is to rent items you need—you will save on the purchase price, pay only when the item is really needed, and the rental cost should be fully tax deductible if you are in business. Note the following points.

● Research possible equipment sources and set up account facilities. Some companies will send items if you live far from their warehouse or depot if you are a known customer, while new customers may need to provide a full-value cash deposit.

● Contact the supplier to reserve the item as soon as you think you might need it.

● Try to pick up the item a day or two early so that you can familiarize yourself with it and fully test it.

● Make sure your insurance covers any rented items.

The world's largest market for secondhand or preowned equipment is eBay, at online at ebay.com. This site offers copious help for the uninitiated, but local retailers are likely to offer stocks of equipment that you can examine in person and return easily if found to be faulty.

Shopping for specific interests
Today's photographer is spoiled for choice, thanks to the numerous camera models with features for every occasion. However, it can take a good deal of research to find the right camera for you.

Challenging conditions Cameras should be sealed against dust and rainfall, and have a rugged construction. Cameras with minimal moving parts are best; avoid those with lenses that zoom forward on turning on.

Collecting Modern digital cameras offer excellent close-up qualities, but many distort the image. Ideally, use a dSLR with a macro lens, and avoid zoom lenses. For flat objects where precision is essential, such as coins or stamps, a flatbed scanner can offer excellent results.

Nature Bridge-type digital cameras with super-zooms are good for nature photography: some offer 35efl of 350 mm or more, allowing high-magnification images of distant animals. dSLRs with long telephoto lenses offer the best results, but at a very high cost. A tripod will be invaluable.

Low light Fast lenses—that is, those with a large maximum aperture—are limited to costly prime optics for dSLRs. A cheaper solution is to use the highest ISO setting available; avoid cameras that have a maximum ISO rating of 400.

Portraiture Cameras with minimal shutter lag are vital. Those with larger chips give the best results, as does using the best-quality lenses. If possible, use full-frame sensors, since digital cameras with small sensors suffer from excessively large depth of field.

Sports Rapid response and long lenses are essential. Many bridge cameras will give excellent results in good lighting. If lighting is poor, you may need a dSLR and fast, long focal length lenses with large maximum apertures. A tripod will save you from having to hold the camera for hours.

Shopping checklist
- Shop with somebody knowledgeable, if you are lucky enough to know such a person.
- Write down the details of your computer model, operating system, and the details of other equipment that needs to work with the item you need.
- If it is secondhand, check that the equipment appears to have been well treated.
- If it is secondhand, inquire about the history of the equipment—for what purpose was it used, and for how long?
- Check that there is a guarantee period and that it is long enough for any likely faults to appear.
- When buying computer peripherals, make sure they will work with your exact computer model and operating system. You may, nonetheless, still need to test equipment at home with your computer, so if any compatibility problems arise, make sure the store will provide you with free technical support. In case these problems prove to be insurmountable, inquire about the store's policy regarding refunds.
- Ask about anything that may be causing you confusion. You will not look foolish—the only foolish thing is to pay for equipment that later proves useless.

Still-life and studio Be sure your digital camera can synchronize with studio flash. Some cameras can be controlled from a computer, and some can even send pictures direct to the computer, through either a cable or a WiFi (wireless network) connection. WiFi is great for heavy-duty, high-volume work.

Travel Bridge cameras offer a winning combination of compact, lightweight bodies, with extensive versatility and freedom from dust. Cameras that use standard AA batteries free you from worries about power, but try to choose cameras with long-lived batteries. For wide-angle views you may need supplementary lenses—awkward on location.

Underwater Housings are available for several models, from entry-level to professional, allowing you to reach all controls. The least expensive are flexible plastic bags but access to controls is limited.

Disabilities

Compared with film-based photography with its chemical processes, many of the features found on modern digital equipment make photography more accessible to people with some forms of disability. The reduced need for darkroom or workroom processes, for example, as well as the greater level of automation of equipment, means that it is altogether easier to produce good-quality, satisfying results.

On the whole, however, any advantages that disabled photographers may enjoy from using digital equipment have been incidental rather than as a result of the industry taking their needs into account at the design stage.

Accessibility is all about accommodating the characteristics a person cannot change by providing options. For example, a person who has impaired dexterity could control equipment via voice commands. The whole subject of photography for disabled people is a complicated one, but some points can be summarized here (*see also p. 215 for Web resources*).

Physical dexterity

Digital cameras could, almost without exception, be designed to make life easier for those with impaired dexterity. In reality, however, buttons are usually tiny, and at times two have to be pressed simultaneously; sockets need connectors that are small and have to be aligned precisely if they are to marry up; and so on. The Kodak DC 5000 stands out from other digital cameras for its larger-than-normal controls and its sturdy, chunky design, which makes it easy to grip and manipulate. In addition, the larger SLR digital cameras, such as the Nikon D1 or Kodak DCS range, are in general far easier to handle than compact models. However, on the downside, they are considerably bulkier and heavier.

Some digital cameras allow remote release—the camera can be set up on a rig or support while the release is conveniently located some distance away. While the remote controls are usually very small, it should be possible to adapt them by attaching a large hand-grip. Most digital cameras

are small and light enough to be easily mounted on a helmet or metal bracket attached to a wheel-chair. If so, the mounting should have some type of self-leveling mechanism to keep the camera horizontal even if the chair is tilted out of plumb by an uneven surface.

On the computer side, some software features voice-activated commands, which help to reduce reliance on the the keyboard. With sufficient programming, this software can be used to perform basic image manipulation as well as produce text for captioning or record-keeping notes. There is a wide range of Windows-based software that offers improved access to computing.

Visual ability

The relatively large LCD screens found on digital cameras may help the visually impaired: the Ricoh RDC-i700 is notable for its unusually large LCD screen with touch-screen controls allowing you to select menu items using a pointer.

Back at home, viewing images on a large-sized monitor offers considerable advantages over the traditional prints from most film processors. Selecting a low resolution—say, 640 x 480 dpi, on a 17-in (43-cm) screen—renders palettes and labels very large and far easier to read. Many software applications employ symbols rather than words to indicate options, which can also be an advantage. There are software utilities, such as KeyStrokes, that place an easy-to-read keyboard on the monitor screen: mouse clicks on the screen have the effect of typing letters. Keyboards with extra-large keys are also available.

Hearing ability

Most digital cameras give feedback on actions and functions with visual confirmation, so people with hearing difficulties will not be affected. However, with digital cameras, there is no physical sensation of a traditional shutter release being triggered. It may be important to find a camera that indicates shutter release with some form of visual signal: many do so indirectly, using a light to indicate that an image is being written to disk.

Survival guide

The care and preparation for photography are not glamorous, but if you ignore simple precautions, you may find yourself unable to engage in photography at all. The central problem is that every element in digital technology—right down to a battery charger or cable—is mission-critical, and its failure can cripple the system entirely.

Tips for trouble-free photography

Consider these points, whether you are planning a big trip away or preparing for an important event such as a wedding.

- Test all equipment before leaving for a major journey or important assignment. Make sure it all works. Make sure sensors on dSLRs are clean, all batteries are charged, and all memory cards are clear of all material (preferably newly formatted). Shoot some test pictures and check them on the computer; if the trip is really important, do this in time to have any problems corrected.
- Be sure you can continually power your digital camera: always have a spare battery in the camera bag, and always travel with the battery charger. If your travel is international, carry plug and voltage adapters. If your camera can be powered by standard batteries, take these as a backup.
- When you buy a new rechargeable battery, charge it fully and use it until it is completely exhausted before you next charge it. This appears to help preserve battery life.
- Equip yourself with as many memory cards as you can afford. Use the large, fast cards if your camera has a high pixel count, but avoid the largest cards: losing one means losing many images.
- Take a portable hard disk or picture storage device that can read memory cards directly. For major trips, take a backup to the storage device.
- If possible, take a laptop computer on long trips, so you can check, review, and even start to catalog and caption images while on the road.
- Take a memory card reader and all the cables you will need if traveling with a laptop. Take spares of all crucial items—for example, FireWire or USB cables and power cords—so there are at least two ways of emptying the camera of its images.

- Cover LCD panels with protective film. These are highly transparent and have a light adhesive covering on one side that should leave no residue when removed. They do not seriously impede the clarity of the LCD display but do a great deal to preserve the screen from scratches and abrasions.
- Obtain insurance to cover all risks while traveling with your equipment.
- Take a small toolkit or universal tool: small screws may need to be tightened (especially after long journeys on rough roads), and small parts may need to be bent back after minor knocks.

While on location

- Do not allow your camera to get too hot—for example, by leaving it in full sunlight or in the glove compartment of a car in the tropics.
- Keep all optical surfaces clean: blow dust off with a blower, and wipe smears off gently.
- Batteries are the most common problem for digital cameras: if the camera is not working, check that the batteries are inserted the right way around, and that they are fresh or newly charged.
- Keep dust out of enclosed spaces such as the memory card and battery compartments and the sockets for connectors. Keep these parts covered when not in use and blow them out with compressed air occasionally.
- Digital cameras are prone to condensation problems because of the electrical contacts inside. A cool camera coming into humid conditions is likely to become misted up. If water forms on electrical contacts, the camera may freeze up, or worse. A camera entering an air-conditioned interior on a hot day may also mist up. In both cases, enclose the camera fully before a sudden change in environment, ideally keeping it so until it has partially reached the new temperature.
- In cold weather, keep batteries as warm as possible. Hold the camera close to your body (but not inside your coat, since the exposure to cold will be too sudden). Keep spare batteries inside your coat. To preserve battery power, turn off all functions that aren't absolutely necessary, such as the flash, autofocus, and image stabilization.

Glossary

24x speed The device in question reads data from a CD-ROM at 24x the basic rate of 150 KB per second. As a guide, modern CD players may reach speeds of 48x or greater.

24-bit A measure of the size or resolution of data that a computer, program, or component works with. A color depth of 24 bits produces millions of different colors.

2D Two-dimensional, as in 2-D graphics. Defining a plane or lying on one.

3D Three-dimensional, as in 3-D graphics. Defining a solid or volume, or having the appearance of a solid or volume.

35efl 35-mm equivalent focal length. A digital camera's lens focal length expressed as the equivalent focal length for the 35-mm film format.

36-bit A measure of the size or resolution of data that a computer, program, or component works with. In imaging, it equates to allocating 12 bits to each of the R, G, B (red, green, blue) channels. A color depth of 36 bits gives billions of colors.

5,000 The white balance standard for prepress work. Corresponds to warm, white light.

6,500 The white balance standard corresponding to normal daylight. It appears to be a warm white compared with 9,300.

9,300 The white balance standard close to normal daylight. It is used mainly for visual displays.

A

aberration In optics, a defect in the image caused by a failure of a lens system to form a perfect image.

aberration, chromatic An image defect that shows up as colored fringes when a subject is illuminated by white light, caused by the dispersion of white light as it passes through the glass lens elements.

absolute temperature A measure of thermodynamic state, used to correlate to the color of light. Measured in Kelvins.

absolute colorimetric A method of matching color gamuts that tries to preserve color values as close to the originals as possible.

absorption Partial loss of light during reflection or transmission. Selective absorption of light causes the phenomenon of color.

accelerator A device that speeds up a computer by, for example, providing special processors optimized for certain software operations.

accommodation An adjustment in vision to keep objects at different distances sharply in focus.

achromatic color Color that is distinguished by differences in lightness but is devoid of hue, such as black, white, or grays.

ADC Analog-to-Digital Conversion. A process of converting or representing a continuously varying signal into a set of digital values or code.

additive A substance added to another, usually to improve its reactivity or its keeping qualities, especially in lengthening the life span of a print.

additive color synthesis Combining or blending two or more colored lights in order to simulate or give the sensation of another color.

address Reference or data that locates or identifies the physical or virtual position of a physical or virtual item: for example, memory in RAM; the sector of hard disk on which data is stored; a dot from an inkjet printer.

addressable The property of a point in space that allows it to be identified and referenced by some device, such as an inkjet printer.

algorithm A set of rules that defines the repeated application of logical or mathematical operations on an object: for example, compressing a file or applying image filters.

alias A representation or "stand-in" for the continuous original signal: it is the product of sampling and measuring the signal to convert it into a digital form.

alpha channel A normally unused portion of a file format. It is designed so that changing the value of the alpha channel changes the properties—transparency/opacity, for example—of the rest of the file.

analog An effect, representation, or record that is proportionate to some other physical property or change.

antialiasing Smoothing away the stair-stepping, or jagged edge, in an image or in computer typesetting.

aperture The size of the hole in the lens that is letting light through. *See* f/numbers.

apps A commonly used abbreviation for application software.

array An arrangement of image sensors. There are two types. *1* A two-dimensional grid, or wide array, in which rows of sensors are laid side by side to cover an area. *2* A one-dimensional or

Glossary continued

linear array, in which a single row of sensors, or set of three rows, is set up, usually to sweep over or scan a flat surface—as in a flatbed scanner. The number of sensors defines the total number of pixels available.

aspect ratio The ratio between width and height (or depth).

attachment A file, such as a PDF or JPEG, that is sent along with an email.

B

back up To make and store second or further copies of computer files to protect against loss, corruption, or damage of the originals.

bandwidth *1* A range of frequencies transmitted, used, or passed by a device, such as a radio, TV channel, satellite, or loudspeaker. *2* The measure of the range of wavelengths transmitted by a filter.

beam splitter An optical component used to divide rays of light.

bicubic interpolation A type of interpolation in which the value of a new pixel is calculated from the values of its eight near neighbors. It gives superior results to bilinear or nearest-neighbor interpolation, with more contrast to offset the blurring induced by interpolation.

bilinear interpolation A type of interpolation in which the value of a new pixel is calculated from the values of four of its near neighbors: left, right, top, and bottom. It gives results that are less satisfactory than bicubic interpolation, but requires less processing.

bit The fundamental unit of computer information. It has only two possible values–1 or 0—representing, for example, on or off, up or down.

bit depth Measure of the amount of information that can be registered by a computer component: hence, it is used as a measure of resolution of such variables as color and density. 1-bit registers two states (1 or 0), representing, for example, white or black; 8-bit can register 256 states.

bit-mapped *1* An image defined by the values given to individual picture elements of an array whose extent is equal to that of the image; the image is the map of the bit-values of the individual elements. *2* An image comprising picture elements whose values are only either 1 or 0: the bit-depth of the image is 1.

black *1* Describing a color whose appearance is

due to the absorption of most or all of the light. *2* Denoting the maximum density of a photograph.

bleed *1* A photograph or line that runs off the page when printed. *2* The spread of ink into the fibers of the support material. This effect causes dot gain.

BMP Bitmap. A file format that is native to the Windows platform.

bokeh The subjective quality of an out-of-focus image projected by an optical system—usually a photographic lens.

brightness *1* A quality of visual perception that varies with the amount, or intensity, of light that a given element appears to send out, or transmit. *2* The brilliance of a color, related to hue or color saturation—for example, bright pink as opposed to pale pink.

brightness range The difference between the lightness of the brightest part of a subject and the lightness of the darkest part.

browse To look through a collection of, for example, images or webpages in no particular order or with no strictly defined search routine.

Brush An image-editing tool used to apply effects, such as color, blurring, burn, or dodge, that are limited to the areas the brush is applied to, in imitation of a real brush.

buffer A memory component in an output device, such as printer, CD writer, or digital camera, that stores data temporarily, which it then feeds to the device at a rate the data can be turned into, for example, a printed page.

burning-in *1* A digital image-manipulation technique that mimics the darkroom technique of the same name. *2* A darkroom technique for altering the local contrast and density of a print by giving specific parts extra exposure, while masking off the rest of the print to prevent unwanted exposure in those areas.

byte Unit of digital information: 1 byte = 8 bits. A 32-bit microprocessor, for example, handles four bytes of data at a time.

C

C An abbreviation for cyan. A secondary color made by combining the two primary colors red and blue.

cache The RAM dedicated to keeping data recently

read off a storage device to help speed up the working of a computer.

calibration The process of matching characteristics or behavior of a device to a standard.

camera exposure The total amount of the light reaching (in a film camera) the light-sensitive film or (in a digital camera) the sensors. It is determined by the effective aperture of the lens and the duration of the exposure to light.

capacity The quantity of data that can be stored in a device, measured in MB or GB.

cartridge A storage or protective device consisting of a shell (a plastic or metal casing, for example) enclosing the delicate parts (film, ink, or magnetic disk, for example).

catch light A small, localized highlight.

CCD Charge-coupled device. A semiconductor device used as an image detector.

CD-ROM Compact disc–read-only memory. A storage device for digital files invented originally for music and now one of the most ubiquitous computer storage systems.

characteristic curve A graph showing how the density of a given film and its development relate to exposure.

chroma The color value of a given light source or patch. It is approximately equivalent to the perceived hue of a color.

CIE LAB Commission Internationale de l'Éclairage LAB. A color model in which the color space is spherical. The vertical axis is L for lightness (for achromatic colors) with black at the bottom and white at the top. The a axis runs horizontally, from red (positive values) to green (negative values). At right angles to this, the b axis runs from yellow (positive values) to blue (negative values).

clipboard An area of memory reserved for holding items temporarily during the editing process.

CLUT Color lookup table. The collection of colors used to define colors in indexed color files. Usually a maximum of 256 colors can be contained.

CMYK Cyan–magenta–yellow–key. The first three are the primary colors of subtractive mixing, which is the principle on which inks rely in order to create a sense of color. A mix of all three as solid primaries produces a dark color close to black, but for good-quality blacks, it is necessary to use a separate black, or key, ink.

codec co(mpression) dec(ompression). A routine or algorithm for compressing and decompressing files; for example, JPEG or MPEG. Image file codecs are usually specific to the format, but video codecs are not tied to a particular video format.

cold colors A subjective term referring to blues and cyans.

color picker The part of an operating system (OS) or application that enables the user to select a color for use—as in painting, for example.

color synthesis Recreating the original color sensation by combining two or more other colors.

color temperature The measure of color quality of a source of light, expressed in Kelvins.

colorize To add color to a grayscale image without changing the original lightness values.

ColorSync A proprietary color-management software system to help ensure, for example, that the colors seen on the screen match those to be reproduced by a printer.

color *1* Denoting the quality of the visual perception of things seen, characterized by hue, saturation, and lightness. *2* To add color to an image by hand—using dyes, for example—or in an image-manipulation program.

color cast A tint or hint of a color that evenly covers an image.

color gamut The range of colors that can be reproduced by a device or reproduction system. Reliable color reproduction is hampered by differing color gamuts of devices: color film has the largest gamut, computer monitors have less than color film but more than inkjet printers; the best inkjet printers have a greater color gamut than four-color CMYK printing.

color management The process of controlling the output of all the devices in a production chain to ensure that the final results are reliable and repeatable.

color sensitivity A measure of the variation in the way in which film responds to light of different wavelengths, particularly in reference to black and white films.

complementary colors Pairs of colors that produce white when added together as lights. For example, the secondary colors—cyan, magenta, and yellow—are complementary to the primary colors—respectively, red, green, and blue.

Glossary continued

compliant A device or software that complies with the specifications or standards set by a corresponding device or software to enable them to work together.

compositing A picture-processing technique that combines one or more images with a basic image. Also known as montaging.

compression *1* A process by which digital files are reduced in size by changing the way the data is coded. *2* A reduction in tonal range.

continuous-tone image A record in dyes, pigment, silver, or other metals in which relatively smooth transitions from low to high densities are represented by varying amounts of the substance used to make up the image.

contrast *1* Of ambient light: the brightness range found in a scene. In other words, the difference between the highest and lowest luminance values. High contrast indicates a large range of subject brightnesses. *2* Of film: the rate at which density builds up with increasing exposure over the mid-portion of the characteristic curve of the film/development combination. *3* Of a light source or quality of light: the difference in brightness between the deepest shadows and the brightest highlights. Directional light gives high-contrast lighting, with hard shadows, while diffuse light gives low-contrast lighting, with soft shadows. *4* Of printing paper: the grade of paper used—for example, high-contrast paper is grade 4 or 5, while grade 1 is low contrast. *5* Of color: colors positioned opposite each other on the color wheel are regarded as contrasting—for example, blue and yellow, green and red.

copyright Rights that subsist in original literary, dramatic, musical, or artistic works to alter, reproduce, publish, or broadcast. Artistic works include photographs—recordings of light or other radiation on any medium on which an image is produced or from which an image may by any means be produced.

CPU Central processor unit. The part of the computer that receives instructions, evaluates them according to the software applications, and then issues appropriate instructions to other parts of the computer system. It is often referred to as the "chip"—for example, Pentium III or G4.

crash The sudden and unexpected non-functioning of a computer.

crop *1* To use part of an image for the purpose of, for example, improving composition or fitting an image to the available space or format. *2* To restrict a scan to the required part of an image.

cross-platform Application software, file, or file format that can be used on more than one computer operating system.

curve A graph relating input values to output values for a manipulated image.

cut and paste To remove a selected part of a graphic, image, or section of text from a file and store it temporarily in a clipboard ("cutting") and then to insert it elsewhere ("pasting").

cyan The color blue-green. It is a primary color of subtractive mixing or a secondary color of additive mixing. Also, the complementary to red.

D

D65 The white balance standard used to calibrate monitor screens. It is used primarily for domestic television sets. White is correlated to a color temperature of 6,500 K.

daylight *1* The light that comes directly or indirectly from the sun. *2* As a notional standard, the average mixture of sunlight and skylight with some clouds, typical of temperate latitudes at around midday, and with a color temperature of between 5,400 and 5,900 K. *3* Film whose color balance is correct for light sources with a color temperature between 5,400 and 5,600 K. *4* Artificial light sources, such as light bulbs, whose color-rendering index approximates to that of daylight.

definition The subjective assessment of clarity and the quality of detail that is visible in an image or photograph.

delete *1* To render an electronic file invisible and capable of being overwritten. *2* To remove an item, such as a letter, selected block of words or cells, or a selected part of a graphic or an image.

density *1* The measure of darkness, blackening, or "strength" of an image in terms of its ability to stop light—in other words, its opacity. *2* The number of dots per unit area produced by a printing process.

depth *1* The sharpness of an image—loosely synonymous with depth of field. *2* A subjective assessment of the richness of the black areas of a print or transparency.

depth of field The measure of the zone or distance over which any object in front of a lens will appear acceptably sharp. It lies both in front of and behind the plane of best focus, and is affected by three factors: lens aperture; lens focal length; and image magnification.

depth perception The perception of the absolute or relative distance of an object from a viewer.

digital image The image on a computer screen or any other visible medium, such as a print, that has been produced by transforming an image of a subject into a digital record, followed by the reconstruction of that image.

digitization The process of translating values for the brightness or color into electrical pulses representing an alphabetic or a numerical code.

direct-vision finder (or **viewfinder**) A type of viewfinder in which the subject is observed directly—for example, through a hole or another type of optical device.

display A device—such as a monitor screen, LCD projector, or an information panel on a camera—that provides a temporary visual representation of data.

distortion, tonal A property of an image in which the contrast, range of brightness, or colors appear to be markedly different from those of subject.

dithering Simulating many colors or shades by using a smaller number of colors or shades.

d-max *1* The measure of the greatest, or maximum, density of silver or dye image attained by a film or print in a given sample. *2* The point at the top of a characteristic curve of negative film, or the bottom of the curve of positive film.

dodging *1* A digital image-manipulation technique based on the darkroom technique of the same name. *2* A darkroom technique for controlling local contrast when printing a photograph by selectively reducing the amount of light reaching the parts of a print that would otherwise print as too dark.

down-sampling The reduction in file size achieved when a bitmapped image is reduced in size.

dpi Dots per inch. The measure of resolution of an output device as the number of dots or points that can be addressed or printed by that device.

driver The software used by a computer to control, or drive, a peripheral device, such as a scanner, printer, or removable media drive.

drop shadow A graphic effect in which an object appears to float above a surface, leaving a fuzzy shadow below it and offset to one side.

drop-on-demand A type of inkjet printer in which the ink leaves the reservoir only when required. Most inkjet printers in use today are of this type.

drum scanner A type of scanner employing a tightly focused spot of light that shines on a subject that has been stretched over a rotating drum. As the drum rotates, the spot of light traverses the length of the subject, thus scanning its entire area.

duotone *1* A photomechanical printing process in which two inks are used to increase the tonal range. *2* A mode of working in image-manipulation software that simulates the printing of an image with two inks.

DVD-RAM A DVD (digital versatile disk) variant that carries 4.7 GB or more per side that can be written to and read from many times.

dye sublimation Printer technology based on the rapid heating of dry colorants that are held in close contact with a receiving layer. This turns the colorants to gas, which then solidifies on the receiving layer.

dynamic range The measure of spread of the highest to the lowest energy levels that can be captured or reproduced by a device, such as a scanner or film-writer.

E

edge effects Local distortions of the image density in a film due to the movement of the developer and developer products between regions of different exposure. Similar effects can be seen with some image-processing techniques.

effects filters *1* Lens attachments designed to distort, color, or modify images to produce exaggerated, unusual, or special effects. *2* Digital filters that have effects similar to their lens-attachment counterparts, but also giving effects impossible to achieve with these analog filters.

engine *1* The internal mechanisms that drive devices such as printers and scanners. *2* The core parts of a software application.

enhancement *1* Change in one or more qualities of an image, such as color saturation or sharpness, in order to improve its appearance or alter some other visual property. *2* The effect produced by a

Glossary continued

device or software designed to increase the apparent resolution of a TV monitor screen.

EPS Encapsulated PostScript. A file format that stores an image (graphics, photograph, or page layout) in PostScript page-description language.

erase To remove, or wipe, a recording from a disk, tape, or other recording media (usually magnetic) so that it is impossible to reconstruct the original record.

EV Exposure value. A measure of camera exposure. For any given EV, there is a combination of shutter and aperture settings that gives the same camera exposure.

exposure *1* A process whereby light reaches light-sensitive material or sensor to create a latent image. *2* The amount of light energy that reaches a light-sensitive material.

exposure factor The number indicating the degree by which measured exposure should be corrected or changed in order to give an accurate exposure.

F

f/numbers Settings of the camera diaphragm that determine the amount of light transmitted by a lens. Each f/number is equal to the focal length of the lens divided by diameter of the entrance pupil.

fade The gradual loss of density in silver, pigment, or dye images over time.

fall-off *1* The loss of light in the corners of an image as projected by a lens system in, for example, a camera or a projector. *2* The loss of light toward the edges of a scene that is illuminated by a light source whose angle of illumination is too small to cover the required view. *3* The loss of image sharpness and density away from the middle of a flatbed scanner whose array of sensors is narrower than the width of the scanned area.

false color A term usually applied to images with an arbitrary allocation of color to wavebands—for example, with infrared-sensitive film.

feathering The blurring of a border or boundary by reducing the sharpness or suddenness of the change in value of, for example, color.

file format A method or structure of computer data. It is determined by codes—for example, by indicating the start and end of a portion of data together with any special techniques used, such as compression. File formats may be generic—

shared by different software—or native to a specific software application.

fill-in *1* To illuminate shadows cast by the main light by using another light source or reflector to bounce light from the main source into the shadows. *2* A light used to brighten or illuminate shadows cast by the main light. *3* In image manipulation, to cover an area with color—as achieved by using a Bucket tool.

film gate The physical aperture in a camera that lies close to the film and masks the image projected by the lens. Its size defines the shape and size of the image that is recorded on the film.

filter *1* An optical accessory used to remove a certain waveband of light and transmit others. *2* Part of image-manipulation software written to produce special effects. *3* Part of application software that is used to convert one file format to another. *4* A program or part of an application used to remove or to screen data—for example, to refuse email messages from specified sources.

fingerprint Marking in a digital image file that is invisible and that survives all normal image manipulations, but one that can still be retrieved by using suitable software.

FireWire The standard providing for rapid communication between computers and devices, such as digital cameras and CD writers.

fixed focus A type of lens mounting that fixes a lens at a set distance from the film. This distance is usually the hyperfocal distance. For normal to slightly wide-angle lenses, this is at between 6½ and 13 ft (2 and 4 m) from the camera.

flare Non-image-forming light in an optical system.

flash *1* To provide illumination using a very brief burst of light. *2* To reduce contrast in a light-sensitive material by exposing it to a brief, overall burst of light. *3* The equipment used to provide a brief burst, or flash, of light. *4* The type of electronic memory that is used in, for example, digital cameras.

flat *1* Denoting a low-contrast negative or print in which gray tones only are seen. *2* The lighting or other conditions that tend to produce evenly lit or low-contrast image results.

flatbed scanner A type of scanner employing a set of sensors arranged in a line that are focused, via mirrors and lenses, on a subject placed face down on a flat, glass bed facing a light source. As the sensors traverse the subject, they register the varying light levels reflected off the subject.

flatten To combine multiple layers and other elements of a digitally manipulated or composited image into one. This is usually the final step of working with Layers prior to saving an image in a standard image format; otherwise, the image must be saved in native format.

focal length For a simple lens, the distance between the center of the lens and the sharp image of an object at infinity projected by it.

focus *1* Making an image look sharp by bringing the film or projection plane into coincidence with the focal plane of an optical system. *2* The rear principal focal point. *3* The point or area on which, for example, a viewer's attention is fixed or compositional elements visually converge.

fog Non-image-forming density in a film or other light-sensitive material.

font A computer file describing a set of letter forms for display on a screen or used for printing.

foreground *1* The part of scene or space around an object that appears closest to the camera. *2* The features in a photographic composition that are depicted as being nearest the viewer.

format *1* The shape and dimensions of an image on a film as defined by the shape and dimensions of the camera's film gate. *2* The dimensions of paper on which an image is printed. *3* The orientation of an image: for example, in a landscape format, the image is oriented with its long axis running horizontally, while in a portrait format the image is oriented with its long axis running vertically.

fractal A curve or other object whose smaller parts are similar to the larger parts. In practice, a fractal displays increasing complexity as it is viewed more closely and where the details bear a similarity to the whole.

frame *1* A screen's worth of information. *2* An image in a sequence replicating movement.

G

gamma 1 In photography, a measure of the response of a given film, developer, and development regimen to light—for example, a high contrast results in a higher gamma. *2* In monitors, a measure of the correction to the color signal prior to its projection on the screen. A high gamma gives a darker overall screen image.

GIF Graphic interchange format. This is a compressed file format designed for use over the Internet. It uses 216 colors.

grain *1* In film, it is the individual silver (or other metal) particles that make up the image of a fully developed film. In the case of color film, grain comprises the individual dye-clouds of the image. *2* In a photographic print, it is the appearance of the individual specks comprising the image. *3* In paper, it is the texture of its surface.

graphics tablet An input device allowing fine or variable control of the image appearance in an image-manipulation program. The tablet is an electrostatically charged board connected to the computer. It is operated using a pen, which interacts with the board to provide location information and instructions are issued by providing pressure at the pen tip.

grayscale The measure of the number of distinct steps between black and white that can be recorded or reproduced by a system. A grayscale of two steps permits the recording or reproduction of just black or white. The Zone System uses a grayscale of ten divisions. For normal reproduction, a grayscale of at least 256 steps, including black and white, is required.

greeking The representation of text or images as gray blocks or other approximations.

H

halftone cell The unit used by a halftone printing or reproduction system to simulate a grayscale or continuous-tone reproduction. In off-set lithography, the halftone cell is defined by the screen frequency: continuous tone is simulated by using dots of different sizes within the halftone cell. With desktop printers, the halftone cell consists of groups of individual laser or inkjet dots.

hard copy A visible form of a computer file printed more or less permanently onto a support, such as paper or film.

highlights The brightest (whitest) values in an image or image file.

hints Artificial intelligence built into outline fonts, which turn elements of a font on or off according to the size of the font. Intended to improve legibility and design.

histogram A statistical, graphical representation showing the relative numbers of variables over a

Glossary continued

range of values. Usually used in image-manipulation software, histograms are also available to view on some digital cameras

HLS Hue, lightness, saturation. A color model that works well for representing a visual response to colors, but one that is not satisfactory for other color reproduction systems. This model has been largely superseded by the LAB model.

hot-pluggable A connector or interface, such as USB or FireWire, that can be disconnected or connected while the computer and machine are powered up.

hue The name given to the visual perception of a color.

I

IEEE 1394 A standard providing for the rapid communication between computers and devices, and between devices without the need for a computer, such as between digital cameras and CD writers. It is also known as FireWire and iLink.

image aspect ratio The comparison of the depth of an image to its width. For example, the nominal 35-mm format in landscape orientation is 24 mm deep by 36 mm wide, so the image aspect ratio is 1:1.5.

indexed color A method of creating color files or defining a color space based on a table of colors chosen from 16 million different colors. A given pixel's color is then defined by its position, or index, in the table (also known as the "color lookup table").

inkjet Printing technology based on the controlled squirting of extremely tiny drops of ink onto a receiving layer.

intensity *1* A measure of energy, usually of light, radiated by a source. *2* A term loosely used to refer to the apparent strength of color, as in inks or the colors of a photograph.

interpolation The insertion of pixels into a digital image based on existing data. It is used to resize an image file, for example, to give an apparent increase in resolution, to rotate an image, or to animate an image.

J

jaggies The appearance of stair-stepping artifacts.
JPEG Joint photographic expert group. A data-compression technique that reduces file sizes with loss of information.

K

k *1* An abbreviation for kilo, a prefix denoting 1,000. *2* A binary thousand: in other words, 1024, as used, for example, when 1024 bytes is abbreviated to KB. *3* Key ink or blacK—the fourth color separation in the CMYK four-color print reproduction process.

Kelvin (K) A unit of temperature that is relative to absolute zero, and is used to express color temperature.

kernel A group of pixels, usually a square from 3 pixels up to 60, that is sampled and mathematically operated on for certain image-processing techniques, such as noise reduction or image sharpening.

key tone *1* The black in a CMYK image. *2* The principal or most important tone in an image, usually the midtone between white and black.

keyboard shortcut Keystrokes that execute a command.

L

layer mode A picture-processing or image-manipulation technique that determines the way that a layer, in a multilayer image, combines or interacts with the layer below.

light *1* That part of the electromagnetic spectrum, from about 380–760 nm, that stimulates the receptors of the retina of the human eye, giving rise to normal vision. Light of different wavelengths is perceived as light of different colors. *2* To manipulate light sources to alter the illumination of a subject.

light box A viewing device for transparencies and films consisting of a translucent, light-diffusing top illuminated from beneath by color-corrected fluorescent tubes in order to provide daylight-equivalent lighting.

lightness The amount of white in a color. This affects the perceived saturation of a color: the lighter the color, the less saturated it appears to be.

line art Artwork that consists of black lines and black and white areas only, with no intermediate gray tones present.

load To copy enough of the application software

into a computer's RAM for it to be able to open and run the application.

lossless compression A computing routine, such as LZW, that reduces the size of a digital file without reducing the information in the file.

lossy compression A computing routine, such as JPEG, that reduces the size of a digital file but also loses information or data.

lpi Lines per inch. A measure of resolution or fineness of photomechanical reproduction.

LZW Lempel-Ziv Welch compression. A widely used computer routine for lossless file compression of, for example, TIFF files.

M

Mac Commonly used term for Apple Macintosh computers and their operating system (OS).

macro *1* The close-up range giving reproduction ratios within the range of about 1:10 to 1:1 (life-size). *2* A small routine or program within a larger software program that performs a series of operations. It may also be called "script" or "action."

marquee A selection tool used in image-manipulation and graphics software.

mask A technique used to obscure selectively or hold back parts of an image while allowing other parts to show.

master *1* The original or first, and usually unique, incarnation of a photograph, file, or recording: the one from which copies will be made. *2* To make the first copy of a photograph, file, or recording.

matrix The flat, two-dimensional array of CCD sensors.

matte *1* The surface finish on paper that reflects light in a diffused way. *2* A box-shaped device placed in front of camera lens to hold accessories. *3* A board whose center is cut out to create a window to display prints. *4* A mask that blanks out an area of an image to allow another image to be superimposed.

megapixel A million pixels. A measure of the resolution of a digital camera's sensor: a 7-megapixel camera has a 7-megapixel sensor.

moiré A pattern of alternating light and dark bands or colors caused by interference between two or more superimposed arrays or patterns, which differ in phase, orientation, or frequency.

monochrome A photograph or image made up of black, white, and grays, which may or may not be tinted.

N

native *1* The file format belonging to an application program. *2* An application program written specifically for a certain type of processor.

nearest neighbor The type of interpolation in which the value of the new pixel is copied from the nearest pixel.

node *1* A computer linked to others in a network or on the Internet. *2* A word or short phrase that is linked to other text elsewhere in a hypertext document.

noise Unwanted signals or disturbances in a system that tend to reduce the amount of information being recorded or transmitted.

Nyquist rate The sampling rate needed to turn an analog signal into an accurate digital representation. This rate is twice the highest frequency found in the analog signal. It is applied to determine the quality factor relating image resolution to output resolution: pixel density should be at least 1.5 times, but not more than 2 times, the screen ruling. For example, for a 133 lpi screen, resolution should be between 200 and 266.

O

offline A mode of working with data or files in which all required files are downloaded or copied from a source to be accessed directly by the user.

online A mode of working or operating with data or files in which the operator maintains continuous connection with a remote source.

operating system The software program, often abbreviated to OS, that underlies the functioning of the computer, allowing applications software to use the computer.

optical viewfinder A type of viewfinder that shows the subject through an optical system, rather than via a monitor screen.

out-of-gamut The color or colors that cannot be reproduced in one color space but are visible or reproducible in another.

output *1* The result of any computer calculation—any process or manipulation of data. Depending on the context, output may be in the form of new

Glossary continued

data, a set of numbers, or be used to control an output device. *2* A hard-copy printout of a digital file, such as an inkjet print or separation films.

P

paint To apply color, texture, or an effect with a digital Brush or the color itself.

palette *1* A set of tools, colors, or shapes that is presented in a small window of a software application. *2* The range or selection of colors available to a color-reproduction system.

peripheral A device, such as a printer, monitor, scanner, or modem, connected to a computer.

Photo CD A proprietary system of digital-image management based on the storage of image files on CDs, which can be played back on most types of CD players.

photodiode A semiconductor device that responds very quickly and proportionally to the intensity of light falling on it.

photograph A record of physical objects, scenes, or phenomena made with a camera or other device, through the agency of radiant energy, on sensitive material from which a visible image may be obtained.

photomontage A photographic image made from the combination of several other photographic images. Also known as a composite.

PICT A graphic file format used in the Mac OS.

pixel The smallest unit of digital imaging used or produced by a given device.

pixelated The appearance of a digital image whose individual pixels are clearly discernible.

platform The type of computer system, defined by the operating system used—for example, the Apple Macintosh platform uses the Mac OS.

plug-in Application software that works in conjunction with a host program into which it is "plugged," so that it operates as if part of the program itself.

posterization The representation of an image using a relatively small number of different tones or colors, which results in a banded appearance in flat areas of color.

PostScript A programming language that specifies the way in which elements are output: it uses the full resolution of the output device.

ppi Points per inch. The number of points that

are seen or resolved by a scanning device per linear inch.

prescan In image acquisition, it is a quick view of the object to be scanned, taken at a low resolution for the purposes of, for example, cropping.

primary color One of the colors—red, green, or blue—to which the human eye has a peak sensitivity.

process colors Colors that can be reproduced with the standard web offset press (SWOP) inks of cyan, magenta, yellow, and black (CMYK).

proofing The process of checking or confirming the quality of a digital image before final output.

Q

quality factor The multiplication factor—usually between 1.5 and 2 times the screen frequency—used to ensure a file size that is sufficient for good-quality reproduction.

QuickDraw An object-oriented graphics language native to the Mac OS.

R

RAM Random access memory. The component of a computer in which information can be temporarily stored and rapidly accessed.

raster The regular arrangement of addressable points of any device, such as scanner, digital camera, monitor, printer, or film writer.

read To access or take off information from a storage device, such as a hard disk, Zip disk, or CD-ROM.

resizing Changing the resolution or file size of an image.

refresh rate The rate at which one frame of a computer screen succeeds the next. The more rapid the rate, the more stable the monitor image appears.

res The measure of the resolution of a digital image expressed as the number of pixels per side of a square measuring 1 x 1 mm.

RGB Red–green–blue. A color model that defines colors in terms of the relative amounts of red, green, and blue components they contain.

RIP Raster image processor. Software or hardware dedicated to the conversion of outline fonts and vector graphics into rasterized information—in other words, it turns outline instructions such as "fill" or "linejoin" into an array of dots.

S

scanner An optical-mechanical instrument that is used for the analog-to-digital conversion, or digitization, of film-based and printed material and artwork.

scanning The process of using a scanner to turn an original into a digital facsimile—in other words, a digital file of specified size.

screengrab An image file of the monitor display or part of it. Also called a screenshot.

scrolling The process of moving to a different portion of a file that is too large for it all to fit onto a monitor screen.

SCSI Small Computers Systems Interface. A standard for connecting devices, such as scanners and hard disks, to computers.

shadows The dark (or black) areas of an image or digital image.

soft proofing The use of a monitor screen to proof or confirm the quality of an image.

stair-stepping A jagged or steplike reproduction of a line or boundary that is, in fact, smooth.

subtractive color synthesis Combining of dyes or pigments to create new colors.

SWOP Standard web offset press. A set of inks used to define the color gamut of CMYK inks used in the print industry.

system requirements The specifications defining the minimum configuration of equipment and operating system needed to run application software or a device. It usually details the type of processor, amount of RAM, free hard disk space, oldest version of the operating system, and, according to the software, any specifically needed device.

T

thumbnail The representation of an image in a small, low-resolution version.

TIFF Tag image file format. A widely used image file format that supports up to 24-bit color per pixel. Tags are used to store such image information as dimensions.

tile *1* A subsection or part of a larger bitmapped image. It is often used for file-storage purposes and for image processing. *2* To print in small sections a page that is larger than the printing device is able to output.

tint *1* Color that is reproducible with process colors; a process color. *2* An overall, usually light, coloring that tends to affect areas with density but not clear areas.

transparency *1* Film in which the image is seen by illuminating it from behind—color transparency film, for example. Also known as a slide. *2* In image manipulation, the degree to which background color can be seen through the foreground layer.

transparency adapter An accessory light source that enables a scanner to scan transparencies.

TWAIN A standardized software "bridge" used by computers to control scanners via scanner drivers.

U

undo To reverse an editing or similar action within application software.

upload The transfer of data between computers or from a network to a computer.

USB Universal serial bus. A standard for connecting peripheral devices, such as a digital camera, telecommunications equipment, or a printer, to a computer.

USM UnSharp Mask. An image-processing technique that has the effect of improving the apparent sharpness of an image.

V

variable contrast A coating formula that mixes emulsions of different speeds and sensitivities to light, with the effect that the midtone contrast can be varied by changing the spectral qualities of the illumination.

vignetting *1* A defect of an optical system in which light at the edges of an image is cut off or reduced by an obstruction in the system's construction. *2* Deliberately darkened corners—used to help frame an image or soften the frame outline.

VRAM Video random access memory. Rapid-access memory that is dedicated for use by a computer or graphics accelerator to control the image on a monitor.

W

warm colors A subjective term referring to reds, oranges, and yellows.

watermark *1* A mark left on paper to identify the maker or paper type. *2* An element in a digital image file used to identify the copyright holder.

write To commit or record data onto a storage medium, such as a CD-R or hard disk.

www.resources

NEWS, INFORMATION, REVIEWS

www.creativepro.com
Great source of news, techniques, and issues of image manipulation, digital photography, design, and graphics. Highly recommended.

www.dcresource.com
Dedicated to thorough reviews of consumer cameras, and featuring useful comparison charts. An enormous number of cameras is covered.

www.dpreview.com
Digital Photography Review: up-to-date, highly detailed, and informative reviews of digital cameras, as well as news and information.

www.getty.edu
Authoritative references on digital collections, including an excellent book-length introduction to digital imaging. Highly educational, and not only to museum people. While you are there, browse the collection of marvelous photos and artwork.

www.letsgodigital.org
Extensive news and reviews of equipment, as well as a regularly updated picture gallery.

www.normankoren.com
Dedicated to the technically inclined photographer, this site offers much to ponder: from printing to scanning and digital photography. Good links.

http://photoshopnews.com
Much more than a site for news about Photoshop, this offers high-quality material on a wide range of issues relating to the Photoshop user. It covers not only the software but also the technical market, as well as legal issues, news, and recommended links.

www.shortcourses.com
Online books on digital photography and instruction books for digital cameras, with links to other resources.

www.shutterbug.net
Wide-ranging photography resource from the great eponymous magazine, with a section on digital photography.

www.zonezero.com
A mixture of photography and digital photography, with text in English and Spanish.

COPYRIGHT SITES

www.benedict.com
Wide coverage of copyright issues with relevant case law. It is heavily US-based, since many of the new laws are being created in the United States.

www.intelproplaw.com/copyright
Useful reference material, articles, and discussion on copyright issues. Good links for news, too.

www.tilj.com
The *Internet Law Journal* site is an excellent source for changes in law and cases relating to Internet law in general, particularly copyright matters.

PORTFOLIO SITES

www.fotolog.com
Online digital gallery/community, with a huge number of pictures from around the world.

http://photos.fotango.com/cgi-bin/index.cgi
Photo-processing services, and a site that hosts portfolios of images free of charge.

www.printroom.com
Free membership makes online albums available for viewing. Prints can be ordered from the site.

TECHNICAL INFORMATION

While technical information is easy to obtain on the Internet, the quality can be variable. Visit the manufacturer of your equipment or software (*see pp. 217–19*) before you visit any others.

Digital photography

www.ephotozine.com
General digital photography website with serious content and useful news, reviews, and help pages.

www.imaging-resource.com
Up-to-date reviews of digital cameras.

www.luminous-landscape.com
High quality of varied content, with essays on a wide range of photographic topics.

www.photocourse.com
Online digital photography textbook-cum-educational resource.

www.steves-digicams.com
This well-known site has a large amount of information on a wide range of subjects. Also, reviews, technical features, and news.

http://www.updig.org/guidelines/
Guidelines for the creation, supply, and transmission of digital images.

Inkjet printing

www.epson.com
Technical guides to common printer problems and how to achieve the best results.

www.inkjetmall.com
Equipment, supplies, and services relating to inkjet products, plus helpful technical support pages.
www.wilhelm-research.com
Reports of tests on inks and papers.

Underwater photography
www.aquapac.co.uk
Suppliers of underwater housings for cameras.
www.divernet.com/photog/photog.htm
A rich source of articles on all matters relating to underwater photography from *Diver* magazine.
www.underwaterphotography.com
Includes information on underwater photography and video-making, a picture gallery, and forums, as well as retailer of specialty equipment.
www.wetpixel.com
Information for underwater digital photography, including specialty equipment, diving updates, and portfolios of images.

Photojournalism
www.digitaljournalist.org
A first-rate site with excellent features by leading photographers—a superb gallery of modern photojournalism. Must be visited.
www.foto8.com
A superb showcase of current photojournalism, with extracts from the unique, cogent magazine *Ei8ht*. Well worth regular visits.
www.robgalbraith.com
An invaluable site by the guru of digital photojournalism, offering a wealth of technical information, with links to the latest information and software upgrades.

Business forms
www.ibiblio.org/nppa/biz/forms
Sample forms from various organizations, covering estimates, invoices, property and model releases, and so on. Although they are intended for US conditions, many of the forms can be adapted for use in other territories.

Web authoring
www.builder.com/graphics
A site packed with very useful, mostly intermediate to advanced, information, complete with tutorials and tips on website and application building.

www.webmonkey.com/kids
This excellent site provides a very easy and clear introduction to website construction and associated technologies.
www.webreference.com/graphics
A Web resource that covers a range of relevant issues—from scanning and formats, to animation.
www.wpdfd.com/wpdhome.htm
This site—Web Page Design for Designers—is devoted to design issues and has excellent links.

SOFTWARE ON THE INTERNET
See also pp. 218–19 for commercial software websites.
www.creativepro.com
Provides free online version of Extensis Intellihance Pro, working through Internet browser to manipulate images to improve overall quality (*see also Online image editing, below*).
www.versiontracker.com
Premier site for checking for updates of a vast array of software applications. An essential resource.

ONLINE IMAGE EDITING
www.dotphoto.com
www.fflive.reallusion.com
www.freephotoediting.com
www.gifworks.com
These sites allow you to edit images for the Web without owning your own image-manipulation software. Obviously it is not as fast as working with the application on your own computer; nor can you expect elaborate effects. Files should be kept small.

RESOURCES FOR THE DISABLED
http://joeclark.org/access
www.ability.org
www.madentec.com
http://store.prentrom.com
The first site offers information about ensuring media access for the disabled, while the second offers a wide range of information about disabilities with links, in alphabetical form. The other two detail and offer for sale technologies designed to improve accessibility of computing to those with disabilities.

Picture sources

Thanks to two parallel developments—the Internet and the universal adoption of the CD-ROM drive on computers—it is easier than ever before to access reproduction-quality images. The total number of pictures available runs into the millions, rivaling the great picture agencies, if only because some of the largest agencies now have their collections in electronic form. Listed below is a selection of different categories of usage and rights management.

FREE IMAGES

Many sites offer images free of charge, as long as they are used solely for personal purposes—for example, as screensavers or to practice image-manipulation techniques. The AltaVista AV Photo Finder is a search engine designed to find images according to keywords that you enter. Be aware that if you find an image this way, copyright notices may not be obvious; nor can you assume that the website owner has permission to use the image. If you were to download it, you could be infringing copyright (*see pp. 196–7*).

You should visit websites of major photographic enterprises, too—for example, the Kodak site (www.kodak.com) is generous with both information and pictures. Also try visiting websites for universities, research centers, museums, and galleries, where you will find a wealth of interesting images—from archaeological treasures, to pictures of deep space; from satellite images from remote sensing, to electron micrographs of viruses and insects. Another source is agencies promoting an industry or country. Images of, for example, steel-making, airplanes, or shipbuilding, of tourist spots and national costume, are often available for free use, even in a professional context such as a magazine article, provided credit is given.
www.freeimages.co.uk
www.gimp-savvy.com/PHOTO-ARCHIVE
http://images.jsc.nasa.gov
www.panda.org

ROYALTY-FREE IMAGES

Once you pay for the CD or downloaded image, you have no further fees to pay for unlimited use. However, some contracts require you to pay extra if the image is used for marketing purposes, such as a book cover or other form of packaging. While delivery was formerly primarily on CDs, now it is increasingly done over broadband connections. This enables you to search through all the major image collections, consisting of many millions of images, from the comfort of your desk. Some sites offer free images for nonprofessional use.
www.alamy.com
www.comstock.com
www.creativegettyimages.com
www.istockphoto.com
www.jupiterimages.com
www.stockbyte.com

ONLINE PRINTING

The following are examples of websites that offer printing services to customers who either download image files or send in their film or images stored on removable media. But this is only the core of the service: several sites allow registered customers to manage their own album, which is used to store image files but may be accessed by others for viewing and sharing. Payments are usually made by credit card. It is advisable to check on shipping costs if the printing service is based outside of your country of residence: it is easy to access websites internationally, but the delivery of prints may be a different matter. Some sites also function as a visually linked community, encouraging comments on each other's images, discussions relating to photography, and more.
www.easymemories.com
www.fotolog.com
www.kodakgallery.com
www.photos.fotango.com
www.shutterfly.com
www.snapfish.com

Manufacturers

Many of the multinational manufacturers host different websites for each of their sales regions. It may be worth visiting those outside your region, since the quality and information can vary between sites: some, for example, simply present pages of their product catalogs, while others are a rich resource of practical tips and technical resources, as well as offering product information. The following is a selection of photographic manufacturers, but inclusion does not imply recommendation.

EQUIPMENT MANUFACTURERS

Apple Computers, displays, picture storage
www.apple.com

Canon Cameras and lenses and accessory system, digital cameras, printers, scanners
www.canon.com

Casio Digital cameras, projectors
www.casio.com

Epson Printers, digital cameras, scanners
www.epson.com

Fujifilm Digital cameras, film cameras, medium-format cameras, accessories
www.fujifilm.com

Hasselblad Medium-format cameras with lenses and accessory system
www.hasselblad.com

Hewlett-Packard Printers, ink-jet papers, scanners, digital cameras, computers
www.hp.com

Imacon Scanners, digital backs
www.imacon.dk

Jobo Picture storage, darkroom and other accessories
www.jobo.com

Kodak Digital cameras, film cameras, film, printers
www.kodak.com

KonicaMinolta Digital cameras, film cameras, film, paper
www.konicaminolta.com

LaCie Storage drives and media, displays
www.lacie.com

Leica Cameras and lenses and accessory system, digital cameras
www.leica.com

Lexar Memory cards and readers for digital cameras
www.lexar.com

Lexmark Printers, including multi-function models
www.lexmark.com

Microtek Scanners, digital projectors, cameras
www.microtek.com

Nikon Cameras and lenses and accessory system, digital cameras, film scanners
www.nikon.com

Nixvue Digital album for computerless storage of files from memory cards
www.nixvue.com

Olympus Cameras and lenses, digital cameras, printers, removable storage
www.olympus.com

PalmOne Personal data assistants (also called PDAs or electronic organizers) and accessories
www.palm.com

Pentax Cameras (including digital and medium-format) and lenses
www.pentax.com

PhaseOne Digital backs, conversion software
www.phaseone.com

Ricoh Digital and film-based cameras
www.ricoh.com

Samsung Digital cameras
www.samsung.com

Smartdisk Picture storage, portable hard disks
www.smartdisk.com

Umax Scanners
www.umax.com

Software sources

IMAGE-MANIPULATION SOFTWARE

Despite the dominance of Photoshop, there are many software applications that are capable of excellent results. The simpler programs are better suited to the beginner or those who do not wish to commit a large amount of time to learning how to use the software.

Photoshop
This is the industry-standard software, thanks to professional features such as color control and a vast range of features, but it is difficult to master and still burdened by some weak features. It is costly to purchase, and at its best when used on very powerful computers with enormous RAM allocations. For Windows and Mac.
    www.adobe.com
Photoshop Elements
An extremely capable image-manipulation application that is easy to use yet has functions that are missing from Photoshop. For Windows and Mac.
    www.adobe.com
PaintShop Pro
Affordable, powerful software with good layers features. It is suitable for most requirements, including Web work. Windows only.
    www.corel.com
Painter
Enormous range of Brush tools with highly controllable painting effects and powerful cloning tools. An excellent supplement to Photoshop. For Windows and Mac.
    www.corel.com
PhotoImpact
Very good range of tools that are strong on features for Web imagery, in an affordable package that is easy to use. Layers-based work is cumbersome. Windows only.
    www.ulead.com
PhotoPaint
Powerful, comprehensive features, with good Layers and cloning elements. Usually part of the CorelDraw suite of graphics applications but also available as an affordable standalone program. Windows only.
    www.corel.com

PhotoRetouch Pro
With powerful correction tools, this highly color-management-aware software is suitable for professional work. Mac only.
    www.binuscan.com
PhotoSuite
Inexpensive, tutorial-based software with a good range of tools and Layers handling, together with good functions for Web work. Windows only.
    www.roxio.com

PHOTOSHOP PLUG-INS

Plug-in software adds functions to the primary software, appearing in its own dialog box for settings to be made. Many of these will work with applications such as Painter, which accept Photoshop-compatible plug-ins. Check with the supplier prior to purchase.
Andromeda 3D
Powerful and able to wrap images around basic 3-D objects, but tricky to learn.
    www.andromeda.com
Eye Candy
With more than 20 different filters to create a wide range of effects, this is an excellent introduction for the filter enthusiast—and it is easy to use.
    www.alienskin.com
Genuine Fractals
Industry-standard image-enlargement software.
    www.ononesoftware.com
Image Doctor
Handy tools for cleaning up images. Easy to use.
    www.alienskin.com
Intellihance
Automatic enhancement of images through color balance, saturation, sharpness, and contrast.
    www.extensis.com
Knoll Lens Light Factory
Extends Photoshop's lens-flare filter for impressive effects—but it's limited to this one trick.
    www.redgiantsoftware.com
KPT
Kai's Power Tools offers powerful sharpening, texturizing, distorting, lens-flare, and perspective-

distortion tools, as well as the ability to create skies, complicated lighting, and so on. It can be tricky to use but is well worth installing.

www.corel.com

Noise Ninja

Powerful and effective reduction of noise, with a high level of control.

www.picturecode.com

Paint Alchemy

Includes a wide range of paint textures that can be produced and controlled easily. Far superior to Photoshop's range, and worth investigating.

www.xaostools.com

PhotoAnimator

Part of the PhotoTools set of applications, this is excellent for creating GIF animations for use on the internet.

www.extensis.com

Terrazzo

Creates tesselated patterns, sometimes of great beauty, from any image. Well worth investigating.

www.xaostools.com

Xenofex

Wide range of highly controllable effects, such as adding elements or distorting the image.

www.alienskin.com

DESIGN AND OTHER SOFTWARE

BBEdit

HTML editor with many useful features, beloved of experts working on Mac OS. The Lite version is available as freeware.

www.bbedit.com

Dreamweaver

Professional, full-featured software for designing webpages and managing websites. For Windows and Mac.

www.macromedia.com

Flash

Powerful software for drawing, animation, and multimedia creation. Flash animation is widely readable on the Internet. For Windows and Mac.

www.macromedia.com

FotoStation

Simple and effective tool for creating sets of pictures and management, with multiple printing and webpage-output options. For Windows and Mac.

www.fotostation.com

FrontPage

Fairly easy-to-use software for the creation of webpages, but it lacks the power features for top-quality designs. Windows only.

www.microsoft.com

GoLive

Industrial-strength design tool for webpage and website management, with a full range of features but difficult to learn. For Windows and Mac.

www.adobe.com

InDesign

Very powerful page-design software with an excellent feature set. However, it is difficult to learn and demands heavy computer resources. For Windows and Mac.

www.adobe.com

Mask Pro

This software offers highly controllable tools for masking difficult objects such as hair and glass. For Windows and Mac.

www.extensis.com

Photo Mechanic

Very speedy picture management, oriented toward digital photographers. Easy to use. For Windows and Mac.

www.camerabits.com

Portfolio

Powerful tool for the management of picture libraries, with the ability to publish on the Internet. It also has search facilities. Suitable for use over network but can be slow. For Windows and Mac.

www.extensis.com

QuarkXPress

This well-established page-design application can be made very powerful with extension software and is relatively easy to learn. However, it is expensive to buy and can be unreliable. For Windows and Mac.

www.quark.com

Index

Index continued

Acknowledgments

Author's acknowledgments
My first thanks go to Judith More for commissioning this book.

Thanks to Adobe and Corel for keeping me up to date; to my editors on *MacUser* magazine, whose commissioning has given me the opportunities to keep up with the industry, and to *What Digital Camera* magazine and its knowledgeably genial editor, Simon Joinson, for keeping me informed.

The greatest and deepest are, however, my thanks to Wendy for all she has done for me. The three little letters spelling the word "all" are a Zen-like concentrate that encapsulates a universe of support, help, and inspiration, which has made possible the enormous project that has been the completion of this book.

Tom Ang
London 2006

Publisher's acknowledgments
Previous editions produced by: **Senior Editor:** Neil Lockley; **Project Editor:** Richard Gilbert; **Senior Art Editors:** Kevin Ryan, Alison Shackleton; **DTP Designers:** Sonia Charbonnier, Adam Shepherd; **Production Controller:** Heather Hughes; **Managing Editors:** Sharon Lucas, Adèle Hayward; **Managing Art Editor:** Karen Self; **Art Director:** Carole Ash.

Dorling Kindersley would like to thank the following for their contributions:
Editorial: Georgina Garner; **Design:** Derek Coombes, Simon Webb, Lee Riches, Simon Wilder, Marianne Markham, Paul Drislane, and Janis Utton; **Index:** Christine Bernstein; **Picture Research:** Anna Bedewell, Samantha Nunn, Carlo Ortu; **Picture library:** Richard Dabb; **Illustrator:** Patrick Mulrey.

Picture credits
The publisher would like to thank the following for their kind assistance and for permission to reproduce their photographs:
ACDSee, Adobe, Agfa UK, Louise Ang, Apple, Aquapac International Ltd., Belkin Components Ltd., Better Light Inc., M. Billingham & Co. Ltd., Bite Communications Ltd., Blitz PR, Broncolor, Calumet International, Canon UK Ltd., Casio UK, Casio Electronics Co. Ltd., Centon, ColorVision Europe, Companycare Communications, Compaq UK, Contax, Corel, Andy Crawford, John Curno, Epson UK, Extensis, Firefly Communications, Fuji, Fujifilm UK, FutureWorks, Inc., Gateway, Goodmans Industries Ltd., Gossen, Hasselblad, Heidelberg USA, Hewlett-Packard, IBM, Ilford Imaging UK Ltd., Iomega, JASC, Johnsons Photopia Ltd., courtesy of Kodak, Konica Minolta Photo Imaging (UK) Ltd., Kyocera Yashica (UK) Ltd., LaCie, Leica, Lexar, Lexmark, Linho, Linhof, Logitech Europe SA, Lowepro UK Ltd., Macromedia Europe, Mamiya, Manfrotto, Megavision, Mesh, Metz, Micron, Microsoft, Microtek, Mitsubishi, Nikon UK Ltd., Nikkor, Nixvue Systems, Nokia, Olympus UK Ltd., Packard Bell, Panasonic Industrial Europe Ltd., Peli Cases, Pentax UK Ltd., Phillips, Ricoh EPMMC UK, Rollei, Roxio, Sigma Corporation, Smartdisk Europe, Sony United Kingdom Ltd., Tamrom UK, Tenba Quality Cases, Tokina, Ulead, Umax, Wacom.

All other images © Dorling Kindersley. For further information see **www.dkimages.com**

Jacket picture credits
Front and spine: Getty Images. **Back:** Tom Ang.